The Canadian Indian:
A History Since 1500

The Canadian Indian: A History Since 1500

E Palmer Patterson II

Collier-Macmillan Canada, Ltd.

Cover Design: Hugh Michaelson Ltd.
Cover Illustration: Gordon McLean.
Maps: Frank Zsigo.

Library of Congress Catalog Card
Number 71-178596.

SBN   2.976570.6 (paperback)
      2.976580.3 (case)

Collier-Macmillan Canada, Ltd.,
1125-B Leslie Street, Don Mills, Ontario.
The Macmillan Company, New York.

Printed and bound in Canada.

1   2   3   4   5
72   73   74   75   76

To Nancy-Lou

Acknowledgements.

For permission to use material in this book grateful acknowledgment is made to the following:

American Anthropological Association and Harold Hickerson: For material reprinted from "The Southwestern Chippewa" by Harold Hickerson. Reproduced by permission of the American Anthropological Association from *AAA Memoirs 92*, Vol. 64, No. 3, Pt. 2, 1962. For material reprinted from "The Sociohistorical Significance of Two Chippewa Ceremonies" by Harold Hickerson. Reproduced by permission of the American Anthropological Association from *American Anthropologist*, Vol. 65, No. 1, 1963.

British Columbia Provincial Archives: For material reprinted from "British Columbia Dispatches" 1864. Deposited in Special Collections Division, University of British Columbia Library.

Mrs. John Collier: For material reprinted from *From Every Zenith* by John Collier.

Department of Anthropology, Yale University: For material reprinted from *Notes on the Indians of the Great Slave Lake Area* by J. A. Mason, published by the Department of Anthropology, Yale University, 1964. For material reprinted from "Contributions to the Ethnography of the Kutchin" by Cornelius Osgood from *Antrhopology* No. 14 published by the Department of Anthropology, Yale University, 1936.

Exposition Press Inc: For material reprinted from *Chief Pushmataha* by Anna Lewis.

Faber and Faber Ltd: For material reprinted from *British Imperial Trusteeship* by G. R. Mellor.

Harper & Row, Publishers, Inc: For material reprinted from "Mexico Since Cardenas" by Oscar Lewis from *Social Change in Latin America Today* by Richard Adams and others.

Historical Society of Alberta: For material reprinted from "An Opinion of the Frog Lake Massacre" by Edward Ahenakew from *Alberta Historical Review*, Vol. VIII, #3.

Indian-Eskimo Association of Canada: For material reprinted from Indian-Eskimo Association *Bulletin*, Vol. 8, No. 5, December 1967.

Manitoba Historical Society: For material reprinted from "Eastern Cree Indians" by J. W. Anderson from Manitoba Historical Society *Transactions*, Series III, #2, 1956.

McClelland and Stewart Limited: For material reprinted from *Winter Studies and Summer Rambles in Canada* by Anna Burwell Jameson. Reprinted by permission of The Canadian Publishers, McClelland and Stewart Limited, Toronto. For material reprinted from *Forty Years in Canada* by S. B. Steele. Reprinted by permission of The Canadian Publishers, McClelland and Stewart Limited, Toronto.

Miss K. McLennan: For material reprinted from *Louisbourg from its Foundations to its Fall 1713-1758* by J. S. McLennan.

Ontario Department of Lands and Forests: For material reprinted from *Indians of Ontario* by J. L. Morris.

Oxford University Press, Canadian Branch: For material reprinted from *A Study of History* by Arnold J. Toynbee. Published by Oxford University Press (London). For material reprinted from *The Dilemmas of Trusteeship* by Kenneth Robinson. Published by Oxford University Press (London).

Penguin Books Ltd: For material reprinted from *A History of Christian Missions* by Stephen Neill. Copyright Stephen Neill 1964.

Prentice-Hall, Inc: For material reprinted from *New Zealand* by William J. Cameron, © 1965. Reprinted by permission of Prentice-Hall, Inc., Englewood Cliffs, New Jersey.

Province of Saskatchewan, Archives Office: For material reprinted from "The Story of the Ahenakews," Ruth M. Buck (ed.) from *Saskatchewan History*, Vol. 17, #1, Winter 1964.

Ross & Haines, Inc: For material reprinted from Edward D. Neill in *History of the Ojibway Nation* by William W. Warren. (Minneapolis: Ross & Haines, 1970)

Professor George F. G. Stanley and the Canadian Historical Association: For material reprinted from "The Indian Background of Canadian History" from the *Canadian Historical Association Annual Report*, 1952.

The American Museum of Natural History: For materials reprinted from David Mandelbaum's article "The Plains Cree" from *Anthropological Papers of The American Museum of Natural History*, Vol. XXVII, (N.Y. 1940).

The Geographical Magazine: For materials reprinted from Douglas Botting's article "Demoralized Indians of Brazil" from *The Geographical Magazine*, Vol. 12, April 1967.

The Macmillan Company: For material reprinted from *The Conspiracy of Pontiac* by Francis Parkman. Copyright © 1962 by The Crowell-Collier Publishing Company.

The University of Arizona Press: For material reprinted from *Cycles of Conquest: The Impact of Spain, Mexico and the United States on the Indians of the Southwest 1533-1960* by Edward H. Spicer, Tucson: The University of Arizona Press. Copyright 1962.

The University of Chicago Press: For material reprinted from *Indian Life in the Upper Great Lakes, 11,000 BC to AD 1800* by George I. Quimby. Published by the University of Chicago Press. © 1960 by the University of Chicago. For material by Helen Codere, "Kwakiutl" reprinted from *Perspectives in American Indian Culture Change*, Edward H. Spicer ed. Published by the University of Chicago Press. © 1961 by the University of Chicago. For material reprinted from *Indian Families of the Northwest Coast: The Impact of Change*, by Claudia Lewis. Reprinted by permission of the University of Chicago Press and Claudia Lewis. Published by the University of Chicago Press. © 1970 by the University of Chicago.

University of Nebraska Press: For material reprinted from *Wilderness Politics and Indian Gifts: The Northern Colonial Frontier 1748-1763*, by Wilbur Jacobs.

University of Toronto Press: For materials reprinted from *Pioneer Public Service: An Administrative History of the United Canadas 1841-1867* by J. E. Hodgetts. Published by University of Toronto Press. Copyright (C) Canada, 1956 by University of Toronto Press. For material reprinted from *The Birth of Western Canada* by George F. Stanley Published by University of Toronto Press. Copyright © , Canada, 1960 by University of Toronto Press.

A. P. Watt & Son: For material reprinted from *The Colonial Reckoning* by Margery Perham. Reprinted by permission of Margery Perham, William Collins Sons & Co. and Alfred A. Knopf, Inc. Copyright 1963.

For permission to reproduce the photographs in this book grateful acknowledgment is made to the following: Alberta Native Communications Society, 17; Department of Indian Affairs and Northern Development, 14, 22; Indian-Eskimo Association of Canada, 16, 18, 20; Information Canada, 24; H. A. McCue, 21; National Indian Brotherhood, 15, 23, 25; Public Archives of Canada, 1, 2, 4, 5, 6, 7, 8, 9, 10, 11, 12, 13; The Fine Arts Publishing Co. Ltd., 3; The Native Voice, 19.

Contents

I. THE COLONIAL PARALLEL:
A VIEW OF
CANADIAN INDIAN HISTORY

When we Westerners call people "natives" we implicitly take the cultural colour out of our perception of them. We see them as wild animals infesting the country in which we happen to come across them, as part of the local flora and fauna and not as men of like passions with ourselves. So long as we think of them as "natives," we may exterminate them or, as is more likely today, domesticate them and honestly. . .believe that we are improving the breed, but we do not begin to understand them.

Arnold Toynbee, *A Study of History*

Introduction

With the passage of time, events sometimes take on an aspect of inevitability. In Canada the relations of the Indians with the white population have this quality about them. The naturalness which characterizes the situation from the white point of view allows us to think of Indians as one more ethnic minority to be assimilated to the national whole. In Canada we may have to speak of two founding nations, but neither of these is Indian. Rather we assume that the Indian is a minority assimilating to an overwhelming majority and a European norm. The same situation pertains to some extent in Latin America, where the Hispanic and Portuguese variants of Western civilization are the norm and the aborigines are thought to be assimilating to these, although the very high percentage of Indians in some regions of Latin America creates certain complications which are absent in the countries north of the Rio Grande.

Other parts of the world—Asia, Africa, and Oceania—have undergone European colonialism and colonization. Except in Australia, New Zealand, and some other Pacific Islands, especially Hawaii (the Republic of South Africa presents further complications), the aborigines have reasserted themselves. In so doing they have employed organizational and technological skills learned from the West, as well as ideologies which they are blending with their indigenous cultures to create a synthesis uniquely theirs. They have created or are creating new cultures, and they are doing so within the context of independent political entities. Thus they are relatively free to shape their own political and cultural futures, with the exception of the problems raised by "neo-colonialism."

At the time of first contact, Indians were treated as separate states or nations in much the same way as were their African or Asian counterparts. The later course of events has resulted in sharply differing situations for the Indian as compared with the other non-European peoples. The former have become a numerically overwhelmed people. Immigrants have continued to increase the numerical disparity and have reduced the Indian to the status of stranger or tolerated guest within his aboriginal homeland. While the mosquito prevented the European from settling West Africa, and the "White Highlands" have reverted to the black man, the Indian seems to have found himself resurging too few and too late. In Canada the Indians will never be able to expel the white man or subdue him in their efforts to create an Indian synthesis in their own "new" nation. Instead the impetus will remain with the conqueror. The Indian, biologically and culturally swamped, has been forced to shape his renewal in a world dominated by white men, even within his own reserve community.

1. The Colonial Parallel

In analysing the position of the Indian in contemporary Canada, and in examining the sequence of events which brought him there, there are two viewpoints possible. Neither is valid to the exclusion of the other; rather, both are true, and full understanding of the Indian's present and past cannot exclude either view.

The first view of the Indians has been that they are one of the many ethnic groups which together constitute the cultural background of Canadians. According to this view, Indians, like other ethnic minorities, contribute to Canadian culture their element of the Canadian whole. Within this variety there is a Canadian nation and culture to which all elements are assimilating as they contribute. Terms such as "the cultural mosaic" and "the multi-cultural society" have been coined for this concept. A still more restricted view, as far as Indians are concerned, is the common assumption that there are but two cultures in Canada—French and English—and everyone, Indians included, must adjust to one or the other of these two alternatives.

Whatever other variations there may be on this theme, the Indian comes out pretty much in the same position. This second "bi-cultural" view is the one held by most whites in regard to Indians, including the Indian Affairs Department. It is fostered by public school textbooks, popular history of the sort used in Centennial advertising, and most public statements by persons referring to "the problem of Canada's Indians." The single unwavering intention in dealing with Indians, since the early nineteenth century at least, has been that they should acculturate—sooner or later, but ultimately altogether—to the "Canadian" norm.

Another way of thinking about the history of Indians in Canada is to see them as a people with a distinct past of their own; to see that the coming of the whites does not change the Indian's continuity with his own past, that his story must be told in terms of his own experience with the white man, placing him at the centre of the narrative, regardless of the fact that he has ceased to occupy the centre of Canadian affairs. The shift in control of the land and in numerical and cultural balance is then seen as part of the experience of the Indian. The territory is not the theme of the story, and the narrative does not centre on the people who constitute either the majority, or the most dynamic and dominant group in that territory. The Indian is the centre, no matter how many people displace him or how deeply he is driven into the remote areas of the land, or to what extent he is forced to conform to the invaders in order to survive. The story still centres on him and his surviving identity.

✗   In this approach, his conquest by the whites is merely the latest series of events in his experience. The Indian is the norm; the others are outsiders. He is the native. If he goes into the white man's world he is expanding his identity to include aspects of the new life introduced by the outsider. This view or something like it is the one held by many Indians, especially the younger militants. Without the "Indian" and the "Canadian" view together, the story will not reach the heart of Indian history. Especially, if the Indian viewpoint is not understood, many of his actions and attitudes will continue to seem obdurate, misguided, and inexplicable, as indeed they do to the majority. [1]

The dichotomy of Indian-*versus*-Canadian is not a new invention; in most references to him the Indian is called "Canadian Indian," not just Canadian, and this is the way the Indian seems to prefer it. In the minds of most Canadians, to be Canadian is to be white, Westernized, and/or conformable to the pattern of life held by those who are white and Westernized. When applied to the Indian, "Westernization" implies that he has set aside his previous identity to accept a new one. Thus Indian culture is seen as largely static, something which can be left behind and replaced by a new "Western" identity. The white man has made himself the norm against which must be tested those who are to be considered Canadians—has in fact declared himself to be the new native—and has defined the Indian into outsider status. The Indian in many cases continues to see the white man as the person who has intruded himself, no matter how many and how dominant. He continues to hold the evaluation of himself (as first introduced by the earliest European colonists) as the native.

It is here that the colonial and post-colonial experience of other non-Western poeple is useful in defining the Indian situation. The black Ghanaian and the black Kenyan, too, are the natives of the lands they occupy. They have survived colonialism, though changed, and have re-emerged as the centre of the history of their own areas. They are still African, even though modified considerably in their culture. In South Africa the black men are the descendants of the original natives of the continent, even though the issue is complicated in that some parts of South Africa were occupied by Hottentots and Bushmen in the seventeenth century when the Europeans arrived. Some of the whites in South Africa have called themselves Africans (Afrikaners), thus urging themselves as natives, or at least as having as great a claim to the land as the black peoples. In this way South Africa offers an interesting middle posture between the re-emergence of an indigenous people to control of their own territory and the complete takeover of the territory— physically, numerically, and culturally—by whites. In South Africa, *apartheid* is, among other things, a perverted vestige of the notion that each culture had and should be allowed to have integrity and respect and should not be destroyed, but allowed to continue in its own right. This still implies that culture is static.

In the three examples—Ghana/Kenya, South Africa, and Canada—assimilation to Western civilization for the previous occupants (original "natives") of a territory has been encouraged and disputed in various ways, and, due to differing historical factors, the results have varied. In South Africa, where the whites dominate although numerically inferior, it is expedient for them to forestall the day when the vast majority have acquired the skills and education necessary to exercise authority for the whole territory. In Canada the indigenous population, though resurging both in numbers and in education, has done or will do so too few and too late. Their effort will be regarded as foolish, inadequate, delaying, or whatever, by those who interpret Indian experience primarily in terms of their adjustment to the white world. The presence of white domination will not allow the Indian to pick and choose in an atmosphere of political independence as in Kenya and Ghana, that is certain. Thus the Indian, though his colonial experience was parallel in its early phases, has become, culturally and numerically, a stranger in his own country, and is likely to remain so. One is reminded of Jomo Kenyatta's parable of the elephant, who thrust into the hut first his trunk, then his head, then his whole body, with obvious results to the smaller original occupant.

The white man of Western culture, then, sees himself as the norm in Canada, the United States, Australia, and New Zealand, in relation to the aborigines of those nations. In the total world picture, however, white civilization and the white man himself, while very influential and penetrating everywhere, are not the norm. The non-white and non-Western peoples in the white-dominated areas can thus find a corrective or counterweight to their situation by looking outside their own boundaries to the total world picture. There is some evidence that those of them who are doing so are deriving moral, if not physical, consolation and inspiration from what they see.

Most of the histories of the nations which include a greater or smaller aboriginal population have been written by the descendants of the conquerors. Their emphasis has been on the white majority (or the white population, even where it is in the minority), and in Canada, as we have seen, Indians are treated as one factor in the history of that majority. In New Zealand, the aborigines, while not totally excluded, are treated, someone has said, as part of the natural environment which had to be overcome. After the conquest—and this is especially true in the United States—the harshness and repression by which it was accomplished have been lost from the popular accounts. The outrages were too many and too great to be admitted. The "salt water fallacy" has further contributed to the frequent failures of Canadian historians to see the Indians as a colonial people. The contiguity of one occupied area with another, from the Atlantic to the Pacific, has minimized the sense of a foreign adventure of imperialism, and made the process "Manifest Destiny" instead. The inevitability about it seemed ample justification.[f]

Although we can find differences in Indian policy on the national and local levels, there was none of the contrast between the frontier and the metropolitan centre which caused the British to vacillate in West Africa between 1805 and 1875. Margery Perham comments in *The Colonial Reckoning* on the differences in treatment of natives by distant and nearby governments:

> Almost all native races have been quick to recognize the difference between a distant imperial government and its all too nearby emigrant subjects. Even the Red Indians knew that and the attempts of the British Government to protect them from the lawless advance of the white frontiersman was one of the several causes of the American Revolution. The Maoris knew it. So did the famous Chief Khama, father of Tshekedi, who bought a top hat and a frock coat, and went to London to protest to Mr. Joseph Chamberlain about the goings on of Cecil Rhodes—and won his case.[1]

With plenty of settlers and no impeding disease, the westward impulse of the white population in Canada went unarrested, as more and more settlers pushed westward. The intensity of pressure for land in the United States contrasts with the Canadian experience, where certain mitigating factors were at work. In the northern territories of Canada, reserves were never created, and in the treaties that alienated most of the Prairies from Manitoba to Alberta, Indians were generally allowed to hunt and fish over land they surrendered to the Crown as long as settlement had not occurred. The Indian population in Canada had always suffered less pressure than that in the United States, because the whites were fewer, the land vast, and the Indians less numerous than in the corresponding areas to the south (with the exception, in the latter case, of the Northwest Coast).

Comparisons of Indians with other aborigines, general accounts of their treatment by the white conquerors, and descriptions of their present status are by no means uncommon. For example, various writers have seen the parallels between the situations of the Australian Aborigines, the New Zealand Maoris, and the Canadian and United States Indians. Some have also included the South African blacks in studies with one or more of these peoples. Sir A. Grenfell Price's study, *White Settlers and Native Peoples*[2] is such a work. The native peoples in each country are the conquered and subordinate, the white settlers in the ascendancy. This present book suggests the comparison of the Indians not only with other subject native peoples, but also with native peoples who are no longer subject.

Parallels in the practices of Europeans have been noted by a variety of witnesses. Price describes Russian and American behaviour in Siberia and North America respectively as greedy and ruthless, the work of adventurers with weapons superior to those possessed by the sparse and frequently mutually antagonistic people with whom they dealt. The letter of Lord Glenelg, Colonial Secretary, to Governor D'Urban at Capetown (26 December 1835), may serve as a general description of [the results of European impact on non-Europeans in much of the world.]This letter has been paraphrased as follows:

> The general question of contact between whites and natives was also reviewed. It was a melancholy and humiliating, but an indisputable, truth that the contiguity of the subjects of the natives of Christendom with uncivilized tribes had invariably produced the wretchedness and decay, and not seldom the utter extermination of the weaker party. This uniform result must be attributed, not to any necessary cause, but to the sinister influence of those evil passions which in such circumstances found but too much to provoke, and too little to restrain them. Of all the chapters in the history of mankind, this was perhaps the most degrading; nor was there any one course of events on which every humane mind dwelt with such settled aversion and shame, as on that which recorded the intercourse between the Christian states of Europe and the heathen nations of Africa and America. "I know not that a greater real calamity could befall Great Britain than that of adding Southern Africa to the list of the regions which have seen their aboriginal inhabitants disappear under the withering influence of European neighbourhood. It is indeed a calamity reducible to no certain standard or positive measurement, but it invokes whatever is most to be dreaded in bringing upon ourselves the reproaches of mankind and the weight of national guilt."[3]

Thus similar practices by the Europeans created similar experiences for the various indigenous peoples. It is not surprising then that Indians had experiences similar to others, or that they responded similarly in many cases. Nevertheless, it seems frequently to be unnoticed that these similarities exist, because the emphasis of most histories subordinates or ignores the Indians' experience and treats them as an ethnic minority comparable to the emigrant peoples who have come to constitute the bulk of the population.

Of the European impact on land, William Woodruff remarks, "In the name of economic efficiency, by fair means or foul, the peasant and the tribesman were dispossessed of their individual, family, or tribal ownership of land."[4] This having occurred, the dispossessed peasant was obliged to go to work for money wages in the plantations, estates, or mines of the Europeans. The innovations of a money economy frequently proved revolutionary to the social as well as the economic order. Woodruff continues, "Where tribes were reluctant to become involved with the European idea of cash crops and market economies, laws were enacted obliging each tribal community to grow cash crops where produce could be marketed."[5] Studies such as Woodruff's, dealing in broad generalizations and characterizations, have implicit in them the idea of parallels and uniformities in the colonial experience of various peoples. The problem in regard to the New World is that the Indians are, or tend to be, ignored, since they are not the most significant population segment. Thus the generalizations, as they are made about majority elements, tend to exclude the Indian, particularly in America north of the Rio Grande.

The Philippines under Spanish rule offers striking examples of the parallelism of Indian experience with that of another colonial people. This occurred despite the fact that Spain attempted to profit from her mistakes in Mexico and to apply that knowledge to the administration of the Asian colony. The Hispanization of the Philippines resulted in the creation of political authorities, "kings," where they were unknown to the indigenous culture, and the institution of indirect rule, through Filipinos. Efforts were also made to "protect," by isolation, the native peoples from secular white contact and to resettle populations in order to accelerate cultural change. This is a practice recognizable in the reserve and reservation systems in Canada and the United States, and in the *reducción* and *aldeias* in Latin America. Nevertheless, that the bulk of the cultivated land remained in the hands of the Filipinos may offer a partial explanation for what has been referred to as an "orderly" culture change.[6]

Robert K. Thomas, a Cherokee and an anthropologist, has examined several elements of the colonial parallel in his essay, "Pan-Indianism." He has provided illustrations of the growing sense of a common Indian identity in the face of the European presence which resulted in the Indian alliance under Pontiac and Tecumseh. The Plains area Thomas finds to be particularly important in the creation of Pan-Indianism. The mobility of the Plains Indians made possible the occurrence of wide-ranging contacts and associations among various Indian linguistic and cultural groups. Furthermore, the attractiveness of their way of life after the coming of the horse drew sedentary or partially sedentary peoples onto the Plains also. The significance of the Plains culture in the creation of Pan-Indianism is to be found also in the prominent place which Plains culture items hold in the Pan-Indian synthesis, the feather bonnet and teepee, for example.[7] Although the proportions of these ingredients may be different in Canada, certain outstanding artefacts of Prairie culture also figure prominently.

In addition to mobility and increased contacts, the boarding school experience of nineteenth- and twentieth-century Indians generated greater knowledge and concern about each other's character and interests, and a consequent sense of common identity. More recently summer workshops and conferences have been conscious attempts to effect the same result. In other parts of the world, urbanization, plantations, mines, schools, and even prisons served to accomplish the creation of an awareness of common interests and purposes. All of these factors demonstrate the effect of the presence of the whites and the growing tendency to collective resistance. The grouping of different peoples on a single reservation was another practice encouraging the growth of Pan-Indianism in the United States.

One of the most interesting points made by Thomas has to do with the existence of Pan–Indianism among the young and the urban Indian. Pan–Indianism seems to give cohesion to the "marginal acculturated" and the "conservative Indian" within its loose and comprehensive fold. Thomas writes, "...the general problem of loss of identity and community in America may mitigate against even very urban Indians cutting their ties with other Indians altogether." As if this were not

sufficiently contrary to the melting pot tradition of inevitable assimilation of minorities, he adds, "One could even imagine a resurgence of
local tribal identity in response to these conditions."[8]

✗ |Pan-Indianism is called a nationalist movement, which Thomas
thinks "may be very productive, as nationalist movements often are, in
literature and the arts, but it is also developing institutions which deal
with people outside the community.'⁊ Pan-Indianism facilitates Indian
participation in the larger society. Dating as it does from the nineteenth
century, thus predating the nationalism of some of the newly independent countries of Asia and Africa, Pan-Indianism, Thomas suggests,
instead of being a latter-day parallel to movements in Asia and Africa,
in fact has already passed through processes which the Africans and
Asians have yet to experience in their "nationalism-building" efforts.
From this it follows that Pan-Indianism may give us insights into the
possible future course of movements in already independent countries.
This is a provocative thought and more daring than the one proposed
here for the usefulness of the study of parallelism. Thomas has in effect
reversed the emphasis of the study of Indian colonial parallels and does
not use the parallels to understand Indians better through the context
of their colonial experience in the light of similar colonial experiences
in Africa and Asia. Instead, he studies the experience of the Indian's
embryonic and maturing nationalism to see what is possibly in store for
the new ex-colonials. A more fruitful approach might be to use Pan-
Indianism to parallel not Nigerian nationalism or similar attempts
within a nation to unite their disparate tribal groups, but rather to
Pan-Africanism in general (or Afro-Asian solidarity) vis-à-vis the still
predominant white Western world (including the United States, the
People's Republic of China, and the U.S.S.R.), with which they have to
✗ deal for their economic and social development. ⸀Thus Pan-Indianism
may be seen as an attempt at unity to resist the white community of
Canada and the United States in a similar way.⸝

In Kenya and central Africa, as in the New World, white settlers
justified their takeover on the grounds that they would use the land
more effectively than the Africans. Once the Africans had been forced
off the land coveted by the settlers, the whites demanded local self-
government. In the New World, however, white population, technology,
disease first determined the Indian's subordinate status. Then a
variety of factors, including self-doubt on the part of the whites,
colour-consciousness, the socialist critique of imperialism, and the rise of
the non-Western world began to work to his benefit. In pre-1945
Canada no Indian Jomo Kenyatta wrote his ethnographic *apologia*, nor
did an Indian John Sarbah and Joseph Casely-Hayford (as in the late
nineteenth century or early twentieth century Gold Coast/Ghana) com-
bine a detailed knowledge of traditional culture with an understanding
of Western culture to further colonial protest by the employment of
Western organizational techniques. None, that is, who have reached the
international press or the pages of standard history texts. There were

groping and unselfconscious attempts to play these roles in areas such as British Columbia, in regard to the land question, and these early stirrings of Indian resistance deserve serious investigation.

While not concerned with the subject of colonial parallels as suggested in this paper, Edward H. Spicer, in his *Cycles of Conquest*, has indicated a comparative colonialism of near-Spenglerian or Toynbee-like proportions. He compares what he describes as the "expansion and withdrawal" of conquest in the American Southwest with the expansion and withdrawal of the Roman Empire in Western Europe. Thus he argues that just as differing kinds and degrees of Roman presence left varying kinds and degrees of assimilation to Rome, a similar pattern is to be found in the contact between Europeans and Indians in the Southwest. Such a scheme opens immense vistas for exploration, including comparisons of aims and techniques of administration, intensity and length of contact, congeniality of culture, and the role of individuals. He even speaks of native elites, though he fails to include the unifying and identity-creating factor of native resistance, and he does not explore the crystallization of anti-imperialist sentiment due to Roman exploitation and rapacity: e.g., "They make a wilderness and call it peace."

Also present is the moralist who uses the primitives as a stick with which to beat the wayward and degenerating society of an imperial nation or state, summoning it back to its high ideal, for example, in the writings of Tacitus. Would nineteenth century artists think that 'the "Orontes flowing into the Tiber" had its parallel in African and Oceanian influences in European fine arts? The Roman poet Juvenal's concern about the evils of Asiatic influence in Rome were remembered and paralleled by Richard Cobden, English anti-imperialist, when he remarked "Is it not just possible that we may become corrupted at home by the reaction of arbitrary political maxims in the East upon our domestic politics, just as Greece and Rome were demoralized by their contact with Asia?"[9] The exploration of this kind of comparative colonialism with other empires might prove interesting and fruitful. Spicer gives a glimpse of the possibilities.

Again drawing upon broad parallels from antiquity and medieval times, Spicer writes of the unevenness and variety of influences spread by expanding cultures. It is sufficiently thought-provoking to warrant quoting at length:

> The Romanization of western European tribes, which never was completed, took place over periods of four to five hundred years. The spread of Arab civilization attendant on conquests beginning in the 700's went on for five hundred years in the vast area from Spain to the Philippines, and Moslemization like Romanization left a great variety of independent and unevenly influenced groups in its wake. The Hinduization of tribes in southern Asia has been going on for two thousand years. The Europeanization of peoples in Africa and Oceania has likewise been in process for more than four hundred years. These processes of cultural assimilation based on conquest and rarely resulting in the complete assimilation of any people have gone on at markedly

A History Since 1500

different rates. How fast they have proceeded has depended on the kinds of conditions set up by the conquerors, the political institutions through which they have maintained dominance, the kinds of organizations permitted or stimulated by the invaders among the native peoples, the compatibility of the cultures thrown into contact, and a host of other circumstances. The speed of assimilation of American Indians has not been measured by any careful comparisons with other situations in which the contact condition was similar. Hence it remains meaningless to speak of cultural assimilation in the Southwest as rapid or slow. We may merely point out the nature and results of those particular processes of assimilation which came into operation, namely, the processes of Hispanicization, Mexicanization, and Anglicization.[16]

Spicer has vaulted the bounds of comparisons of Africa vis-à-vis the New World or the New World vis-à-vis Oceania. Parallels or even the uniformities of practice of missionaries around the world, or comparative studies of administrative techniques in dealing with aborigines, and the political, economic, and social responses and resulting developments, all are left behind and below such a vision.

The recession of European physical contact, the recession of European self-confidence and ethnocentrism has left invigorated and adaptable cultures around the world, including the New World. The inevitable, linear progression, of which John Collier speaks in his debate with Robert Manners,[11] the uniformity of all cultures, sinks away before Spicer's time- and space-hurdling view. Others have compared themselves to past empires—Britain to Rome, Napoleon to Caesar—and they have sometimes thought of themselves as imitating or even improving upon Rome. This kind of comparison predates the modern era, of course. Caesar's enemies accused him of modelling himself upon Alexander, not only for his imperial dreams, but even to the epileptic seizures. Thus Spicer's significant contribution has not been just to call attention to a larger area of comparative imperial studies, but to introduce the Indians into his comparisons. As a scholar of Indian history and culture he is able to do what few outside the circle of Indian specialists can do, to see the parallels and potentials for generalizations about imperialism and colonialism to be found in the Indian experience.

It is important to note, finally, that during the era of imperial control from London and in the eyes of the imperial administration in London, Indians were as much part of the colonial situation as were Africans, Australian Aborigines, or Maoris. The quotation given earlier from the correspondence of Lord Glenelg clearly illustrates this point of view. The shift in perspective comes with the emphasis upon national history as opposed to imperial history. When the histories of individual states, which had emerged from the Empire, began to be written, the shift to a concern with the European caused the Indian or other aboriginals to recede into the background until the resurgence of the mid-twentieth century. There occurred a process not dissimilar to that of the written histories of newly independent countries—that is, a concern to examine the mainstream of the origins and development of the

11

new states. In such histories the aborigines' part was confined to the early days and a few specialized topics thereafter. An emphasis on political and constitutional history also aided in their exclusion from accounts, whereas concern with military affairs seemed to keep them in the narrative for the early phase of the account. Since the imperial history aspect dealt with topics of first contacts and adjustments, early settlement, and military campaigns and alliances, aborigines were more likely to figure in the story. Humanitarians viewing native affairs with concern and the detachment of distance had their effectiveness sharply reduced with the advent of self-government, and local humanitarians had a hard job overcoming local interests, although they continued to work, and received aid and comfort from the mother country.

The colonial parallel continued to be made, however, by the Indians of Canada. After World War II, the Canadian government was involved with concerns in various parts of a world where racial discrimination was becoming unfashionable, and was experiencing continuing Indian agitation at home. In 1946, therefore, a Special Joint Committee of the Senate and House of Commons was created "to examine and consider the Indian Act."[12] A successor Committee, composed of essentially the same members, was constituted in 1947 and again in 1948 "to continue and complete the examination and consideration of the Indian Act."[13] The Committee heard testimony from Indian organizations, Indian individuals of note, government officials, religious bodies, a United States Indian Bureau official, and from experts on a variety of subjects related to Indian affairs, including agriculture, animal husbandry, irrigation, and health.

Continuously faced with specific situations of reserves across Canada, the Committee had the New Zealand treatment of the Maoris set before it repeatedly as a model for future government policy. The Indians' problems were not specifically compared with those of the Maoris. Rather, the Maoris served as a kind of inspirational example of the ideal in aboriginal relations. The University Branch No. 72, B.C., of the Canadian Legion of the British Empire Service League, the government anthropologist Diamond Jenness, and the ordained Indian clergyman, the Rev. Dr. Peter Kelly (as well as others) referred favourably to the Maori example. The Canadian Civil Liberties Union submitted a brief in which it called on the government to examine the New Zealand system of dealing with the Maoris, deciding, however, against the Maori form of communal representation, and emphasized race over ability.

The Rev. Dr. Peter Kelly, a Haida chief who had been active for many years on behalf of Indians and was long a leader in the Native Brotherhood of British Columbia, then the major Indian organization of Canada, spoke out strongly for the Maori system of communal representation. Referring to the *New Zealand Yearbook*, 1944, as a source for his remarks, Kelly asked, "Why cannot this be done in Canada?"[14] He pointed out that the Maoris were growing and prospering under the system. None of the Indian spokesmen seem to have shared the ill opinion of communal representation held by the Canadian Civil Liberties Union. Earlier in the same session of the Special Joint Committee of 1947, the anthropologist Diamond Jenness, when questioned about the Maoris, had called attention to the pride of race among them and to their degree of progress in political and social matters, referring also to the question of their physical location. They had had set aside for them an area where they dominated the population, but were free to come and go as they pleased, he testified.[15] One Indian band, replying to the invitation sent by the Committee requesting briefs from Indian band councils, organizations, and other parties of individuals interested in Indian affairs, called upon the government to secure for the Indians of Canada representation like that of the "Maori Indians of New Zealand."[16]

The present writer, curious about the influence of the Maoris and the way their example had apparently captured the imagination of many Indians, asked Dr. Kelly in the summer of 1960 how it happened that the Maoris had become a model. Had any of the Indians been to New Zealand? He replied that information about Maoris had been gained through reading, and that the system seemed equitable and suited to the Indian situation in Canada.

During the 1950's, the topic appeared again from time to time. In *The Native Voice* (August, 1950), official organ of the Native Brotherhood of British Columbia, the Maori system of communal representation was cited as a model for Canadian Indians. In the March 12, 1951, issue of *The Vancouver Daily Province*, the nationally known Indian figure, Andrew Paull, was reported to have called for direct representation by Indians in both Houses of Parliament. He referred to the four seats representing 90,000 Maoris (but not to the contrast between the four Maori seats and the 76 seats held by Pakehas), and called attention to the Indian population, which he estimated at about 170,000. In 1959, Paull prepared a new brief for the Joint Committee of Parliament appointed to review again the Indian Act. In this paper, which he did not live to submit, he again called for application of the "Maori system" of representation for Canadian Indians.

In the case we have been illustrating, the influence of one aboriginal people upon another did not end in the granting to the one of the political status of the other. It is necessary to remember, of course, that the decision was not made by the Indians, but by the representatives of the white electorate. The white majority was, if not indifferent to the opinion of the Indians about their own status, nevertheless unprepared to accept it. We have here an interesting, though perhaps minor and ultimately fruitless instance of the colonial parallel in a situation of intra-commonwealth influence, in which a displaced minority tried to rescue some advantage from its situation by calling for emulation of the superior situation of another minority in its struggle with the expansionist European. As the study of aboriginal response advances—and it now is doing so at an accelerating rate, due to the emergence of the many countries again governed by their own aborigines—such minor incidents will be given a place in the story of the development of aboriginal self-awareness.

FOOTNOTES:

[1] Margery Perham, *The Colonial Reckoning* (London: 1963), p. 74.

[2] Sir A. Grenfell Price, *White Settlers and Native Peoples* (Melbourne: 1950). See also G. R. Mellor, *British Imperial Trusteeship* (London: 1951), for a study of the treatment of native peoples in British colonies in the nineteenth century.

[3] Mellor, *op. cit.*, p. 251.

[4] William Woodruff, *Impact of Western Man—A Study of Europe's Role in the World Economy, 1750-1960* (London: 1966), p. 10.

[5] *Ibid.*, p. 12.

[6] J. L. Phelan, *The Hispanization of the Philippines* (Madison, Wisc.: 1959); see p. 135 for orderly change: see p. 121 for discussion of indirect rule through headman, which characterized Spanish practice in Mexico and the Philippines.

[7] Robert K. Thomas, "Pan-Indianism," *Midcontinent American Studies*, Vol. 6, No. 2, (Kansas: 1965), pp. 78-83.

[8] *Ibid.*, p. 81.

[9] Rita Hinden, *Empire and After* (London: 1949), p. 51: quoted from John Morley, *The Life of Richard Cobden* (1883), p. 532.

[10] Edward H. Spicer, *Cycles of Conquest, the Impact of Spain, Mexico, and the United States on the Indians of the Southwest, 1533-1960* (Tucson: 1962), p. 569.

[11] See John Collier v.s. Robert A. Manners, "Divergent Views on Pluralism and the American Indian," in Roger C. Owen, James J. Deetz, and Anthony D. Fisher (editors), *The North American Indians*, a Sourcebook (New York: 1967).

[12] Canada, Parliament, *"Special Joint Committee of the Senate and House of Commons appointed to examine and consider the Indian Act, "Minutes of the Proceedings and Evidence*, Nos. 1-20, Select and Standing Committees of the Senate and House of Commons, Vol. VI, 1946 (Ottawa: 1946).

[13] Canada, Parliament, *"Special Joint Committee of the Senate and House of Commons appointed to continue and complete the examination and consideration of the Indian Act, " Minutes of the Proceedings and Evidence*, Nos. 21-41, Select and Standing Committees of the Senate and House of Commons, Vol II, pts. 1 and 2, 1947 (Ottawa: 1947). Also, for 1948, see Ibid., Nos. 1-5, Vol II, 1948 (Ottawa: 1948).

[14] *Special Joint Committee* (1947), Vol. 2, Pt. 1, p. 766.

[15] *Ibid.*, pp. 308-313, *passim*.

[16] *Ibid.*, Appendix BD, p. 52.

2. A Catalogue of Parallel Experiences

We may begin to see Indians more clearly as a colonial people when we study the colonial scene in other parts of the world. Recurrent themes appear in the examination of Indians as they do in Africa and Asia. One of the most frequently occurring and frequently observed aspects of the colonial situation is cross-cultural misunderstanding and conflict. Attitudes and practices concerning land are a striking and recurring illustration of this phenomenon. The English, for example, arrived in Africa and the New World with land tenure concepts totally foreign to their hosts. At first tolerated as useful or welcomed as guests, they soon forced themselves upon their hosts in greater numbers. The king had already granted lands to the settlers before they left home; to detach the Indians from these lands, they negotiated treaties for sales in which it is now thought the sellers frequently had neither the right to sell (in terms of traditional authority) nor any clear concept of what they were being asked to do. Thus land was acquired with the same zest and in as vast amounts as those meant to accrue to Germany through the enthusiastic efforts of Dr. Karl Peters in late-nineteenth-century East Africa.

Internecine rivalries and wars have for the Indians, as for many other colonial peoples, contributed to their subordination to the European invader. The European practice of allying themselves with a given tribe or state against a second indigenous people is universal in the history of Western expansion. In North America the Iroquois-Huron dichotomy and their respective English-French alliances is an obvious example. Cortez's alliance with the Tlaxcalans, traditional enemies of the Aztecs, is well known. From India and Africa further illustrations are available.

The impact of new diseases on Indians and other aborigines is another phenomenon which is so well known as to require no new exposition. In fact these inroads upon the Indian population made such an impression upon the white settlers that only in the recent decades of the twentieth century was it realized that aboriginal populations and populations of mixed race were increasing rapidly. The increase has been due to the application of medical and hygienic knowledge in all of the colonial world. Thus disease, both old and recently introduced, is being checked, and we have witnessed an explosion of population not only in Asia and Africa, but in Latin America and among Canadian and American Indians as well. In this way the Indian is participating in yet another aspect of the resurgence of the non-European peoples, even though many of the new generation are in fact of "mixed" race.

The creation of missionary havens for aborigines is another common feature of the colonial experience, as in the case of Paraguay and the *aldeias* of Brazil. The Jesuits were also active in Canada, attempting to "shield" the Huron from the worst aspects of white civilization. Less well known was the establishment of an indirect-rule theocracy: the Durieu system in British Columbia under Bishop Paul Durieu of the Oblates of Mary Immaculate. Here, too, the fathers saw themselves serving as buffers for the disadvantaged red men until they had acquired the skills to operate on their own in the new world of the white man. William Duncan's two Metlakatlas—British Columbian and Alaskan—are other illustrations of the same impulse, sponsored by a nominally Anglican missionary. What the missionaries saw themselves as doing, and what the Indians found, or believed that they found themselves to be experiencing, were often sharply at variance. We will return to this aspect of the topic later.

These efforts have their parallels in South Africa, where the London Missionary Society, an ecumenical Protestant group led by J. T. Vanderkemp and John Phillip, sought to protect the Hottentots from the depredations of the Boer settlers. In the nineteenth-century Gold Coast, the Wesleyan missionary, Thomas B. Freeman, with the aid of George MacLean, established farm settlements, in this case to shelter and aid slaves, and to introduce them to Christianity, which to the nineteenth century missionary involved Western technology, apparel, and social customs. Villages for freed slaves had been created in India, Mauritius, and the Seychelles. These in turn became the models for comparable Anglican and Roman Catholic settlements in East Africa. In Australia, the Church Missionary Society and the London Missionary Society were active in creating havens for aborigines. In Tasmania a Methodist bricklayer, B. A. Robinson, directed an ultimately unsuccessful effort to spare the Tasmanian aborigines from destruction by white newcomers and to introduce them to a sedentary, agricultural (and therefore "civilized") way of life. The protected status which Europeans attempted to give converts in China is a reminder that these new Christians sometimes needed protection from their non-Christian fellows, protection both against relapse into former beliefs and practices and from physical abuse. Scholars have pointed out that this led to the same kind of cleavage between Christians and non-Christians in Africa and China as occurred in the New World. The Christian/non-Christian rift between the Hurons is an example.

It is perhaps not too far-fetched to suggest another example of parallels involving the missionary. There has come about a degree of rehabilitation of missionaries as contributors to the development of Africa. This contribution, recognized by African historians, for example, has not been seen primarily in religious terms, but as significant in education, medicine, and other elements of Western culture such as political and social ideas. Their students became the leaders of the nationalist-independence movements. A similar contribution may be seen in the case of missionaries among Indians. Anthropologists have attacked them for their bigotry, narrowness, and destructiveness. Traders and administrators have cursed them as nuisances or worse. But evidence suggests that as in Africa they have at times, however inadequately, provided aid and advice to the Indian in resisting the encroach-ments of white injustice.

Obviously the missionaries also had ends they were working toward, and these they intended to reach, and indeed formulated, in the context of their European Christian beliefs and biases. Nevertheless, they did give some aid and comfort to the Indians with whom they were associated, in the attempt to deal with new and unfamiliar circumstances created by the increasing pressures of the white man, themselves included, even in the remotest areas, in the late nineteenth century. In the process of experiencing this missionary-imposed educa-tion, the Indians were able to resist pressures while gaining knowledge of and self-assurance in the new world into which they were being forced. This process was neither comfortable, efficient, consistent, nor always consciously directed to this end. Nevertheless, particularly in the more remote areas, Indians were able to gain time and perspective to mitigate the severity of the impact and to achieve a degree of selectivity in adjusting to the many facets of European culture.

In Kenya, missionaries helped frame letters of protest and were instrumental in calling together the meeting of rural African leaders which led to the formation of the Kikuyu Association. In 1921 a Church of Scotland missionary helped draft a petition to the govern-ment outlining various grievances. The missionaries served as catalysts in the more generalized sense that they helped to create a class of Westernized or semi-Westernized people. These were particularly the young people of their mission churches. Commenting upon this factor in the development of Kenyan nationalism, C. G. Rosberg Jr. and John Nottingham state, "The missions' gift of literacy brought them the possibility of great power."[1]

The employment of a system of reserves for natives is such a familiar pattern in a number of colonial countries that it need only be mentioned in passing. The havens described above were reserves, whether privately or governmentally sponsored. The *reducción* or *con-gregación* of Mexico and the reserve system in Africa, including the Bantustans, provide further illustrations of the extent to which, through Canadian reserves and American reservations, the Indian ex-perience may be seen as part of the spectrum of colonial experience. The reserves were not intended in each case to perform the same functions. Aboriginal removal, creation of labour pools, concentration for more efficient acculturation were among the motivations for creating these designated areas. Unlike examples in Africa and Latin America, most Canadian and American reserves were not labour pools for white industry, mining, and agriculture, but a means of removing Indians from desired land. As such, some Indians were willing to accept them as a refuge. For example, Spokan Garry is credited by his biographer, Thomas Jessett, with wanting "a reservation for his people where they could continue to live as a tribal group while they adjusted to the ways of the white man."[2] Even the policy of removal, as in the infamous "Trail of Tears," seemed justified in the eyes of some Indian leaders, if it could provide protection during a period of transition. The biographer of the Choctaw leader, Pushmataha, indicates that he was influenced by a similar hope that western migration would give his people time to learn new ideas without severe pressure; [3] Boudinot of the Cherokee also assigned the treaty of removal with the same rationale. Charles M. Johnston shows that in coming to Canada the Iroquois were prompted by a similar motivation:

> In spite of Brant's arguments, a number of Sachems, including John Desoronto, had already rejected the Grand as a refuge, choosing instead the site allocated at the Bay of Quinte, convinced that in such a relatively remote area they could live undisturbed by the Americans. [4]

A pattern in the colonial situation which has been studied extensively is the appearance of certain religious manifestations in the face of colonial domination and restriction. Frustrated in political and social channels, some colonial peoples have exhibited their protest through religious movements. These movements have varied from peaceful withdrawal and quietism to militant and insurgent groups seeking by violence to expel the white man and to restore the golden days before colonialism. At times they incorporated elements of the European's religion and culture into messianic and millenarian religions. John Slocum of the Shaker religion on the West Coast, Wowoka of the Ghost Dance on the Plains, Handsome Lake of the Longhouse religion among the Iroquois, and a less well-known prophet, Uzakle, of British Columbia, are examples in North America. Ruth Underhill, in *Red Man's Religion*, has proposed two categories of prophets in this connection: those of hostility, and those of co-existence. R. Bastide's comment on messianic religions, although made in the context of Africa and Asia, is equally applicable to North America:

> Messianism may be regarded as an attempt, not too successful, perhaps, but an attempt nonetheless which deserves to be studied. It represents an effort to sift and filter values, introduced by Europeans, through the various forms of local mythologies or, if you prefer, to pour new wine into old bottles, just as it is an attempt (and this is even more significant) to adjust ancient systems of values to new needs and requirements. [5]

The Cargo movement in Melanesia represents a similar growth and effort toward synthesis in that it is symptomatic of change and itself produces change. Interpretations of the factors precipitating these messianic movements vary. Not only are they regarded as examples of synthesis and an attempt to absorb new concepts, they are also thought by some writers to appear only where the conditions of culture contact create a situation of great pressure and rapid change. Margaret Mead, in *New Lives For Old*, while accepting the idea that they come from a condition of great pressure, treats the cargo cults as a form of extreme rejection of the old culture rather than emphasizing them as synthesizing the old and new.

A.F.C. Wallace illustrated an aspect of parallelism in his foreword to the most recent edition of James Mooney's *The Ghost Dance Religion* by calling attention to Mooney's identification of the Indian struggle against whites with the Irish struggle against the English. Commenting on Mooney's awareness of the larger implication of the Ghost Dance Religion, Wallace says, "Mooney not only provided a vivid and detailed account of a major revitalization movement, but also recognized—albeit in a crudely classificatory way—the essential similarity in process between this one Indian nationalistic movement and the many comparable efforts at cultural renewal among other peoples, both primitive and and civilized."[6] Thus Mooney too saw the colonial experience of the Indians.

Another and related parallel is that of land problems or land questions as a focus or catalyst for the growth of early movements for native unity, native resistance, and proto-nationalism. Passing reference to this phenomenon has been made above. In such varied places as the Ohio Valley under Tecumseh, in nineteenth-century New Zealand's "King movement," in the former Gold Coast of West Africa, in Kenya with the Mau Mau, and in British Columbia in the early decades of the twentieth century, land pressures caused native peoples to engage in protests, peaceful or violent, against the whites, and to resist, if possible the increasing encroachments. In some cases these early manifestations are seen as part of the early growth of nationalism leading eventually to independence. In places where the aborigines have been outnumbered and out-gunned, nevertheless the course of developments has striking parallels to early aspects of nationalism in other colonial situations.

Speaking of the character of the early Kenyan political movements, Carl Rosberg and John Nottingham tell us in *Mau Mau: Myth and Reality*, "The alienation of land to the European settlers was a dominant and unifying theme in the polity."[7] They become even more specific when they credit the founding of the Kikuyu Association to the resistance of a particular family, two of whose members were active in the embryonic nationalist movement, to government efforts to alienate a portion of their land. This occurred when the missionary, Canon Harry Leakey, suggested that the successful protest of an individual case be followed up by a mass meeting of chiefs and people.

Regarding Chief Joseph and the Nez Percé, Alvin Josephy finds, in *The Patriot Chiefs*, that the main factor provoking them to war was a "conflict over land."[8] An article by D'Arcy McNickle, "Indian and European: Indian-White Relations from Discovery to 1887," provides a good summary of the importance of land in the occupation of the United States. He concludes with a comment on the General Allotment Act of 1887 by which Indian land could be assigned as individual holdings, thus alienating much of it for sale to whites:

> In the heat of. . .discussion, it would not have occurred to any of the debaters to inquire of the Indian what ideas they had of home, of family, and of property. It would have been assumed in any case, that the ideas, whatever they were, were without merit since they were Indian.[9]

Again, land was the focal point in the Maori nationalist movement, and their resistance to the threat to their land led to the end of what one authority calls "tribal isolation and uniting to defend the common interest."[10] One is reminded of the remark by Gilbert Murray in the context of ancient Greek tragic drama:

> Unnatural affection, child-murder, father-murder, incest, a great deal of hereditary cursing, a double fratricide, and a violation of the sanctity of dead bodies—when one reads such a list of charges against any tribe or nation, either ancient or in modern times, one can hardly help concluding that somebody wanted to annex their land.[11]

Like other colonial peoples, Indians are attempting to "find themselves," to establish a sense of their own identity. This has led to protest organizations, which in their initial phases were frequently without mass support and lacked clearly defined goals as well as stable financial support. These organizations spasmodically appeared in the headlines and met periodically. They called for greater government aid and greater freedom for self-expression. Their leaders varied from flamboyant individualists to effective manipulators of Western organizational techniques. In some cases the individuals, organizations, and their activities may be compared to earlier phases of nationalist movements in such countries as Ghana or Nigeria. As in the nationalist movements in these countries it has been necessary to create symbols of identity. In the case of the North American Indian, they have, with the aid of the white tourist, begun to bring together a kind of composite of Pan-Indian culture which has been remarked upon by a number of writers. A potpourri of totem poles, birchbark canoes, feather headdresses, war- and rain-dances, tom-toms, teepees, bows and arrows, tomahawks, and buckskin clothing, has amalgamated their culturally various features into an "Indian" culture in which elements of the Eastern woodlands, the Prairies, and the West Coast are merged. Perhaps it will not be straining the search for correspondence of experience if we cite the search for the "African personality" and the African paradigm of former President Kwame Nkrumah and Professor Willie Abrahams as parallels, if not exactly on the same plane. The efforts to manufacture a "national culture" in India described by McKim Mariott as India's "search for inspirational symbols in her tangled pasts"[12] may be a corresponding development.

There is another significant aspect to this development—the emergence of the Pan-Indian organization. These organizations are becoming active as lobbyists and as mechanisms for allowing Indians across the continent, whether in Canada or in the United States, to meet and explore common problems and their solutions. At the same time there is a publicly expressed willingness on the part of the non-Indian to consider redress to grievances. Thus in Canada Indians from Ontario may profit by a legal decision in British Columbia recognizing and alleviating some restriction on hunting or fishing. The Native American

Church (the "peyote cult") also contains, though not by design, the seed of a developing unity among the participating Indians over a wide area. The average man-in-the-street's notion of what is helpful to the Indian frequently not only does not correspond to what the Indian believes to be helpful, but is a further example of coercion, pressure, and failure to give the Indian the initiative for his own life and community. In their early years, to mention a final parallel on the theme of Indian organization, nationalist movements in various parts of the world found, as some Indian groups have done, that between crises it was difficult to maintain membership and enthusiastic support.

The use of indirect rule, a very widespread colonial practice, in the administration of Indians, constitutes another example of the colonial parallel. John Collier, United States Indian Commissioner from 1933 to 1945, clearly states in *From Every Zenith* his ideas that Indians are colonials and that during his administration they were being administered under a form of indirect rule. He idealized this approach as the best means to preserve and extend the Indian's culture. Collier indicates the context and aim of his effort when he asserts:

> These policies, all formulated in general terms in the years preceding 1933, were derived from some knowledge of colonial administration, and a knowledge of the Indian affairs history of the hemisphere from the time of Las Casas onward. They expressed a philosophy intended to reach beyond the United States Indians to all Indians and to all colonial peoples, and generally to the government-citizen relationship. In administration, they related essentially to the equation between government viewed as a necessity, and the Indians viewed as groups thinking and striving in their own being. This entailed a maximum of stimulus and permissiveness between headquarters, the field, and the Indians; and with a minimum of any kind of pressuring or rushing, whether of the Indian Bureau personnel or of the Indians.[13]

Elsewhere in the same work, Collier states, "...the generations of multitudinous disaster for Indians were generations of direct rule by the United States: while the radical methodical shift in the Indian New Deal—a shift to indirect rule, or, better, indirect administration—changed Indian disaster to Indian victory..."[14]

The technique of governing the Indian in Canada through chiefs and band councils has elements of indirect rule in it. Like indirect rule in other places, it also by its very existence created or implied political and social relationships which were new and/or different from previous custom. In the case of Canada, the bureaucracy of Indian administration played the role of the colonial officers in the field.

All of these topics can be examined fruitfully for comparisons and contrasts. Other topics which might produce evidence of colonial parallels may be found in biographical studies, illustrating the nature of contact and adjustment in an individual life, and of personal accomplishment in the context of the contact situation. The importance of economic factors in shaping Indian-white relations and the parallels in the role of Indians in extractive industries during the early contact period may also be examined. Knowledge of these matters may lead to further generalizations about aboriginal response of colonial status. In the independence movements of non-Western countries it may be possible to find analogies for constructing accounts and detecting conformity to a general pattern in Indian agitation for rights and privileges at the local and national level. A comparison, for example, might be drawn between militant anti-European societies. Comparisons of religious leaders and assimilationists among Indians and other colonials or erstwhile colonials would contribute to a broader understanding of the effects of colonialism.

This catalogue, then, while it does not exhaust the list of parallel experiences of Indians and other colonials, does provide an indication of the range of related situations and responses. It also suggests the variety of topics available for study in the field of aboriginal response to colonialism. To sum up the conclusions which may be drawn from this catalogue, then: the hypothesis has been formulated that the Canadian Indian could be studied and his story reconstructed in a way which would show the parallel with the colonial experience of other indigenous peoples, and it has even been claimed that this method would throw light upon the Indian's present-day motivation and self-view. Admittedly this will have more than a few pitfalls; the major difficulty being that which is discussed at the outset—that the Indian became in the nineteenth century hopelessly outnumbered, with his culture accordingly swamped and his biological survival threatened. Even his aboriginal status has been somewhat modified by the fact that he had survived biologically partly because of the creation of a large *mestizo* or *métis* element within the people calling themselves Indians and/or so-called by the Indian Affairs administration.

To understand the reasons for these similarities of experience between the Indian and other non-European people it is necessary to explore the motivations for the Europeans' presence in these "new lands" and the activities which they undertook to satisfy the ends they sought. The motives have been alliteratively summarized as "Gold, God, and Glory." Translated into more particular economic goals, the Europeans sought land, trade, labourers, natural and manufactured resources (already present or capable of being developed and exploited). They sought to bring the Indian into their economic system if possible or to remove him from interference if necessary. These aims led to a variety of relationships, conditions, and linkages between aborigines and Europeans depending on factors deriving from the European and non-European elements in the new situation. Factors of size of population (on both sides), intensity of contact, length of contact, voluntary and involuntary relations, technology of both parties, and congeniality of each to cultural borrowing and flexibility in cross-cultural relations, were among those operating.

The Indians, and others, were not only to be brought into the economic sphere of the newcomers, however. Increasingly from the sixteenth century to the twentieth century the Europeans sought to change the ideology of their non-European subjects. They did not make sharp distinctions among the various aspects of their own culture—e.g. religion, economy, education, customs of dress and speech. They tended to see these as interlocking and in fact inseparable parts of a way of life which they thought, especially after the late eighteenth century, to be superior to the way of life of other peoples. The technological and scientific ascendancy which Europe had gained by the nineteenth century, plus such currents as nationalism and popularization of ideas derived from the work of Charles Darwin, helped to create a self-image among Europeans by which they saw themselves as the advance guard of the unilineal direction of a "mainstream" or "historical process" or "march of progress." The Europeans, secular and religious, had a sense of mission to change the rest of the world— economically, ideologically, physically, and in any other way which might be thought necessary to achieve "progress." The desired changes could be brought about by "educating" the native, "converting" the native, "administering" the native, and generally "enlightening" the native. These activities set in motion or accelerated the changes which have led to the creation of new nations and new nationalisms as well as changing societies and peoples in Asia, Africa, and the New World. They were created by the uniformity of purposes and programs of the colonizers. The non-European peoples in various parts of the world were submitted to European ideas and systems, particularly as illustrated in the nineteenth century by the overseas expansion of France, the Netherlands, Belgium, and Great Britain. In other areas the descendants of European colonizers had taken over the task of expansion and the conquest and control of indigenous populations. In countries such as those of Latin America, the United States, and by the second half of the nineteenth century in Canada, Australia, and New Zealand, the Westernization of the native was under new, but not a very different kind of management. Other colonizers have had less impact perhaps because their term of power was shorter and/or their activities on behalf of controlled change were weaker and less efficient.

The agents of imperialism were drawn from relatively homogeneous segments of the population, though of different nations, and the institutions and organizations through which they carried out their operations were similar in their actions and intentions. Mission societies, for example, framed policies in terms of world-wide efforts, and personnel not infrequently moved from one area to another. Mission journals reveal side-by-side accounts from the "fields" of Japan, India, Africa, and North America. In some cases mission work among Indians was reported in the sections which also dealt with the Far East or foreign missions.

FOOTNOTES:

[1] Carl G. Rosberg, Jr., and John Nottingham, *The Myth of "Mau Mau". Nationalism in Kenya* (New York: 1966), p. 17.

[2] Thomas E. Jessett, *Chief Spokan Garry* (Minneapolis: 1960), p. 183.

[3] Anna Lewis, *Chief Pushmataha, American Patriot* (New York: 1959), p. 133.

[4] Charles M. Johnston, *The Valley of the Six Nations* (Toronto: 1964), p. xxxviii.

[5] R. Bastide, "Messianism and Social and Economic Development," in Immanuel Wallerstein (ed.), *Social Change: The Colonial Situation* (New York: 1966), p. 477.

[6] Foreword by A. F. C. Wallace in James Mooney, *The Ghost Dance Religion* (Chicago: 1965), p. v.

[7] Rosberg and Nottingham, *op. cit., p. xviii.*

[8] Alvin M. Josephy, *The Patriot Chiefs* (New York: 1960), p. 313.

[9] D'Arcy McNickle, "The Indian and European: Indian-White Relations from Discovery to 1887," *The Annals of the American Academy of Political and Social Science* (Philadelphia: 1957), Vol. 311, p. 11.

[10] Harold Miller, *New Zealand* (London: 1955), p. 63.

[11] Quoted in Lewis Hanke, *Aristotle and the American Indians* (London: 1959), p. 48.

[12] McKim Marriott, "Cultural Policy in the New States," from Clifford Geertz (ed.), *Old Societies and New States* (New York: 1963), p. 35.

[13] John Collier, *From Every Zenith* (Chicago: 1963), p. 172.

[14] *Ibid.,* p. 345. See also pp. 348-50 for other comments which show that Collier viewed American policy in the context of world-wide colonialism.

3. Canadian Applications

There remains the question of whether a history of Indians can be studied significantly within the context of the main categories of Canadian history. The answer proposed here is tentative, but it is this: that only in limited places before, say, the mid- or even late nineteenth century can an account following Canadian chronology provide a reasonable reconstruction of Indian history.

By the early twentieth century, most Canadian Indians appeared to be settling into some adaptation to Canadian life or assimilating altogether. Thus the Indian as a separate cultural and biological identity had entered a period of irrelevance. Economically, socially, and politically, he had ceased to be a factor that needed to be reckoned with, and his presumed destiny of absorption or extinction seemed near. This situation is vividly recreated in the following modern account of Brazil:

> In those early days it was possible for the colonists to be the pillars of Indian society rather than the enemies of it. But things changed. The Portuguese grew in numbers, ventured further inland and fought the Indian. In the 17th century the *bandierantes* were used as pacifiers and they brought home strings of ears to Goias, testifying to their prowess in exterminating Goias Indians. The new plantations required Indian land and labour, and when the Indians retreated into the interior to avoid the untender ministrations of the plantation foremen, negro slaves were introduced. Thereafter the Indians ceased to be of economic importance in Brazil.
>
> . . .The Indians who survived the gloomy cycle of massacre, epidemic (like the smallpox epidemic which wiped out three-quarters of the Indians in Bahia), demoralization and suicide in the 17th and 18th centuries, retreated from the coast higher up the tributaries, or, standing their ground, were defeated.[1]

This onset of irrelevance as experienced by Indians in North America is given poignant expression in the following account:

> A great change had taken place in the attitude and policy of the government toward the Choctaws since 1804, when Pushmataha last visited Washington. At that time the Choctaws were needed to divert Indian trade from the Spanish and to be used as soldiers and scouts to combat English and Spanish interest in the South: hence, they were given more consideration and flattered as to their importance. In 1824, the Indians were not needed in any capacity. There was no international complication on the frontier. In fact, the Indians were now only a hindrance to western development. The politicians were interested in securing the friendship of the new democracy in the West. The Indians' friendship was not considered. This change was too great for Pushmataha to understand. He had on all occasions befriended the American people, and he had expected a lasting friendship in return from the American government.[2]

25

Like their Brazilian and American counterparts, the Indians of Canada in the nineteenth century had "ceased to be of economic importance," and "were not needed in any capacity." We shall return to this below.

From 1860 (not until 1862 were the mechanics of administration completed) until 1913 the cost of Indian administration was borne primarily by revenues derived from Indian sources, such as the sale or lease of land. The limited funds available through these sources provides a comment on the "services" which would be made possible. It is necessary to keep in mind, of course, that the era of the late nineteenth and early twentieth centuries predates the Welfare State.

Kenneth Robinson notes that in 1919 the Colonial Office as such employed no medical, agricultural, technical, or scientific staff.[3] Lord Milner is reported as asserting in 1921 that the Colonial Office was the "Cinderella" of the great public departments. When economy measures were the order of the day, the Colonial Office fared even worse. In the colonial empire generally, colonies were expected to finance their own administration, defense being an important exception. Only with the advent of the Colonial Development and Welfare Acts (1940, 1945), does a significant shift in this policy begin to occur.

Diamond Jenness, characterizing Canada's Indian Affairs Branch in the 1920's and 30's, says, "Parallel with this failure to promote the political and economic welfare of the Indians went negligence in providing them with educational facilities."[4] The matter of Indian health was also neglected. This is the kind of charge frequently voiced by the nationalist leaders in the colonial and post-colonial eras of Africa. The Indian administration Jenness believed to have been a holding operation, "more concerned with preserving the *status quo* than with improving the economic and social status of the Indian or with raising their living standard."[5]

J. E. Hodgetts gives the following summary of the development of irrelevance in the Canadian Indian's experience:

The history of the Indian Department affords rather convincing evidence for the cynical view that where there are not votes administrative services are bound to be neglected or starved for funds. The affairs of the aborigines were of paramount importance in 1763 when the Proclamation which transferred control from French to British hands was issued. About one-third of that document was devoted to the future arrangements to be made for the Indians. Eighty years later, Indian affairs had been pushed so much into the back eddies of provincial politics that the Act of Union of 1841 forgot to provide for the annuities to which the Indians were entitled. The omission was discovered and remedied only in 1844. As late as 1850 Lord Grey observed to Elgin that he felt "that less has been accomplished towards the civilization and improvement of Indians in Canada in proportion to the expenses incurred than has been done for the native tribes in any of our other Colonies." From highly useful military assistants they had become expensive impediments to the white man's search for *Lebensraum*. Their degenerate and sometimes depraved state of existence bore embarrassing testimony to the neglect by the Great White Father who operated out of Whitehall.[6]

Commenting on the relation between political power and government attention, Jenness says the same thing in other words:

> Parliament, for its part, contented itself with voting whatever amount of money seemed necessary to fulfill Canada's treaty obligations towards its aborigines and then promptly forgot them, because their number was small and exercised no influence at the ballot box.[7]

The kind of attention received is also a point of similarity between Indian administration in Canada and British Colonial administration. If the Canadian Parliament's obligations to the Indians were protection from exploitation, safeguarding of health, education and training for eventual citizenship, then no one considered the question of the length of time that would be necessary to accomplish these ends. How long were the Indians to be "wards"? Jenness continues:

> The Indian administration did not ask: its job was simply to administer, and, like many a custodian, it was so involved in the routine of its administration that it forgot the purpose of its custodianship, especially since the fulfilment of that purpose would sign its own death-warrant. Neither did Parliament nor the Canadian people ask how long: their attitude seemed to be that the less heard of the Indians the better.[8]

Something like this situation pertained in the relation of the British Parliament to its colonial wards:

> Government in the Colonial Empire was bureaucratic government. Society and economy were shaped most powerfully by other agencies, native and immigrant. But the limits within which those agencies worked, narrow to the point of suffocation, or wide to the point of neglect, depended to an extent which it is now hard to imagine, on the bureaucracy, the hard core of that world apart that made up the Colonial Empire. For that bureaucracy, of course, the limits of manoeuvre were set by the brute economic and social facts as it saw them in each territory and also by its own attempt to work out for itself some rationale of its own activities.[9]

And again:

> Parliamentary intervention was limited not only because Parliament often had "a thousand more pressing interests to attend to" but because not many members of either house had direct personal knowledge of, or interest in, the colonies.[10]

By the mid-twentieth century—that is, since World War II—the Indians, now with some leaders sufficiently Western-educated to be informed of world events and at the same time retaining a sufficiently keen sense of their unique "Indianness," have begun to emphasize their separate identity. Aided by other expressions of self-awareness and anti-assimilationist ideas, they have begun to develop organizational skills in promoting their notion of their identity. It should be stated frankly here that most quotations of expressions of thought by "the Indians" are actually those of the articulate segment, which as in most societies are a minority. Some younger leaders today talk of Indianness, Indian personality, Indian culture, and Indian nationalism with its special contribution to make to world history and culture, and especially to Canada. These new Indian "militants" have their forerunners, though the significance of these precursors is dependent upon the significance of the future direction of events. The term "Indian" is used by these young men in the sense of Pan-Indian (c. f. Pan-African) and the most grand of their statements refer sweepingly to North and South America.

Of course these men may eventually lose their militancy and uniqueness, but they may not, and there is some evidence to support the latter prognosis. The fact that they exist at all in this day and age, after education and integration programs—many of these leaders function in the majority society—is noteworthy. They cannot be understood within the context of "Canadian history" but must be understood as a part of an on-going and long-developing aspect of the colonial parallel, of the Indian as seen consistently and continuously as the centre of his own history.

The colonial parallel approach has validity by any analysis until well into the nineteenth and even the twentieth century for a large part of the country, even if Indian nationalism, separate culture, and separate identity could not be argued successfully as concepts. If the colonial parallel approach is used as a model for telling the story of Canadian Indians, then an occurence such as the Indian participation in the War of 1812 becomes not only clearly explicable in Indian terms but assumes thereby a different aspect than it has in a strictly "Canadian" historical setting. In this case, Tecumseh, for example, as Josephy has portrayed him, becomes a patriot chief, joining with the British to check the encroachments of the Americans into the lands of the Indians of the Ohio Valley. In so doing he can be seen as trying to create a kind of Pan-Indian state or confederation of all the peoples between the Appalachians and the Mississippi. In attempting this he became a New World example of the kind of movements toward unity which were found in other areas—e.g. Ghana and New Zealand—in an early era of European impact. So Tecumseh prefigures Indian "nationalism."

A seemingly pervasive, but unspoken assumption is that the culture of the New World Indians was entirely static. The counterpart to this view is that any adaptation to the dynamic Western culture is therefore a loss of Indianness. Thus when a comparison of Indian culture in the 1500's is made with Indian culture today, the profound differences, which indicate acceptance of various aspects of Western culture, are taken to show the gradual but ultimately total assimilation of the Indian. However, the Indian can adapt and adjust without loss of his identity and self-awareness as an Indian. It may be relevant to point out that Western civilization has changed considerably since 1500, but it is still thought of as Western civilization. This is due in part at least to the acceptance of the notion that Western civilization is always dynamic, and being so, change is built into the definition. Indian culture, being *a priori* static, cannot, by the alternative definition, adapt. Of course the overwhelming evidence is to the contrary. Indian cultures have changed greatly in the last four hundred years and have kept their identity. We accept this continuity of identity for European culture because we can identify the threads connecting past with present. Indians believe, and the continued existence of their community is evidence, that a similar continuity exists within Indian life. This continuity has preserved certain values, it is asserted, which distinguish Indians from non-Indians.

Indians were also changing in pre-Columbian times. Archaeology, linguistics, and other historical sources reveal that material and non-material cultures were diffused from people to people. The European culture did not breathe life into previously static Indian cultures, though the white man did provide a yeast and a new stimulus for expansion and growth in many areas. He also gave the kiss of death when he embraced the Indian too closely. The scheme of contact (stimulus) and response seems to offer an open-ended approach to the narrative, consistent with the colonial parallel reconstruction. This method provides a basis for writing the history of the Indian in Canada from pre-Columbian times to current events, but it may not be the same as Canadian history.

One holding the popular view, which sees Indians as just another ethnic minority, will find it difficult to understand some of the responses of Indians to the Canadian scene. The Indian has never lost his identity with his own past, let alone with his own native soil, even in the depths of "irrelevance," when in the European view he had been "...reduced to the condition of forlorn aliens in the land of their ancestors," as one commentator put it in 1846.[11] For the most part, Indians have not followed the pattern of other ethnic minorities in seeking to merge their identity with the white majority. This is true for both the "melting pot" United States and the more pluralistic Canada. Obviously many individuals have in fact accepted assimilation, but the existence of several hundred thousand reserve and reservation Indians in the two countries, plus others who do not live on reserves but consider themselves Indians, indicates that most have not blended in either culturally or biologically. The rise of a militant "nationalist" element among Indians is only the latest manifestation which illustrates the colonial parallel.

The equation of assimilationist with progressive and the opposite of assimilationist with retardative or even retrogressive may lose more than just the negativeness of vocabulary if for assimilationist vs. non-assimilationist we substitute ethnic minority vs. nationalist. Not everyone would be willing to agree that nationalism is not retrogressive, but among many non-Western peoples it may represent a step toward great social, political, and economic participation in, even control of, the environment in which they live. For the young militant Indian, to be "nationalistic" may be unrealistic, given the Canadian or American context in which he operates, but it is understandable as a reaction to his experience.

When Indians are compared to an emerging or colonial people, the existence and future of reserves is also put into a different light. They become national homelands, which, if not carefully defended, could cease to exist. For the assimilationist this may not represent a situation to be avoided, but to the "nationalist," it may become a matter of serious concern. The Canadian or American majority may find this colonial interpretation difficult to appreciate or understand. It would certainly seem to pose a more exacting problem for solution, for it supposes more than one loyalty on the part of the Indian. Where it does not seem foolish it may be infuriating, as when Iroquois go to the United Nations seeking redress for alleged grievances.

A study of the policy of the Mexican government and people might make an enlightening contrast to the situation north of the Rio Grande. The Mexican government has made some effort to identify the history of Mexico with the history of the Indian. For Mexico the Indian has become "the symbol of oppression, and the redemption of the Indian has been a major aim of the Mexican Revolution. In sentiment, most Mexicans identify their nation with the Indian rather than the Spanish heritage."[12] The replacement of Las Casas by Cuauhtemoc as the symbol of the defender of the Indian is offered by Oscar Lewis as illustration of the above assertion. The Mexican Congress, on October 10, 1948, formally enshrined the new defender in his role by a decree: "We hereby express categorically that the heroic figure of Cuauhtemoc is the symbol of our nationality and therefore deserves the sincere devotion of the Mexican people."[13] The recovery of the Indian past as Mexico's past has only faint parallels in Canada. The past for Canada, as for the United States, lies primarily in Europe, and this is reflected by the sparse and generally uninformed and unsympathetic treatment of Indians in our history books.

In New Zealand, where the Maoris represent a sizeable minority and are likely to become a much larger one, greater efforts by whites to identify New Zealand history and culture with Maoris seems to be developing. William Cameron says of the situation there:

> Maori and *pakeha* alike must learn (and they seem to be learning) an even greater appreciation of this cultural heritage, both Polynesian and European, if they are to develop and maintain in health all their faculties, an indigenous multisocial culture in which matters of the intellect and of the spirit are prized as much as matters of bodily health and comfort may yet arise from the educational friction supplied by more intimate contact between the two most important cultures at present flourishing in New Zealand.[14]

From the foregoing examples we may see that by working from an examination of specific occurrences in the history of Indians, not in terms of a resistant minority or a minority problem of the majority, but as an example of native reaction to colonialism, a particular case may be better illuminated, the sorting out of motivations made easier, the issues and problems more clearly delineated, and the continuity of the past with the present brought more sharply into focus.

It is desirable, in understanding any self-conscious group, to attempt to see them as they see themselves, but it is also desirable to see the world as they see it. To do this it is useful to have at least for academic inquiry, a multicultural or pluralist view of the world. The point of view held by the group affects events. Without this flexibility of perspective the non-Indian may be continually amazed or perhaps frustrated by the response of the Indian to efforts to deal with him. Statements of irritation or fatigue on hearing of some difficulty of the "poor Indian" reflect the sense of frustration felt by many non-Indians who are unable to understand the Indian point of view.

Originally, of course, the British and French invaders had treated the Indians as nations or separate political identities and this relationship fitted the reality of the Indian situation. When new nations emerged from the old colonies a new situation was created for the whites, but the Indians did not change their status, except insofar as the whites changed it for them by changing their own status and becoming the new administrators of the natives. Laura Thompson summarizes the traditional policy of the United States Indian Bureau, and the changes it underwent, thusly:

> . . .at first the government treated the Indians as members of small nations in treaty relationship with the United States. But as more and more tribes were subdued and the Indians became less of a threat to white settlers, the government changed its attitude toward them. By breaking or amending treaties unilaterally it reduced the Indian tribal lands to a fraction of their former size, regarding the Indians as federal wards to be assimilated into the general population as soon as possible.[15]

Commenting upon the treaties as conventionally conceived of, and also drawing colonial parallels from South Africa and New Zealand, George Stanley observed in 1936:

> In general, the treaty system, as a method of governing the relations between savages and civilized peoples, has not been an unqualified success. Native treaties, intended to preserve native rights, maintain peaceful relations and promote harmony between natives and frontier settlers, have been attended in North America, as well as in South Africa and New Zealand, by misunderstanding, racial hostility, and, oftentimes, bloodshed. Hobson's Treaty of Waitangi with the Maoris, Stockenstrom's with the Kaffirs and those with the American Indians, although designed to meet different conditions, were all based upon the common assumption of free consent and the equality of the contracting parties. This assumption was unsound. The natives seldom understood the full implications of the contract. The disparity in power and interests between the signatories reduced the treaties to mere grants of such terms as the weaker people might accept without active resistance, and such treaties were, accordingly, rather the preparatives and apology for disputes than securities for peace.[16]

In 1871 the United States government ceased the practice of signing treaties with the Indians. Canada signed the last ones in 1923.

The Indian continued to be in a colonial relationship, but by the second half of the nineteenth century, the masters had been changed. The old White Father or White Mother was replaced by one closer to home, and the constituents of the new overlord had interests more frequently clashing with the interests of the Indian. In this situation the Indian may have clung to what he had, for fear of loss of identity, a fear based on an awareness of the new reality which made "Canadian" the norm, the native, the identity in Canada, and destroyed Indian identity as previously established in relation to the former colonial power. This apparent contradiction is to be understood as an effort to retain what tribal or group identity they had when in the earlier relationship. Without this bulwark they would be submerged into the new white nation. Thus the protestations of loyalty to Queen or King became a means to retain separate existence just as refusing to vote has been intended to achieve the same end.

The essay by G. F. G. Stanley, "The Indian Background of Canadian History,"[17] provides an astute summary of several aspects of the Canadian Indian in Canadian history. A sympathetic and concise overview, it illustrates the presentation intrinsic to accounts which take the modern state of Canada as the centre or focus for the historical narrative. In this presentation, in the seventeenth, eighteenth, and first part of the nineteenth centuries (varying geographically with the progress of white settlement), Indians figure prominently in the reconstruction. Government, church, and citizenry find that Indians constitute a large segment of their concern. It is therefore possible to speak of and write about an Indian background in which the Indian is in fact an important consideration in Canadian history.

The idea of the Indian background to Canadian history in the twentieth century is another matter, and is very questionable unless a meaningful synthesis of the history of Indians and whites is taking place. Since it is not, the notion of an Indian background to Canadian history must be expressed with considerable qualification. This was not so in the seventeenth, eighteenth, or early nineteenth centuries, in most parts of what is now Canada, but has become increasingly true since the last quarter of the nineteenth century. To have meaning, therefore, the term must be applied to the period prior to the 1870's and 1880's. Since that time the Indian background has become less and less significant. It is perhaps more valid to speak of various European national backgrounds to Canadian history, or the United States background for the mid-twentieth century, than it is to speak of Indian background. However, for a number of reasons this is ceasing to be so.

With the maturing of the nineteenth century, Indians became increasingly irrelevant, as we have seen above. This is illustrated in Professor Stanley's essay when the emphasis shifts from the "background" to what is only a segmental account of Canadian history. And it is in the nature of the account that this shift in emphasis should occur. From being a significant element in the account, the Indian, by the last quarter of the nineteenth century, has in fact become peripheral to Canada's history. Thus the later nineteenth century and the twentieth century might more accurately be called "The Indian in Canada." Tutelage, farming, disease, ignorance, malnutrition, are the catalogue of Indian "history" during this period. By the mid-twentieth century a "renaissance" among Indians has begun. They have started to regain their voice. The rise of Indian nationalism in Canada, though embryonic, has begun. Pan-Indianism is the international manifestation of this renaissance. All of this Professor Stanley sees and puts together into his provocative essay. In so doing he has been more than a little prophetic (the essay was written in 1952) about the course of Indian response in Canada since World War II.

But is this background? It might more profitably be studied as the proto-nationalism of the aboriginal minority in the midst of a predominant Canadian society. Terms borrowed from the language of colonialism and recent emergent nationalism must be used, and Stanley has used them, though the colonial parallel is not made explicit in his account. Conquest, subjection, colonial administration, degrees of assimilation or acculturation, renaissance, and nationalism or proto-nationalism and Pan-Indianism; this vocabulary is consistent with the colonial parallel. But Stanley's presentation, as we have already seen, must by its very nature come to a shift in emphasis which precludes a consistent narration of "Indian background." Indian history would present its subject neither as background to, not segment of the narrative, but as its centre.

In 1937 Diamond Jenness' essay, *The Indian Background of Canadian History*,[18] was published. Stanley's work may be said to have taken up the discussion about where Jenness left off, except that Stanley, seeing Indian "resurgence," has no framework for it in the Canadian context. Jenness's Indian background flows into Canadian history and then presumably becomes absorbed by it. Thus the wars of the Iroquois and their results "may be gleaned from any *Canadian history.*"[19] His description is of Indian peoples and their movements in the first millenium of the Common Era and of their disposition by the time of the arrival of Europeans. Part II of his essay, in which he deals with these topics is entitled "Prehistory of the Canadian Indian." The term "prehistory" seems to be used in deference to the types of sources employed in the reconstruction, since elsewhere in the essay the terms "prehistory" and "history" are more or less interchangeable. Part I, "Backwardness of the American Aborigines and Its Causes," is clearly aimed at prejudices and misinformation concerning the development or lack of development of Indian cultures. Much could be gained if it were required reading today.

In twentieth century Canada the Indian, though moving into the forefront, is still viewed as a segment. He is making his move in terms like those of emerging colonial peoples in other parts of the non-Western world (and some parts of the Western world too). Thus the

Indian is part of the larger topic of colonialism and imperialism, European expansion, and the story of the "Third World," as well as a segment of the nation in which he finds himself.

In Canada there is a dichotomy between the viewpoints of the Indian and the white majority. The Indian sees himself in the land and state differently from the way the white majority of the nation sees the Indian. And the corollary of this is that the Indian sees the white man differently from the way the white man sees himself in the land and state. Without insisting that we can define exactly either of these outlooks, the suggestion already put forward, that the Indian sees himself as the native and the white as the intruder, usurper, and disturber, seems a generally reasonable statement of an Indian view. The whites, on the other hand, do, among other things no doubt, see the Indian as another ethnic minority to be assimilated, or at least made to adjust to the dominant white society which is the norm and national condition of the country. This is not to say that all Indians or whites can be found to hold these views but as a working generalization of the prevailing attitudes, those outlined above are probably representative.

Given the contrast between the two outlooks and the historical relations between Indians and whites, and in view of the past and present response of the Indians, the notion of the colonial parallel, as has been set forth in various ways by a number of authors, would seem to offer a useful interpretation for understanding not only the historical relations between whites and Indians, but also to enable the student better to understand much of the present response of Indians. In Canada they are defining for themselves the nature of "Indianness," and they are drawn together by the common antagonism to Indian administration and to their inferior position in the society, and by a growing sense of cultural and racial affinity. The Indian is just now emerging from the period of irrelevance in Canadian life. Across Canada, the Indians had been swamped by the whites. This situation, varying in time and place, is changing, and for a variety of reasons. The reasons include philanthropy, guilty conscience, more enlightened views of the whites, as well as pressures resulting from political awareness, urban migration, education and organization, and population explosion on the part of the Indian. The history of the Indian since 1500 can be told as the story of the Indian's retreat from a position in which he had the initiative for the social, political, economic, and other aspects of his life, to a point where he lost the initiative in most of these areas, and where to retain the initiative in some, he was forced to practise them underground. By means of the economic linkage in the fur trade, the Indian was drawn into a relationship which made him lose (or by means of which he lost) the initiative first of all in his economic life, and then in his technological, political, and to some extent social and religious life. This loss of initiative reached its climax when the Indian was moved onto reserves.

On the reserves, particularly with the centralizing and federalizing of the Indian administration and the Indian Act of 1876, the main thrust of administrative policy was assimilation. As we shall see, the inefficiency and inadequacy of understanding the mechanisms of a society prevented this goal from being achieved, if in fact it was ever achievable short of police state methods. In the mid-twentieth century Indians have with growing effectiveness articulated their desire for the return of initiative in these various important facets of their lives to their own hands. This does not necessarily imply separatism or a new state within a state. What the Indians ask is the control of the management and shaping of the direction of Indian communities. The statements of most Indian public figures do not indicate that this recovered identity would be impossible of achievement within the framework of a flexible and understanding Canadian community. Where the present agitation will take the Indian and the white is not forseeable and does not fall within the scope of this essay. However, an attempt to outline the major phases of the relationship to date will be useful.

To attempt to write about Indian history is of course dangerous when documents from the Indian side are unexplored. Therefore the interpretation proposed must of necessity be general, but at the same time sufficiently clear-drawn to allow for more detailed formulation as well as elaboration of factual material as more research into the history of the Indian in Canada is undertaken.

FOOTNOTES:

[1] Douglas Botting, "Demoralized Indians of Brazil," *The Geographical Magazine*, Vol. XXXIX, No. 12 (April, 1967), p. 1002.

[2] Anna Lewis, *op. cit.*, pp. 173-174.

[3] Kenneth Robinson, *The Dilemmas of Trusteeship* (London: 1965), p. 30.

[4] Diamond Jenness, "Canada's Indians Yesterday, What of Today", *Canadian Journal of Economics and Political Science*, *Vol. XX*, No. 1 (Toronto: February, 1954), p. 99.

[5] *Ibid*, p. 96.

[6] J. E. Hodgetts, *Pioneer Public Service—an Administrative History of the United Canadas, 1841-1867* (Toronto: 1955), p. 205. See also Duncan Campbell Scott, "Indian Affairs, 1763-1841," in Adam Shortt and Arthur G. Doughty (eds.), *Canada and Its Provinces*, Vol. IV (Toronto: 1913): "It is a comment on the importance of the Indian question in those days that at least one-third of the Proclamation of 1763 should have been devoted to defining the protection to be accorded to the Indians and their property and trade." (p. 703).

[7] Jenness, *op. cit.*, p. 48.

[8] Jenness, *Ibid.*, p. 98.

[9] Robinson, *op. cit.*, p. 48.

[10] *Ibid.*, p. 50.

[11] The Aborigines Protection Society, *Ninth Annual Report, May 18, 1846* (London: 1846), p. 15.

[12] Oscar Lewis, "Mexico Since Cardenas," in Richard Adams and others *Social Change in Latin America Today* (New York: 1960), pp. 290-291; quoted from Jose E. Iturioga, *La estruction social y cultural de Mexico* (Mexico City: 1951). Lewis' further observation illustrates another aspect of the character of this Mexican identification with the Indian: "Even Mexico psychiatrists reflect the Indianist views with their idealized characterization of the Indian mother as the apogee of maternity, and the Spanish-colonial woman as cold and rejecting. Widespread Mexican hostility toward the Spaniard, and by generalization, toward most foreigners, is explained by the psychiatrists as hostility against the absent father figure. The Spaniard is still the symbol of the oppressor and no statues of Cortez are allowed in the country." (p. 291).

[13] *Ibid.*, p. 291.

[14] William J. Cameron, *New Zealand* (Englewood Cliffs, N.J.: 1965), p. 106.

[15] Laura Thompson, *Culture in Crisis* (New York: 1950), p. 146.

[16] G.F.G. Stanley, *The Birth of Western Canada* (Toronto: 1960), p. 213.

[17] G.F.G. Stanley, "The Indian Background of Canadian History," *Canadian Historical Association Annual Report*, (1952), pp. 14-21.

[18] Diamond Jenness, *The Indian Background of Canadian History*, Bulletin #86, Anthropological Series #21, King's Printer (Ottawa: 1937).

[19] *Ibid.*, p. 46. my italics.

4. A view of Canadian Indian History

The life of the Indian in North America began many millenia ago. Recent research into the question of just how many millenia pushes the date farther into the past, and figures such as 30,000 or 40,000 are seen. Throughout his existence in this continent the Indian has been adapting and changing to meet new environments, physical and social. His culture has not been static, nor has it been lived in total isolation. Archaeological remains provide the evidence for this conclusion.

Indians are known to have traded with one another, to have met and separated from one another as groups and communities, both seasonally and as a result of population movements. Changes in tools, weapons, dress, foods, house styles, and other material elements make it reasonable to suppose, and in many cases apparent, that other alterations, more and less sweeping in character, took place on the plane of non-material culture as well.

The history of the Indians of Canada for the last several hundred years has exhibited an acceleration of change. The impetus for change during this period has shifted from the Indian to the European. More and more, voluntary change has been replaced by coerced change. The Indian of today still finds himself faced with the necessity of adapting. In this respect his story is similar to that of the rest of our society. But the Indian is struggling with the problem of achieving a maximum degree of control over the alterations he will undergo. He is endeavouring to regain the freedom of choosing what, when, why, and how much.

Part of the process of answering such questions necessarily lies in the understanding of his own past and more particularly his past in relation to the non-Indians in Canada. Indians are thinking about and studying their past. They are beginning to write about it. When they do so they will bring insights to it which are not available to the non-Indian historian even though methods and sources may be the same.

Methods and sources are in any case expanding. Archaeological evidence, oral traditions, written accounts by travellers and missionaries are part of the "primary" material which the historian will employ. Historians will also be concerned with identifying and defining topics which best tell the story of the Indians. Topics such as land, treaties, cultural change, economics, will have to be dealt with, as will Indian/non-Indian relations, a broad topic which has significance for all the others. Throughout the research and construction of Indian history the focus will be on the Indian. He will be the central figure, not an assistant or "side-kick" or a background for the non-Indian.

In order to write such a history it will be necessary to propose eras or periods or meaningful subdivisions of the several hundred years of the account which do not conform to, and grow out of, categories or periods of history taken from the political, constitutional, economic, or other aspects of the history of the non-Indians. The usual periodization of Canadian history will most likely not fulfill these requirements, though there will be overlappings or parellels in parts. Most of these considerations will have to be dealt with by the historian of the Indian whether he be an Indian or a non-Indian.

Much has already been written about the history of the Indian in Canada. But much of what has been written does not centre on the Indian. It deals primarily with the non-Indian and the Indian's role in the story of the non-Indian in Canada. As such most of what has been said above about the content and arrangement necessary to Indian history has been lacking. Instead the accounts may be characterized as dealing with "The Fur Trade and the Indian," "The War of 1812 and the Indian," "The Riel Rebellion and the Indian," or "The Settlement of the Prairies and the Indian." These are not primarily concerned with the Indian. They deal with the making of Canada. The Indian is only a small part and so far not an integral part of Canadian history, though he has been more integral in the past than he is today, as we shall see.

The history of the Indian in Canada is a long one and capable of great elaboration and detail. This book presents only an outline of Canadian Indian history. It will attempt to explore topics and divisions of Indian history since the coming of the European.

The history of the Indian in contact with Europeans may be divided into four major phases that occur at different times as one views Canada from east to west and from south to north. Thus the first phase occurs in Nova Scotia and Eastern Quebec before it occurs in the Prairies. Similarly when the Prairies are experiencing the first phase the Maritimes may be experiencing the second or third phase or characteristic period of Indian history. These phases are defined in terms of the Indians' position in relation to the European. This does not imply some kind of rigid, mechanical, or inevitable progression. What we are observing here is simply that as the Indian culture, particularly its economy, was similar from the Maritimes to the Rockies and beyond, and as the European's interest in the Indians tended to begin with fur trading and then change to a desire for the removal of Indians to enable white settlers to practise agriculture, the same process tended to occur, repeating itself as the Europeans came in contact with each new and more westerly or northerly group.

The initial contact between the two peoples frequently led to an era of greater prosperity for the Indian. It was a period when the Indian was independent of the European, politically, socially, and economically. Voluntary acceptance of material objects (and non-material culture if desired) was possible for the Indian and for the Europeans. The Indian made his technology available to the European and accepted some parts of the European technology.

After this period of initial contact, the numbers and the impact of the European grew. The Indians had greeted the white men with hospitality in most cases, and did not realize the aims and intentions of their guests, nor appreciate that the European's coming was to prove to be an invasion, not a visit.

The Indians, of course, did not think of themselves as "Indians"; this category was invented and applied by the Europeans and eventually taken up by the people so denominated. Far from having a common sense of identity and purpose, they were very diverse in their political groupings. Though they were nearly all hunters and gatherers, differences of language and religion meant that they responded to the Europeans according to their own experiences and ambitions. To the Europeans, however, their resemblances outweighed their differences. This may in part be a reflection of the Europeans' notion of the Indians' role in the European economy, which was primarily their ability to provide furs.

Generally Indians were drawn deeper into the economy of the white. They found that the goods of the Europeans were in many instances preferable to their own. As they spent more of their time in the fur trade they spent less time providing for their subsistence by traditional means. They became more dependent on trade goods of all kinds. This trend weakened their political autonomy and tended to make them rely on Europeans for military aid and assistance. At the same time they attempted to resist European displacement of their new-found advantages as suppliers of furs. There was a tendency for competition to grow among the various Indian peoples when they did not work out patterns of co-operation in the acquisition and transportation of furs.

At the same time that they were changing their life through economic, military, and political means, they were being made the object of efforts to change their way of life—explicitly, through religious conversion. This frequently involved efforts to have them settle down to an agricultural life, or if already agricultural (and few Indians of Canada were), it sometimes meant resettling in a new village composed only or mostly of Christian Indians. In this way in the mid-seventeenth century Canada's first reserves were created.

With the creation of reserves and progressive settlement of Indians on them, the third phase of Indian relationship to the newcomers may be said to have begun. However, this situation was not reached all at once by all Indians, and technically some Indians are even now not on reserves. These are the Indians of the northern territories: to the south of the Yukon and the Northwest Territories, however, by the end of the nineteenth century most persons legally designated as Indian in Canada lived on reserves. This third phase (as are the others) is an analytical convenience, since the Indians were passing onto reserves and into political and economic dependence during a period of many decades from east to west. For the sake of convenience, and recognizing the arbitrariness of the choice, we may use the date 1876, that of the first Indian Act, as the beginning of what we may call the "colonial" period. From the point of view of the European, the Indian had become irrelevant. During this period, the European made himself the native and the Indian was transformed into an ethnic group. To themselves, however, though they may not have used the term, the Indians became a colonial people whose continent had been invaded and wrested from their control by foreigners. As a minority in his own land, the Indian saw the Europeans as a coercive and superimposed majority who were not the inheritors of the space they occupied but usurpers of Indian land and destroyers of Indian rights and heritage. /

In this situation they had lost control of the political and economic shaping of their lives. They were encouraged or coerced into continuing social and ideological change as well. And it was at this point that they appeared to be either dying out as a biological entity or as a cultural entity or both. Many Europeans, including Indian affairs administrators, missionaries, and teachers on reserves, spoke of the Indian as undergoing the transition, in isolation and on reduced land, to Westernization. What they did not see was the cohesiveness and tenacity of the Indian community and in most cases the capacity of the Indian to adapt without loss of identity. Because individuals assimilated to Canadian society and because the Indian culture clearly was not what it had been at earliest European contact, non-Indians assumed that Indians were being assimilated. This understanding of the situation served to underscore the prevalent view of Indian culture as static, and encouraged a tendency to interpret all change as evolution toward assimilation rather than as the creation of a new synthesis which continued to be Indian culture.

This third phase of the history of the Indian in Canada began to come to a close at the end of World War II. In the late 1940's and 1950's a fourth phase became apparent which was characterized by a sharp upturning of the Indian population, greater organizational activity, and the emergence of new leaders, not all of whom thought in terms of assimilation. Some Indians had begun to see themselves in a new light, that of non-Europeans elsewhere who in the two decades after World War II had gained political independence from colonial rule. References to the Indian as a colonial became more common, and concern with how to alter this condition began to be exhibited. Government responded to this resurgence. Indians were asserting themselves to regain as much control as possible of the decision-making processes which shaped their political, economic, and social affairs. Leaders and spokesmen emerged who could more and more effectively manipulate organizational techniques for protest. As we shall see, the roots of this fourth period lie deeply within the period preceding it. A closer examination of reports extending as far back as the middle nineteenth century indicate that some of these developments were already taking shape. Indian efforts to develop their own organizations for protest and redress of grievances, though little observed by non-Indians, were already in progress at least as early as the second decade of the twentieth century. As we shall see, issues which have now been brought to the attention of the non-Indian public, such as treaties, land title, hunting and fishing rights, and the preservation of Indian customs and religious practices, have long been features of a catalogue of Indian concern.

From within the structure of this rough framework of interpretation, we shall examine the history of the Canadian Indian.

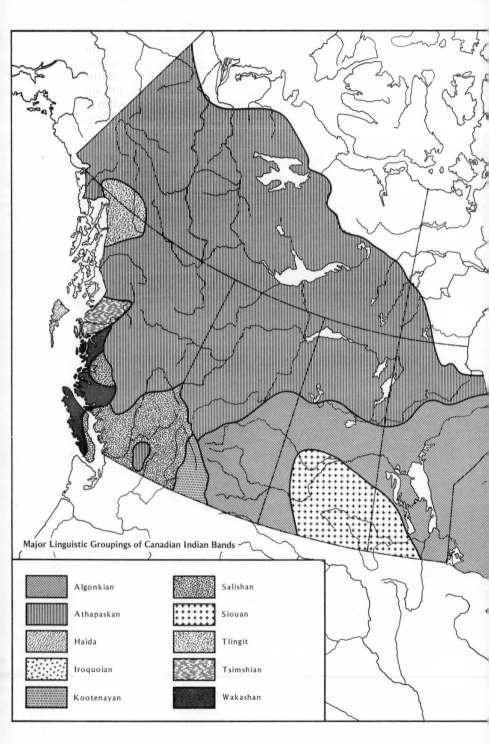

Major Linguistic Groupings of Canadian Indian Bands

Algonkian		Salishan	
Athapaskan		Siouan	
Haida		Tlingit	
Iroquoian		Tsimshian	
Kootenayan		Wakashan	

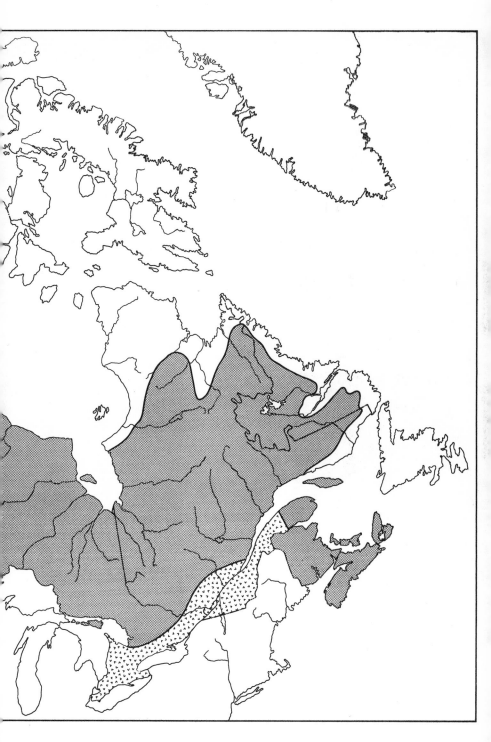

43

Figure 1.
Callicum and Maquilla,
Chiefs of Nootka
Sound, c. 1788

Figure 2.
Crowfoot, Chief
of the Blackfoot.

Figure 3.
Thayendanegea,
Joseph Brant,
Mohawk Chief.

Figure 4.
Kahkewaguonaby
Peter Jones.

44

Figure 5.
The renowned "Beardy"
speaking at pow-wow,
Fort Carlton.

Figure 6.
Waywaysacapo, Chief
of a band of the
Salteaux.

Figure 7.
Pi-A-Pot, a Cree
leader at the time of
the Second Riel Uprising.

Figure 8.
The leaders of the North-West Rebellion and their captors.
In the front row are Horse Child, youngest son of Big Bear;
Big Bear, Cree Chief; A. D. Stewart; Poundmaker, Cree Chief.

Figure 9.
Chief Big Bear,
leader of a band
of Cree in
Saskatchewan,
in chains.

Figure 10.
Chief Poundmaker who
reluctantly joined forces
with Big Bear in
the Métis uprising.

Figure 11.
Nelson's Cornet Band, Tsimshian
Tribe, Port Simpson, British
Columbia, at the turn of the century.

Figure 12.
"Old Sun" and
"Low Horn" of
the Blackfoot.

Figure 13.
Three Cree Chiefs.
Seated, Flying-in-a-circle,
Big Child, and Star
Blanket. Standing,
Chippewa Chief Osoup
and P. Houri.

II. THE PEOPLE AND THE NEWCOMERS

If and when Pan-Indianism seizes the imagination of the 40,000,000 native aboriginal peoples in the western hemisphere, we must not delude ourselves that the ripples at least of this continental movement will not reach the Indian nations living on the periphery. Indian nationalism has not been unknown in our history—the names of Pontiac, Brant, Tecumseh and Big Bear, spring to our minds. It may, under the inspiration of strong leadership, once more become an active factor in Canadian history.

G.F.G. Stanley, *"The Indian Background of Canadian History"*

Introduction

The prehistory and history of man in the New World, like that of the Old, begins with a long initial phase which vastly outweighs all the later phases in terms of simple time span. The later phases are increasingly shorter and increasingly accelerated in the rate of change they represent. Humankind probably entered the continental complex of North and South America before the last ice age. Travelling in small groups and on foot, these "Big-Game Hunters" made their way across the ice-bound corridor connecting Siberia with Alaska, quite unaware that they were in the process of populating a new world. Those other men whose descendant, Columbus, was to "discover" the New World, for the second time, in 1492, were in this early era living the same big-game-hunting life in Europe, somewhat more secure from the pressure of ice and consequent game movements and content for millenia to come with their native campsites.

The Paleo-Indians, as the first occupants of the New World are called, came armed. Their weapons are distinguished from those of their Old World counterparts by the presence on the projectile points of an elegant groove, called a "fluting," which may have served in hafting the little flint point to a wooden spear, which in turn may have been flung with the aid of a spear-thrower. Neither the arms which flung them, nor presumed wooden components have survived, but a variety of fluted points have been found in various parts of North America in sufficient numbers so that different groups and styles can be identified. It is possible that during the last interglacial phase, some of these men hunted the marshes and shores of enormous lakes in the area of what is now Canada, but the returning glacier of the last ice age obliterated whatever record they may have left. Nevertheless, there are a few finds of fluted points in the Great Lakes area to indicate that Paleo-Indian hunters penetrated as far north as they could.

There is another material industry in the leavings of what may have been a later group in the Old Cordilleran area of the West Coast. Canada-to-be was covered in the final phase by two vast glacial masses. One scraped off the Canadian Shield and left most of its former surface along the present northern border of the United States, an uneven frontier marked by the last of the glacial run-off in the form of the present Great Lakes. The other ran a great tongue of ice down the West Coast, culminating in a huge run-off trough at Puget Sound. (The interior run-off produced the gigantic waterfalls of Eastern Washington State and drove the Columbia River straight through the rising coastal mountain ranges.) Between these ice masses there seems to have been a more or less open corridor down which group after group of peoples moved into the New World. Phases of this movement left leaf-shaped points, smooth, rounded "bolas," and other characteristic stone arte-facts, and are thought to be the possible antecedents of the West Coast peoples. Other movements across the roof of Canada brought in the various Arctic peoples whose descendants are the Eskimos.

When the glaciers receded, they brought about changes not only in the topography but in the weather and consequently in the vegetation and animal population. Men were not immune to these changes, but they were affected culturally rather than physically. In other words, they responded to the changes, which were slow, by learning to hunt the new kinds of game, take fish from the huge glacial lakes, and work the new vegetable forms into sources of shelter and food. New kinds of weapons, tools, and equipment of every sort (including women's sewing implements) were developed to cope with new needs. The story of man in the New World as in the Old is the story of his genius at cultural adaptation. It should be added that the Paleo-Indians had brought from the Old World not only physical equipment but psychic equipment as well. There are strong similarities between what is known of the hunting-life-related religions and world-views of the New World and the Old. These express themselves in art as the "X-ray Style" and the "Animal Style," and in religion in the Shamanist elements common to both worlds.

The various cultural phases of the area now Canada included the development of metal-working in the form of cold-hammered copper implements of the Great Lakes region, among the earliest examples of metal-working in the world. Another innovation was introduced as a late wave radiating from the centre of Meso-American culture: a dif-fusion from the agricultural civilizations of Mexico. New World agricul-ture began at approximately the same time as it began in the Near East, at about 7,000 B.C.. It made use of an almost completely different set of vegetable forms: squashes, beans, and corn (maize) especially. The domestication of animals was never carried very far in the New World, and in Canada only the dog served man until the eighteenth century.

Associated with agriculture was cooking; a distinctive method was by boiling from within: vessels full of water and food were heated by plunging red hot stones into the midst of the substance to be cooked. Pottery was developed, based upon basketry and skin-bag prototypes. Associated with these developments was a new psychic set; a religion and world view with new emphasis on the cosmos: the four directions, heavenly bodies and their movements, the seasons, ritual sacrifice, and burial practices of increasing complexity. The use of tobacco for ritual purposes may be part of this complex as well. Attenuated forms of these developments reached what is now Canada, and the Hurons, Neu-trals, Tobaccos, and later the Iroquois people practised agriculture, as did some of their Algonkian-speaking neighbours. Most of Canada's Indians remained hunters, and even the agricultural peoples continued a mixed economy including regular hunting. This did not prevent the development of complex living styles and superb art on the West Coast and indeed among other non-agricultural peoples as well.

The enormously long period of continual development and change treated in this brief summary provides the background for what has ever been of most interest to white historians: the period of contact with Europeans which was brought about by the arrival of these new-comers. This period is one of extreme and continual acceleration of culture change for the Indian. But in the same way that continuities of physical, material, and psychic identity can be discovered in the deep past of the New World's first inhabitants, the Indians of Canada have retained their selfhood and identity in the new synthesis which they are achieving in the face of this latest and perhaps most drastic challenge to their being. They not only survive; they continue to be Indians to this day.

1. Treating with the Newcomers:

From earliest contact to the reserve/treaty period in the Maritimes and Eastern Canada.

The earliest date of contact between Indians and Europeans is uncertain. Perhaps it began with Vikings sailing along the northern coasts of North America. If so this meeting was short-lived and of little or no lasting importance. The beginnings of continuous, though initially sporadic, Indian relations with Europeans seems to have occurred in Newfoundland and the area of Eastern Quebec and the Maritimes. Here the Indians first saw Europeans, traded with them, and assisted them or resisted them according to the behaviour of the Europeans. They may have observed the cutting of their trees for fish-drying racks, firewood, and ship repairs. Exactly when these observations may have begun is uncertain, but the mid-fifteenth century is probably not too early a date.

In 1534 the Indians along Canada's eastern coast already knew what the whites sought in North America. Cartier, in that year, described how Indians held up a beaver skin attached to a stick, indicating their willingness to trade. They also kept their women-folk out of sight.

The impact of the European was often felt before face-to-face contact occurred. Two aspects of the European presence were particularly far-reaching in their effects. One of these was the fur trade and its concomitants, such as the introduction of European tools, weapons, clothes, foods, and the resulting alterations in Indian life which these caused. Another was the spread of European diseases in epidemic forms. These diseases—primarily small-pox, measles, and tuberculosis—to which the European had built up a degree of resistance or immunity, and to which the Indian had never before been exposed, wiped out large segments of Indian population when they struck, and they struck repeatedly.

These and other influences affecting Indian life helped to reshape Indian cultures, which as we have seen were already altered from various previous forms before they were first described by European writers. The earliest extensive descriptions begin in the sixteenth century, though Indians were presumably being influenced by European culture either directly or indirectly for at least seventy years (probably many more) before that time. How existing culture patterns were adapted to new influences is illustrated by the way in which the fur trade was grafted into the life of the Huron Indians. Some historians have suggested that by turning to fur trading some of the eastern Algonkian-speaking Indians largely changed their pattern of gaining a livelihood. It is postulated that in response to the potential wealth available through fur trading, the Micmac Indians, who prior to the arrival of the Europeans had been oriented toward fishing, sealing, and the hunt for sea mammals, changed their pattern to expand their traditional three-month period of hunting over the land. In doing so they may have reduced their food supply and made themselves more susceptible to famine.

An early seventeenth century French writer, Lescarbot, asserts, with what some writers regard as exaggeration, that Indians on the eastern coast of Canada spoke a language which by that time was "half-Basque" as a result of long and intensive contact with Europeans. This suggests that Lescarbot was aware of previous culture changes and was attempting to account for them. Other elements introduced into the Indian vocabulary included French curses and obscenities. Jesuits reported that the Indians gave indecent words to the priests who were trying to learn Indian vocabulary to be used in sermons. On another aspect of the new impact, writers report that Indian-French *Métis* at this early date were sometimes referred to by a term also employed to designate people from St. Malo. Whether this was a generic term for all French-speakers or may indicate a more particular knowledge of local differences among the French is not clear.

The case of the St. Lawrence Iroquoians is another and much written-about topic in Indian history relating to early effects of Europeans on the Indian. When Cartier sailed up the St. Lawrence in 1535 he found two Indian settlements, Stadacona, the site of the present Quebec City, and Hochelaga, the site of the present Montreal. The Indians in these settlements practised agriculture, lived within the palisaded walls of their villages, and possessed a culture and language which scholars agree affiliate them with the Iroquoian cultural and linguistic group. However, when Champlain visited the same vicinities in the first decade of the seventeenth century, he found no villages at these locations. What specifically caused them to disappear may never be known for certain. Many writers speculate that their removal, forced or voluntary, is part of the reshaping of Indian life following upon their aquisition of guns and other trade items. Perhaps, it is argued, these sedentary peoples had been forced out of their places by the now technologically superior, because European-equipped, Algonkians. Prior to this the agriculturalists may have had the advantages inherent in a more stable food source—a larger population and the more elaborate organisation associated with it. Their removal sometime between 1525 and *circa* 1600 was followed by the occupation of those areas by Algonkian-speakers whose economy was based on hunting.

The earliest continuous contact between Indians and Europeans occurred on the shores of the fishing banks of eastern Canada. The Indians of Newfoundland and Labrador met seamen engaged in dry-curing their fish. Dry-curing involved coming ashore to obtain space and tim- ✗ ber, and then remaining on land and building racks and sheds on the areas thus cleared. All of these activities plus additional destruction of forests by fires accidental and deliberate (to aid clearing) seem to have produced a negative response from the local Indians. Their response prompted the Europeans to describe them as "cruel and austere," and "impossible" to have dealings or converse with. Whatever the Indians did to show their unhappiness with the European's behaviour, the latter responded, as he frequently did in later times, by blaming the Indian. Assuming that these Newfoundland aborigines were the ill-fated ✗ Beothuks who by the middle of the nineteenth century had been completely exterminated, we can get some notion of the origins of the early relations which eventually led to their annihilation.

In the second half of the sixteenth century the area of the Gulf of St. Lawrence and southward to Nova Scotia witnessed a shift from wet-curing to dry-curing. Wet-curing had been done for the most part aboard ship, with less frequent activity on land, for it involved the use of salt rather than drying for the preservation of the fish. Greater contact began to occur between Europeans and the Indians of those areas when this shift occurred, and the development of the fur trade followed. It was perhaps at this time that the cultural changes speculated upon above, occurred. It is certainly in this period that the St. Lawrence Iroquoian relinquished their places on the lower St. Lawrence and, as we have seen, this is thought to have been linked to the newly established fur trade.

To follow the earliest history of Indians in contact with the Europeans we must return to the eastern coastal areas.

Elements which were to recur in Indian-white relations appeared in the early-seventeenth-century Maritimes. There, for example, the Jesuit missionaries began their work of converting the Indians—the Micmacs and their allies, the Malecites. Some of these people had been met by Cartier in 1534; one of the Micmac leaders, Membertou, told Champlain that he remembered Cartier's visit. At that time the Micmacs occupied all of Nova Scotia and the coastal areas of New Brunswick. In 1612, Father Biard, a Jesuit missionary to the Micmacs, estimated the combined Micmac-Malecite population at about 3,000. The early attachment of these Indians to the French *via* the Jesuits, and the tenacity and continuity of this connection, became an important factor in shaping the early history of the Maritimes.

The French treatment of Indians, and their racial and cultural attitudes toward them, have frequently been written about. Their relations with the Micmacs, Malecites, and Abenakis, form an early illustration of French behaviour. It is usually pointed out that the French did not look down on the Indians or other non-whites as being racially inferior, an attitude which was the reverse of that often characteristic of the English. The Jesuit evangelists stayed among their flocks as spiritual ✗

leaders and political advisors. Some also seemed to act as military advisors. The religious attachment made it possible for political ends to be served through their personal influence. The government of New France worked through the priests where possible, including using them to prosecute war against the English.

Writers on the conduct of the Indians usually pass derogatory judgements on their method of warfare while describing the same behaviour on the part of the Europeans as deviant from the norm. Referring to the French and English, J. B. Brebner wrote in 1927, with what was meant to be objectivity, that they "frequently allowed the savagery of the Indian methods of warfare to overcome their own more decent and civilized instincts."[1] The assertion of European moral superiority in the face of the record of Indian-European relations is a thesis which most historians have found too congenial to abandon, however one-sided the evidence.

The Indians found themselves threatened by the continual growth of the New England colonies from about the second quarter of the seventeenth century. They formed alliances among themselves, such as the Abenaki confederacy, and sought aid from the French. The French settlers were few in number and the main thrust of the economy was the fur trade. This meant that the Indian was not threatened in his lands as he was in adjacent New England. Warfare between English and Abenaki in the late 1670's led to the Abenaki migration into Canada and Acadia, and into alliance with the French. In the 1680's when their neighbours, the Penobscots, warred with the English, they did so with arms supplied by the French.

Governor Thomas Power of Massachusetts, writing in the eighteenth century, observed that the English,

> ...with an insatiable thirst after landed possessions, have got Deeds and other fraudulent pretences, grounded on the abuses of Treaties, and by these Deeds claim possession, even to the exclusion of the Indians, not only from their Hunting Grounds (which with them is a right of great consequence) but even from their house and home...Upon these pretences they have drove the Indians off their lands: the Indians unable to bear it any longer told Sir William Johnson that they believed soon they should not be able to hunt a bear into a hole in a tree but some Englishman would claim a right to the property of it as being his tree...This is the sole ground of the loss and alienation of the Indians from the English interest, and this is the ground that the French work upon; on the contrary the French possessions interfere not with the Indian's Rights, but aid and assist their interest and become a means of their support.[1]

The Indians, then, for their own advantage became engaged in wars of international scope. The Indians also profited from gifts from their French allies. Since they did not think of themselves as "Indians" but as members of this or that local grouping there were usually Indian allies on both the French and English side. In this way the principle of letting Indians fight Indians became a recurring fact of Indian history from the time of early European contact in Canada. The following quotation illustrates both the moral superiority assumed for and by whites and the rationale which emerged from this attitude to explain and excuse the European's practice of employing Indians. The era described is that of late seventeenth century and early eighteenth century warfare between England and France in upper New England and Nova Scotia: "The Indians, too, saw their opportunity and added the peculiar terror which their presence invariably introduced into American warfare. In 1712 a band of Iroquois *had* [my italics] to be brought in from New York for a time to meet them with their own techniques and weapons."[3] Iroquois conflict with Micmac and Malecite was a recurring phenomenon, and the Micmac and Malecite developed an attitude of strong hostility to the Iroquois, who became for many years a hated and feared real or potential opponent.

While English settlements were small, the Indians resisted their encroachments and carried out raids against them. It was a war for survival for the Indians, too. Though the wars in Europe had assigned Acadia (renamed Nova Scotia) to the English, in the early eighteenth century as one of the terms of the Treaty of Utrecht (1714), the Micmacs were unwilling to see their land slip from them. Their resistance continued into the mid-eighteenth century and produced the figure of a priest-captain in the form of the Jesuit missionary, Father LeLoutre. On a number of occasions he acted as their military commander and spiritual adviser as well.

That the Indians regarded themselves as superior is attested to by reports of the Jesuits. The obvious desire for liaison which the French exhibited reinforced this conclusion of the Indians. Economic interdependence developed quickly as the Indians took up European tools, weapons, clothes, and food. Each became indispensable to the other. Other consequences followed the Indian contact with the Europeans. The heightened rivalry among groups competing for the furs and the resultant conflicts led to population decline. But disease also accelerated this frequent accompaniment to the European presence, as for example the epidemic of 1694 in Acadia. The Indians were not slow to make the connection between disease and the European, though the cause and effect which they supposed differed from our own. The priests' enthusiasm to send people to heaven was impelling them to kill Indians, the Indians concluded. They also noted that the disease broke out wherever the priests went.

The European religious forms into which the Indians entered were interpreted by them as being political as well as spiritual. Baptism they took as a solemnization of their alliance with the French. The advantages of the French connection were obvious. They were "eager to be initiated into the French tribe."[4] Elements of this reaction by the Indians recur across Canada. Conversion also meant the acquisition of French arms: that is, the French provided only Christianized Indians with guns and ammunition. Adherence to Christianity cut across tribal lines and introduced a new tie between peoples. Indians grouped together into intertribal alliances as the rivalry between French and

English grew. As we have seen, the advantages of the French over the English were readily apparent to those eastern Algonkian-speaking Indians who witnessed or received reports of the land occupation of the English.

Perhaps the most notorious of the clerical figures encouraging Indians against the encroaching English was the above-mentioned Father Le Loutre. His ingenuity in creating incentives for Indian antagonism toward the English must have reached an apex when he instructed the Micmac that the English had crucified Christ. It is paradoxical that any Jesuits should have been employed in such work. In the mid-seventeenth century, members of the same order had contributed to the tenacious stereotype of Indian ferocity and barbarity through their relations of Jesuit tribulations at the hands of the Iroquois in what is today southern Ontario.¹ A half-century later, in Acadia, through the exigencies of war, their role had been reversed and they were abetting raids and war parties. In both circumstances the extreme experience and activities of a few men have been formed into the basis of generalizations about many men, Indians and Jesuits alike.

Evidence exists, however, that the Indians attributed their alliance with the French to something more than the influence of the Jesuits. The French connection meant greater liberty to continue their traditional way of life, with selected modifications, and less pressure for their land. They told the Engish Governor of Nova Scotia in 1719: *"Nous voulons avoir notre pays libre."*⁵ A further aspect of Indian-French relations is revealed by Brebner's comment that the Acadians for their part regarded the Indians as a nuisance, and that the Indians made trouble between the *habitants* and the English, "but their visitations and activities were an intermittent, and apparently necessary evil."⁶

To the new colonial government in Nova Scotia after the British takeover, the Indians were a defence problem. The alliance between the Indians and the French continued to be a threat. As we have already seen, the British resorted to engaging the Mohawks against the Micmac and other Indians allied with the French. In 1710 the British threatened to bring in their Indian allies, though the context in which they made the threat was by no means complimentary to those allies. They told the French: ". . .as we abhor the Barbaritys of Your Savage War, so we hope you will give us no Occasion to copy after you in this respect."⁷ In 1711-12 Indians were engaged on the British side. At that time it was thought that the territory would soon be passed back to France.

The British, on the other hand, would have liked to remove the French, but despite the warfare saw them as a kind of check on the Indians. The traditional means employed by the British to win the favour or at least the quiescence of the Indians consisted of sending officials to reserves to reassure or threaten them, or of calling the Indians to Halifax for one of these purposes or for the distribution of presents. The importance of the Indians during this period is illustrated by the constant requests for more money for presents from the home government./

During the war of the Austrian succession the threat of attack led to proposals for the creation of additional forts and increased garrisons as well as bounties on individual Indians killed. By the end of the 1740's some of the Indians changed to the British side. The French were no longer so strong and, with a pragmatism which saw the pointlessness of continued resistance, the Indians changed their alliance. Fighting did continue in the Chignecto Isthmus under the leadership of the Abbé Le Loutre. A price was put on the head of Indian men, women, and children, though they were still regarded as the pawns of the French. R. O. MacFarlane states: "The early success of the French missionaries and traders in comparison with efforts of their British competitors made the Indians willing tools in the hands of the French."[8] This view tends to diminish while not dismissing the fact that even "willing tools" have their own motivation. Could they have been made tools if they had been unwilling? It ignores any idea of the legitimacy of Indian concern since they are in the way of the people who are the "real people" who live in the area and the Indians and French are holding up the "real" course of events and developments. There is a grudging acceptance of Indian motivation in MacFarlane's further statement that the Indians ceased to fight when they found they would be unable to dislodge the British: ". . .thereafter many of them attempted to reconcile themselves to their new masters."[9]

The Indians may be said to have experienced a new challenge to their existence. New means of resistance had to be worked out to meet the new circumstances. A report of 1774, quoted by MacFarlane, stated: "Since the French have been expelled from the neighbourhood of this Province, they [the Indians] have become quiet and well-disposed."[10] The French Governor, Duquesne, had understood the Indian's position better. During the war he had written to Le Loutre:

> . . .we should never permit our Abnakis, Malecites, and Mickmacs to make peace with the English. I regard these savages as the mainstay of the colony, and in order to keep alive this spirit of hatred and revenge, we must remove every occasion of allowing it to be bribed; and the present position of Canada demands that those nations which are strongly connected should strike without delay, provided the order shall not appear to come from me because I have precise instructions to remain on the defensive.[11]

After 1760 the Indians of Nova Scotia found themselves in a new relationship with the government. No longer defenders of their homeland they were still sufficiently numerous in relation to the whites and sufficiently important for the economy to require some special attention. Still they were by no means under close supervision and the main efforts of the government were to keep them happy by setting up a system of trading posts under a provincial monopoly. By this means it was hoped their confidence would be gained and renewal of fighting prevented.

This sytem was ended in 1764 as in its place free trade was provided for European merchants. For the Indian, however, the beginnings of a more elaborate administration were coming into being. A Superintendent of Indian Affairs for the Province was created. Assistant Superintendents were appointed for local areas. In 1768 the Province gained control of Indian Administration. The Indians of Nova Scotia were about to be launched into the sea of Indian administration troubles. Schemes to make the Indians economically viable and pressures on land were in evidence by the 1780's. An influx of loyalists after 1783 reduced the area for hunting and trapping. It also led to encroachments on Indian lands. They responded by requesting tracts for cultivation. The government proposed that they make and sell tools to the immigrants. Unfortunately this scheme proved impractical, as the immigrants did not have the money to buy the tools. A system of relief was instituted.

By the end of the eighteenth century the Micmacs had become economically dependent. As late as the American Revolution, moreover, they were wooed as prospective allies. The Micmacs did not join the Malecites and Penobscots against the British. The role of the chief was bolstered by his being given official recognition. Under the impact of European trade he had suffered some demotion of status. The relief provided by the province was extremely meagre. The Nova Scotia government tried unsuccessfully to get the British government to bear the cost of Indian administration, as the province thought it too heavy to be borne.

As elsewhere around the world when Europeans expanded, land became a major issue of concern to the indigenous people and an article much sought after by the whites. In 1761 and 1762 Indians had been guaranteed land for hunting. In 1783 licences were issued to some Indians for lands they requested for settling on. These, however, were not grants but tickets of location. They were given as confirmation of existing settlements or on promise to farm. The Indian was not acknowledged as owning the land outright. Indian apprehension grew. This situation led to the creation of the first reserve in 1786 at St. Margaret's Bay. The three Indians, including a chief, to whom the plot of five hundred acres was given, received "direct title," and not merely a "ticket of location" or a "license for occupation." After 1786 Indians were encouraged to settle down as farmers. Blankets, seed, and equipment were made available to those interested in cultivation. However, the Indians did not take readily to farming. Elizabeth Hutton says they ". . .often failed to live up to their promises to the authorities of cultivating the soil."[12]

In 1800 a commission was created to study the Indian situation in Nova Scotia. This study led to three recommendations, one of which was the creation of permanent settlements. Not very much came of these recommendations, however, and in 1815 another report on Indian affairs was written. This report dealt primarily with the lands which had already been allotted to the Indians at Shubenacadia River, Pugwash, Antigonish, St. Margaret's Bay, and Chester. The report called for reserving of land frequented by the Indians.

In 1820 the creation of reserves in Nova Scotia reached a new stage when a new report called for grants of land for Indian reserves and for these reserves to be held in trust by local magistrates. Still another report tabled in 1827 provided the system for the allotment of land within a reserve. Elizabeth Hutton finds that this acceleration of interest in Indians was part of the humanitarianism of the ruling classes who were moved to "alleviate" Indian "suffering and destitution."[13] The growth of concern about aborigines around the British Empire in the late eighteenth and early nineteenth centuries thus had its manifestations in Nova Scotia. By the mid-1830's Nova Scotia had generally a "broad outline of the scheme of Indian reserves." The Micmac was forced to settle down or starve: "...to surrender himself to dependency upon the white man and to accept land on a reservation," as Elizabeth Hutton puts it.[14]

Studies made in 1911 showed that the Micmacs retained a memory of warring, particularly with the Mohawks. Though they had various stories of defeating the Mohawks by battle or by magic, they also exhibited an extreme fear of the Mohawks which seems to belie their assertions of unbroken success in combating them. Malecites and Penobscots also had stories of warring with the Mohawks.[15] Tales of Mohawk atrocities can be explained in part by the eighteenth century alliance of Micmacs and Malecites with the French in conflict with the Mohawks and the English. Among the Indians, warfare other than that involving Europeans usually resulted from a drive for revenge or prestige, not for land and property. In the seventeenth century the Micmac, Abenaki, and Malecites were allied against the English. In the mid-eighteenth century the Wabnaki Confederacy was formed by the Micmac, Malecite, Penobscot, and Passamoquoddy, all of whom had been victims of Iroquois attack. In the nineteenth century, however, the Mohawks of Caughnawaga and Oka formed an alliance with the Wabnaki Confederacy and regular meetings were held at Caughnawaga, and the Micmac sent delegates as late as 1872.

To the west, in the St. Lawrence River Valley, several Indian tribes were in contact with Europeans or with European cultural elements a few decades later than the occurence of initial contact on the Atlantic Coast. Indians were in regular trade relations with Europeans at Tadoussac by the middle of the sixteenth century. This settlement became the fur-trading centre on the St. Lawrence River by that date. In the mid-sixteenth century it was being observed that the Indians had gained sophistication from their experience in dealing with the white traders to know that it was more advantageous to wait for two or more ships in the harbour: bargaining for the best price between competing potential buyers brought them better results.

The Montagnais were one of the first peoples of the lower St. Lawrence River to come into contact with the European culture. They were seriously affected by the new conditions this contact created. Scholars believe that, as a result of the new opportunities opened up by the fur trade, the Montagnais changed their tradition of holding land as family or group holdings to individual holdings. They early acquired guns from the French and used these to good advantage against their neighbours. The Eskimos, who as late as the seventeenth century occupied the north shore of the St. Lawrence River down to a point opposite Anticosti Island, were driven northward and off the north shore altogether, up to the Newfoundland coast. In addition, Naskapi Indian neighbours of the Montagnais were driven northward and northeastward by the better armed Montagnais. Indians along the St. Lawrence River may have relied much more heavily on marine sources for their food and other needs, like the Eskimo, prior to the impact of the fur trade. If so, some writers think, they may have been exchanging a more precarious food source for a more stable one in order to get the pelts which, while they lasted, would supply them with everything.

Research on the history of the villages of Stadacona and Hochelaga has left many questions unanswered though most writers agree that the disappearance of the Iroquoian-speaking peoples along the St. Lawrence must be related to the European trade, as stated above. Perhaps Algonkian neighbours wiped out one or both settlements or forced them to withdraw. The Algonkians may, it is speculated, have gained a physical and technological supremacy over the Iroquoians through their acquisition of tools and weapons. (The French were much less willing to trade in guns than other products.) It has been asserted that Stadacona was more dependent on hunting than was Hochelaga. If so, competition with neighbouring Algonkians may have seen the balance tip in the Algonkians' favour, as they were better equipped. On the other hand, the two settlements may themselves have been in competition by the second half of the sixteenth century, so that their own rivalry led to their termination. Their inhabitants may have retreated to join Iroquoian-speakers further west and/or south, e.g., the Hurons.

As in coastal Canada, Indians became middlemen in supplying more remote groups in the interior. The interior peoples received the cast-offs of those closer to the Europeans. The equipment which had been used by those in more immediate contact became the trade items for dealing with the more remote peoples. Indian middlemen were reluctant to lose their markets and sources of supply, and attempted to discourage French penetration into the continent. The Indians at Stadacona, for example, tried to convince Cartier that he should not proceed farther upstream.

The most significant tribe of middlemen in the first half of the seventeenth century were the Hurons. They were a people well suited to trading and had a tradition of having been traders prior to the coming of the European: corn was the main item of that commerce.

Their villages contained a population which is variously estimated as between 15,000 and 30,000 people in the early seventeenth century. This numerical strength, added to their strong economic base, made them a powerful group (more numerous than the French were to be for several decades after Champlain's first important linkage with them in the joint Huron-Algonkian-French expedition against the Iroquois in 1609). Archaeological evidence suggests that the Hurons were already part of a trade in European goods in the second half of the sixteenth century and some connections probably existed with the St. Lawrence Iroquoians. Evidence of aboriginal trade dates back to A.D. 900.

The Huron confederacy may have begun to take shape in the early fifteenth century, but if so the latest additions to it probably did not long antedate the arrival of the French in the area. It is thought that the Rock and Deer Tribes (the Huron consisted of a confederacy of four tribes, the other two being the Bear and the Cord) had joined the Huron confederacy not long before French arrival, and evidence exists that some had come from east of historic Huronia. The most easterly of the four tribes, the Rock people, were also the first to engage in trade with the French.

Huronia was geographically well suited for an important trading position. It was located on the shore of Georgian Bay along established canoe routes, thereby easily accessible to their northern neighbours, the hunting tribes of Algonkian-speakers. The French observed this trading relation in 1615, and twenty years later Huronia was described as the granary of the more northerly tribes. Champlain readily appreciated the importance of these people to French plans for expansion and control, and concluded a treaty with them in 1615. He did this in spite of another middleman group, the Algonkians of the Ottawa River, who saw their position being threatened by the direct contact with the powerful and well-situated Hurons.

After 1615 the Hurons were drawn more and more deeply into the fur trade. Where they could not produce furs from their own territory, they provided them from others who traded furs for corn. The Huron also supplied the French with this necessary foodstuff as well as furs. They in turn successfully prevented the French from trading directly with their two neighbours, the Tobaccos and the Neutrals.

The Hurons and the Europeans practised between themselves the Indian custom of placing young men or boys with friendly tribes, and after 1615 Europeans were to be found living among the Hurons. The main contact in the early years was probably with the Rock Tribe, but in later years the Bear tribe became more closely linked to the Europeans through trade and through large numbers of conversions to Christianity. The presence of French *coureurs de bois* and other adventurers was a source of great discomfort to the Jesuits, who were trying to convert the Hurons. They had succeeded by 1632 in making themselves the main if not the exclusive agents of Christian evangelism.

The Hurons suffered the presence of the Jesuits, so necessary for retention of the trade connection with the French, even when in the 1630's they linked the Jesuits to the epidemic which reduced the Huron nation to about one-half its previous population. The Hurons, perhaps demoralized by the epidemic, were certainly under more intensive influence from Jesuits and other Europeans in the 1630's than they had been in the previous decade. A sizeable minority of Christian converts was to be found among them by the middle of the 1640's. Accompanying these important ideological changes was a polarization of attitudes toward the French linkage which led to efforts to form a trading agreement with the Iroquois or some elements of them. These efforts failed, due to resistance on the part of all parties effected—Hurons, Iroquois, Jesuits, and French. When the attack of the Iroquois came in 1649 and the Hurons were dispersed, many of the Rock and Deer tribes joined the Iroquois. These were the groups which had been the most anti-French. Many of the remaining Hurons moved to Christian Island where they starved due to food shortages on the quickly over-populated island. Some Hurons joined the French further east and settled in communities that have continued into our own day. Others went westward, some joining themselves to the Ottawa Indians, who had been their traditional partners in the fur and corn trade. These people became a successor middleman group when the Hurons ceased to hold their predominant trading position. The fur trade gradually moved westward, drawing more and more Indians into the economic system of the Europeans and permanently altering their material and non-material culture.

In less than three decades, the Hudson's Bay Company was to leapfrog the French trade in the Great Lakes-St. Lawrence area by establishing contact with the Crees. Although the Hurons became less important to the history of the white man in Canada, they did not cease to exist, or to have a separate identity, even when they joined with other groups. A closer examination of their experiences during the subsequent period is therefore called for.

During the first half of the seventeenth century, the Hurons had succeeded in maintaining their position as middlemen in the fur trade, as we have seen. Their settled villages and agricultural base gave them advantages in size and location, as well as in having a staple food to offer nomadic peoples in exchange for furs. This position was not lost until the ravages of disease had greatly reduced their population in the 1630's. Combined with this development was the fact that the Iroquois to the south had by this time exhausted their own beaver resources and were raiding northward in an effort to gain new fur sources. The defeat and dispersion of the Hurons by the Iroquois illustrates the way in which the fashions of Europe and the European rivalries drew the Indians into greater involvement with the white man and made them more destructive of each other in the process. The nature and scope of Indian warfare must therefore be understood in terms of European influences as well as native culture.

The French had feared that an alliance between the Hurons and the Iroquois would take the fur trade away from them and send it down the Hudson River. The events of 1649 ended that threat, but they also broke the pattern of French trading relations. As a result of the Iroquois attack, the Hurons were dispersed—some to amalgamate with the Iroquois, some to Michigan as Wyandots, some to the islands of the Upper Great Lakes, some to Indian settlements in the vicinity of Quebec City, and others to attach themselves to the Ottawa and the more northerly Algonkian-speakers. The attack also ended the possibility of their becoming a Christian Indian nation under Jesuit leadership and direction. The Hurons had seemed to offer the best potential for such a development of any of the Indians so far encountered by the Europeans. They had the particular advantage of being sedentary and agricultural. This meant that they were easier to evangelize and to teach both the Gospel and European agriculture. Here the Jesuits could attempt on a grand scale what they were in the 1630's and thereafter beginning to attempt farther east.

As with other colonial peoples, too close involvement with the Europeans had drawn the Hurons into a complex of rivalries and tensions which destroyed them as a separate political entity. The destruction of Huronia resulted from the impact of European influences which led to the pitting of native people against native people. Whatever influence the presence of the Europeans had in stimulating the creation of Confederacies was counteracted by the fact that the tensions and contradictions arising from the contact situation battered the Indian societies and inter-tribal relations, so that many were shattered and broken and all were altered. Perhaps a united sense of their Indianness, and common political and military action, might have saved them. By the eighteenth and early nineteenth centuries unified action such as that of Pontiac and Tecumseh was too little and too late.

The Hurons were not, however, annihilated in the usual sense of that term (killed off as in genocide), for though many were killed in the attacks, many were also dispersed. Some died of starvation while hiding from the Iroquois in the islands of Georgian Bay, as we have seen. Another group, as mentioned above, made their way east to Quebec City. There they occupied several sites. Their numbers in the early 1650's were about six hundred and dropped to one-quarter of that figure within the next two decades due to defections to the Iroquois and raids by the Iroquois. In the middle of the 1670's the group was bolstered in numbers by the adhesion of Mohawks who had been converted by the Jesuits. This number fell to less than 150 by the mid-1680's but the little group did not die out. In 1697 they made their last transfer of residence. This time it was from Ancienne Lorette to Jeune Lorette, still in the vicinity of Quebec City, indeed on the lands of the same seigneury. In 1793 the land was transferred to the Hurons with the provision that the Indians were not to sell or otherwise alienate it.

By this means some Hurons continued to experience the life of tutelage under the Jesuits. They were now on what amounted to "reserves" and were among the first Canadian Indians to live on reserves— that is, land set aside for Indian residence where the Indian was supervised by the whites in an effort to alter the culture of the Indian. Here the Indians, however, proved to be less eager to be assimilated than the Europeans (in the 1630's) thought they would be. The first reserves, most of which were in what is now the province of Quebec, had already come into existence before the migration of the Hurons.

In order to understand the developments which created these early "reserves," it is necessary to examine the course of events among those Indians along the upper St. Lawrence who were in more or less continuous contact with the French by the early decades of the seventeenth century. Algonkian peoples, especially the Montagnais and Algonquins, had undergone the cultural changes already discussed and had developed strong economic and military links with the French. The French hoped to capitalize upon these relations and assimilate the Indian into French culture. Education was to be the chief means by which this would be done. Plans were made to remove children from their parents and what the Jesuits thought of as the retrograde influences of their Indian culture. Some were sent to France, though most were to be schooled in New France. The implementation of the plan foreshadowed the later results, though the Jesuits, whose task it was to accomplish the assimilation, did not perceive this.

On the contrary, they were optimistic, though few young Indian scholars appeared at the school to be instructed. Promised twelve, after the first class only three arrived, and these found it difficult to adjust to the living conditions and routine of seventeenth-century Western education. The Jesuits showed some sensitivity to these cross-cultural conflicts. Hurons, Algonkians, and Montagnais constituted the enrollment, but at the end of five years the experiment was abandoned. No student had stayed more than one or two years and they all returned to their people. It is difficult to assess what impact the experience had on them or how much it changed their lives or, through them, the lives of other Indians.

Parallel efforts by Ursuline nuns with Indian girls apparently proved to be equally ineffective in bringing about the hoped-for changes. Although initially they were adjudged to be more docile and were pictured as exhibiting manners and attitudes which indicated their assimilation to the values and life-style of their teachers, they tended to become depressed and ill in their new environment. This at least is how their guardians interpreted their behaviour. A. G. Bailey[16] is more accepting of the Jesuit and Ursuline reports of significant culture change taking place among the students, especially the girls, than is G.F.G. Stanley.[17] In view of the cultural tenacity of the Indians and the abandonment of the projects, Stanley's view seems the more reasonable one.

In the 1660's the efforts at systematic assimilation of the neighbouring Indians went into a second phase. Again it was the youth who were to be changed, as they were the leaders of the future. The object was to unite Indian and French under one law and one government, and make them one people. Although the impetus for this new effort seems to have come from the government in France, the means by which it was to be done were to be the clergy—Jesuits and Sulpicians. A seminary for boys was founded in Quebec City under the authority of Bishop Laval. It was the foundation of Laval University. Within two decades the government's interest in this project seems to have vanished. Frontenac blamed the Jesuits for not making a really rigorous effort. He charged that they wanted to keep the Indians under their control and so were not working very hard at changing them. Little or no account was taken, either by Frontenac, or Colbert back in France, or by the Jesuits, of the likelihood that the Indians had a culture which they found meaningful and satisfying, and hence saw no necessity for wholesale embracing of the new culture with which they were confronted. Indian life, however, continued to be attractive to young Frenchmen and not a few went to live among the Indians.

By 1700 the government was willing to accept the idea that any formal effort to change the Indians was to be left to the church. To accomplish this task the Jesuits employed the pattern already tried in Huronia of creating Christian villages of Indians under the tutelage of themselves. This approach had its forerunner in Paraguay and adjacent areas of South America at the beginning of the seventeenth century. The Indians, for reasons on which we can only speculate, settled in these new village sites, and communities were formed or existing communities were re-established in new locations. In this way the reserves which have continued down to the present time came into existence in the late seventeenth and mid-eighteenth centuries, such as Caughnawaga (1696), St. Regis (1750's), Lorette (1697), and Becancourt (1680, 1708).

These reserves were composed primarily of Huron and Iroquoian peoples who were agricultural and sedentary prior to European arrival. Indeed, these and their immediate Algonkian-speaking neighbours were the only Indians in pre-European Canada who practised agriculture, and it was among them that the only succesful agricultural communities were created until well into the nineteenth century. It seems apparent that they did not immediately abandon their practice of moving their villages periodically about once every twenty years in order to cultivate new land not depleted of nutrients. The inhabitants of these villages were Roman Catholic converts of the Jesuits, sometimes of more than one generation, and this fact, combined with greater French acceptance of Indians, made living with the French more agreeable to them than perhaps experiencing pressures from their non-Christian neighbours. Economic linkages through the fur trade and employment as military allies presumably also influenced their decision to dwell among the

French. The indigenous leadership was much prized as converts by the Jesuits and these people were the basis of a trend of indirect rule in the villages.

The Abenakis, like the Micmacs further east, found that the French were less destructive of them than were the English, and they fled from harassment by the New Englanders to ally with the French and settle in French territory. In each case both the Indian and the French, or more particularly the Jesuits, found the arrangements to be of mutual advantage. The Indian may be said to have been fighting a rear-guard action to retain what he could of his culture. In these reserves in varying degrees of isolation from the European communities the Indian languages continued to be spoken, agriculture and hunting formed a mixed economy with agriculture, and the process of Westernization was mitigated. Indians had resisted the various efforts to change their culture in residential schools and the attempts to teach them to speak and dress like Frenchmen. Neither did they assimilate under the revised plan which isolated them from general European society and attempted to provide a selected segment of that society to which they were to assimilate. The Christian Indian state proved to be very difficult to create.[18]

The Ottawas were the neighbours and friends of the Hurons. Resident to the south and west of the Hurons in the mid-seventeenth century, they were reported as inhabiting Manitoulin Island and the south shore of Lake Huron. When the Hurons were dispersed, their allies and trading partners, the Ottawas, fled westward, accompanied by some Hurons. They went to the shore of Lake Michigan, Green Bay, Mackinac Island, and some as far as the headwaters of the Mississippi River.

At the end of the eighteenth century some were resident in the area of Detroit. Like the Hurons they were an agricultural people and middlemen in the fur trade. When the Hurons' position as middlemen was ended by the Iroquois attacks, the Ottawas succeeded to the role of chief middlemen in the French fur trade. The Hurons became their assistants. The westward movement of the Ottawas opened new markets for French goods and new sources of furs. The more remote interior peoples were happy to receive even the used tools, weapons, and utensils of the French. The Ottawas became the major suppliers. Centres at Michilimackinac and Green Bay were the new depots for the collection of furs to be taken down to Montreal. The Sioux, Nipissings, and Assiniboines were drawn into the trade.

In the second half of the seventeenth century the Ottawas were the pivotal people between the interior and the French. Unfortunately for them, they were not permitted to retain this position, due to English competition from Hudson's Bay and French efforts to bypass their middlemen to control the trade more securely. Among other things they feared that the Ottawas might forsake them in favour of the English. The Ottawas, like other middlemen before them, resented the threat to their position. At the same time the interior Indians would trade directly with both the English and the French. As an instrument for bypassing them, LaSalle's ship, the *Griffin*, was viewed with alarm by the Ottawas.

The Ottawas, not to be outdone, made deals with the English and the Iroquois by which at least some of their furs were sent through Albany and sold to the English. Generally speaking, however, the Ottawas remained allies of the French. In the 1730's we find them selling enslaved Sioux to Montreal buyers. The Sioux in turn were given to eastern Indians to replace English captives who were to be set free.

In the early eighteenth century under Huron influence, the Ottawas were practising agriculture. Their crops included corn, beans, squash, peas, and melons, all typical of North American Indian agriculture. Their summer houses and the accompanying fortifications were like those of the Hurons. However, the houses they built when on the move resembled those of their more nomadic neighbours, the Ojibways and Potawatomi. In addition to furs they also sold birchbark canoes to the French and served as oarsmen in the transport of the furs eastward to Montreal.

By the end of the seventeenth century many of them had become Christians, as had their Huron allies before them. It is noteworthy that they did not have a large supply of firearms before about 1670. Whether their more obvious adherence to French influences through accepting Christianity in any way affected the willingness of the French to sell them arms is not clear, but it was the French policy, as we have seen, to arm only Christian Indians. On the other hand competition between the French and English for their friendship may have contributed to this increase in arms. As happened with other tribes before them, they gradually abandoned the use of tools and utensils of their own making in favour of European trade items. Thus their role as middlemen declined at the same time that they were becoming more dependent on the French for trade goods.

By the eighteenth century the Ottawas had drifted eastward again. They continued to be staunch allies of the French and received from them gifts and presents. This relation with the French was cut off by the outcome of the Seven Years' War and it is generally thought that the British policy of cutting back on gifts and presents to the Indians provoked the Pontiac uprising. The British wanted to end this practice or control it, and force the Indians into a trading pattern regulated to British convenience.

The Ottawas requested gunpowder and other commodities from Sir William Johnson, who in 1755 was appointed the Indian Commissioner for the Northern Colonies. Johnson promised them aid but tried to convince them to conform to a pattern more suited to British interests. This interest was basically that the Indians bring in furs and ask for less in the form of presents. British policy met with a sharp reaction from the Ottawas. Wilbur Jacobs says: "...the Ottawas, Hurons, and Chippewas...had long been accustomed to French finery for their women." Apparently their desire for goods extended well beyond the dressing of their women. He adds that "...no less an authority than William Johnson declared that Pontiac's Indian war was caused largely by the lack of presents from both the French and English."[19] He asserts:

> ...it is clearly established in Johnson's writings that an outstanding cause of the rebellion was the failure to supply the Western Indians with goods. Francis Parkman recognized this factor...as did Peckham in his more recent study of the Pontiac rising. .... The western tribes expected to partake of British gifts after the "reduction" of Canada. But the British were especially cautious about giving ammunition to the French Indians. [This would have included the Ottawa.] This refusal of the English to grant goods—even those items which were absolutely essential for hunting—led the Indians to believe the rumors that the British meant to make slaves of them. Here was an opportunity for Pontiac to make the most of Indian discontent. It was an opportunity he did not overlook.[20]

Pontiac "...urged Ottawas, Hurons, and Foxes to attack the English who refused supplies to the sick, made no condolence for the dead, and gave no credit for trade."[21]

The French had avoided the need for an army by making alliance attractive to the Indians. The British were obliged to do the same. The importance of the Indian as an ally for both French and British is perhaps reflected in the effort at biological warfare on the part of the British commander, General Jeffrey Amherst. He urged that blankets taken from a hospital for smallpox patients be distributed among the Indians. This was done, according to Wilbur Jacobs.[22] In a more specific account, William Hagan states that Amherst took a very dim view of Indians in opposition to British interests, and under his orders some blankets and handkerchiefs from the smallpox hospital at Fort Pitt were passed to Delaware Indians. Soon afterwards an epidemic of smallpox broke out among them.[23]

The single most important event of the Pontiac rising was the seige of Detroit, which lasted from May to October of 1763. This was an unusual military operation for an Indian force and is frequently commented upon in accounts of the rising. Various tribes, Mississaugas, Potawatomi, Ojibways, Hurons, and others, joined the Ottawas in the fight. Most of the fighting occurred in what is today the United States. Indians seized nine forts extending westward from Fort Pitt, though Fort Pitt itself did not fall.

Pontiac's call for war developed out of the messianic message of a Delaware prophet. The Delawares were a more easterly tribe who had already experienced not only the cultural impact of the European, but the more particular pressures on their land which resulted from westward expansion. The message of the prophet contained a synthesis of the new and the old. Pontiac reinterpreted the burden of the instructions given by the Great Spirit, emphasizing the destructive impact of the English. The Great Spirit, according to Pontiac's version, exhorted the Indians, all Indians, to resist the invaders and to continue to adhere to the French. The Great Spirit had told him, he asserted:

And as for these English,—these dogs dressed in red, who have come to rob you of your hunting-grounds, and drive away the game,—you must lift the hatchet against them. Wipe them from the face of the earth, and thus you will win my favour back again, and once more be happy and prosperous. The children of your great father, the King of France, are not like the English. Never forget they are your brethren. They are very dear to me, for they love the red men, and understand the true mode of worshipping me.[24]

This account appears in Francis Parkman's mid-nineteenth century classic, *The Conspiracy of Pontiac*.

Pontiac attempted, unsuccessfully in the long run, to convince the French Canadians in the Detroit vicinity that his cause was theirs. He hoped and believed that the French would send aid, but by the autumn of 1763 his allies were disengaging themselves. French representatives informed him that no French aid would come, and advised him he would do well to cast his lot with the new masters, the English. Parkman, whose treatment of Indians is not generally to be emulated, says of Pontiac at one point that he was "...not a stranger to the high emotion of the patriot hero, the champion not merely of his nation's rights, but of the very existence of his race."[25]

European penetration into the upper Great Lakes in Canada continued. Long after the Pontiac rising its chief form was still that of the fur traders and a few missionaries. Pressures on Canadian land lay in the future. The Ottawas continued to live by hunting and agriculture. Their material culture had in the seventeenth and eighteenth centuries absorbed much of European origin, a fact attested to by archaeological finds.[26] The result was the creation of a certain degree of cultural uniformity, at least in material objects, among the Indians of the Great Lakes area. George Quimby has used the term "Pan-Indian culture" to describe this development.[27] The Indians manifesting the "Pan-Indian culture" after 1760 still lived primarily by hunting and trapping and exchanged their catch for trade items. Apparently they did give up, presumably under missionary influence, some elements of their religious culture. In any case, the Ottawa ceremony of the Feast of the Dead was last celebrated in 1682.

Allied to the Ottawas, and culturally closely akin to them, are the people known as the Ojibway, whose native territory lay along the north shores of Lakes Huron and Superior. Their own name for themselves the nineteenth century part-Ojibway historian William Warren translates as "the Spontaneous People." Diamond Jenness uses the term "Ojibway" generally to include the Ottawa, as well as the Saulteaux (those Ojibway at the Sault Saint Marie), the Potawatomi, and the Mississauga. Living along the upper Great Lakes as they did (and still do), elements of the Ojibway are to be found in the United States as well, where they are known as the Chippewa. Culturally, one group shades into another along a continuum of cultural variation.

The Saulteaux branch of the Ojibway are thought to have come into existence as a distinct unit in the first half of the seventeenth century.

They consisted of people identified before this time by their indigenous groupings, who lived by hunting, fishing, and gathering in the vicinity of the Sault. These various local groups joined together as a new political, social, and economic unit consequent upon their involvement in the fur trade. Harold Hickerson writes:

> The Saulteaux themselves, like their Nipissing congeners to the east, appear very early to have formed a heterogeneous or amalgamated group at a pivotal trading locale accessible to Huron middlemen and/or their Nipissing agents. Thus, when the French first arrived at Sault Ste. Marie in 1640, and later on a permanent basis in about 1667, they found the pretrade organization of local exogamous kindreds in part destroyed, so much had Sault Ste. Marie become a commercial magnet for the scattered local groups.[28]

By the last quarter of the seventeenth century the local groups were nearly extinct as independent political units. After the destruction of Huronia and the westward movement of the Hurons and Ottawas, the Saulteaux were drawn more deeply into the fur trade. Not only did their political organization and their economy change, but they also expanded the territory of their habitation.

The desire for furs and the acquisition of arms motivated these Ojibway to move westward to what is today northern Minnesota. Conflict between the Ojibway and the adjacent Dakota (Sioux) people forced the latter southward, and the Ojibway engaged in selling as slaves the Indians captured in the fighting. These were sent east to Montreal. Moving northwest, the Ojibway linked in alliance with the Cree and Assiniboine, who were also at odds with the Sioux. By the end of the seventeenth century, however, they agreed to make peace with the Dakota, and marriages were performed to seal the peace treaty. It was at about this time (1680) that the Saulteaux established the village of Chequamegon on the south shore of Lake Superior at Chequamegon Bay. This village was to become the largest and most important Ojibway (Saulteaux) centre in historic times. Another village linked historically to Chequamegon was, according to Hickerson,[29] the nearby Keweenaw.

Earlier efforts by Ottawas and Hurons to settle at Chequamegon—in 1660—had resulted in their ejection by the neighbouring Dakota. Now the Saulteaux had made good the attempt, presumably as a result of their superior organization and technology. Their cultural changes had led to further changes, and changes in one sphere had increased the possibilities for changes in other spheres.

Hickerson has shown how specific features of the religious life of the Saulteaux can be linked to political, social, and economic changes which were occurring in the seventeenth and eighteenth centuries:

> The accretion of new wealth through the fur trade was at the base of the Feast of the Dead. If relationship ties (marriage ties) had the effect of deterring competition and friction among contiguous related peoples, the Feast, through exchanges of wealth newly available, had the effect of creating a framework for active co-operation among those peoples. The significance of

the Feast, then, was the shift, founded in altering political and economic factors from the mutual tolerance of the hegemony of related peoples to the active co-operation of those same peoples as allies.[30]

Hickerson sees another important Ojibway ceremony as also reflecting the successful reorganization by the Ojibway of an aspect of their life to suit a new social environment:

The Midewiwin (which on the surface represented the assumption by a new priesthood of the rights to ancient magical and medicinal practices erstwhile the property of shamans) came into existence as the Chippewa developed their village organization, based upon tribal affiliation. The embosomment of the kindreds within the village, the abrogation of authority vested in the kindreds or in their derivative partri[sic]-lineages, in a word, the radical changes which had taken place in civil life, resulted in the transformation of ceremonial emphasis. The Feast of the Dead had fostered alliances among separate people, stressing the particularity of the totemic kindred; the Midewiwin bolstered the solidarity of a single village people, among whom the gens had no independent political authority.[31]

In 1763 the Saulteaux-Dakota peace ended and war broke out again. Not until 1844 did the Saulteaux and the Dakota again make peace. The general success of the former against the latter made possible their expansion southward. In the mid-eighteenth century, Ojibway were also moving westward and by the early nineteenth century were in the Red River area. In the Prairies as in the upper Great Lakes, they continued to play a part in the fur trade. To the east of Sault Ste. Marie other Ojibway were expanding eastward in the second half of the seventeenth century. The Iroquois threat had diminished and the power of the French grew. The Ojibway were firm friends of France.

The Ottawas, also allied to the French, were returning eastward at the same time as were the Ojibways. These two peoples and a third, the Potawatomis, were linked together into a loose association referred to as the Council of the Three Fires. Rivalries to the east and west made such an alliance useful. Probably Thomas Forsyth was referring to this alliance when he wrote:

Early in the eighteenth century an alliance was formed by the Wyandotts (Hurons) Chippewa, Ottawas, and Potawatomis for their mutual protection against the incursions of hostile western tribes; the French made a fifth party to this alliance—which before many years fell through. About 1720 those four tribes made an arrangement as to the respective territories which they were to occupy—each tribe, however, to have the privilege of hunting in the territory of the others. The Wyandotts were made the keepers of the international council-fire (a figurative expression, meaning their international archives), and arbiters, in their general council, of important questions that concerned the welfare of all four tribes.[32]

William Warren speaks of the "allied Ottawas, Potawatomis, and eastern Ojibways" at the time of the War of 1812.[33] Again, Parkman in his Introduction to *The Conspiracy of Pontiac*, speaks of Ojibways, Potawatomis, and Ottawas as being "banded into a sort of confederacy."[34]

The Mississauga, an element of the eastward-moving Ojibway, had, prior to 1700, occupied the area of Manitoulin Island and the mainland coast north of the island. There they were in contact with the Nipissing and the Ottawa—culturally speaking, their near-relations. As their expansion westward was marked by clashes with the Dakota, so in the east they were in frequent battles with the Iroquois. By the mid-eighteenth century the Mississauga had secured for their own territory much of the area of southwestern Ontario which had been occupied by the Huron and Tobacco until about 1650, then passed to the Iroquois in the second half of the seventeenth century. After they had driven off, destroyed, or absorbed the Hurons, Neutrals, and Tobaccos, the Iroquois themselves used that territory for hunting purposes, so that it was from them that the Ojibways had to wrest the land. J. L. Morris tersely summarizes this Ojibway expansion to the east and south: ". . .after 1736, the Chippewas forced the Iroquois out of the Peninsula between Lakes Huron and Erie."[35] The last important clash between Ojibway and Iroquois took place in the 1750's.

Although the culture of the Ojibway was undergoing various changes, some unique, as well as some similar to those of other Indians, the changes were generally speaking not imposed by the European. The Indian retained a high degree of autonomy. The nature of his linkage with the European culture obliged the European to desire relatively less change in the Indian way of life than was to be true in the era and areas of reserves. Nevertheless, Indian culture was undergoing important changes as a result of the fur trade and contact with the white man's culture and goods.

Prior to the coming of the European there were undoubtedly conflicts between tribes and peoples. These, however, took on a new scope and intensity with the material changes introduced by European trade and commerce. For example, the highly stylized warfare patterns of the aboriginal practice now involved smaller units but caused the destruction of larger numbers. The Indians repeatedly showed the pragmatic basis of their alliances in their willingness to alter them and their refusal to act concertedly. They attempted to carefully weigh offers in deciding their best course of action.

In another sense, however, they were becoming dependent on the European and losing their freedom of action. By the end of the seventeenth century the Indians of the St. Lawrence River area, as we have seen, had become entirely dependent on trade goods for tools and weapons, and as beaver gave out they relied more on their role as middlemen to the interior fur sources. By 1800, George Quimby shows, the Indians of the Great Lakes were dependent on European trade for tools, arms, and other items. An Indian told Father Le Clerq: "In truth, my brother, the beaver does everything to perfection. He makes for us kettles, axes, swords, knives, and gives us drink and food without the trouble of cultivating the ground."[36]

George Quimby comments on the flowering and decay of the Indian culture in the Great Lakes area before 1800:

> The Pan-Indian culture of the Upper Great Lakes region was in part an adjustment to the fur trade of the white men; and when the fur trade ended in the region, the pan-Indian culture began to disintegrate. The Indian livelihood was almost completely dependent upon the trapping and hunting of fur-bearing animals. As these animals became scarce, the fur traders moved westward. Also white settlers were moving into the Upper Great Lakes region.
>
> The Indians were left without livelihood. They no longer had the means of purchasing their supplies, and much of their old way of life was lost to them. A great many Indians moved into areas where wild rice could be harvested, some tried farming, others moved westward, and many were kept in a rather hopeless condition on the frontier. It was these Indians, deprived of their aboriginal culture and left in a badly depressed economic situation who made the last futile but bloody attempts to delay white settlement of the Upper Great Lakes Region. A cultural continuity that had lasted about 13,000 years was destroyed by the advance of the Old World civilization.[31]

Thus the Indians, from being a desirable or even necessary element in the survival and/or prosperity of the whites, became an impediment to the continued expansion of the Europeans. In the case of the Hurons, they became victims of the larger struggles of the Europeans in which aboriginal fought aboriginal as allies of the French and English.

There were other aspects of the white-Indian contact besides the trade itself which are usually considered to have been destructive as well. Much has been written about the liquor trade or the part played by liquor in the trade and general contact of the Indian and European. Besides causing drunkeness and fights, liquor has been credited by some writers with causing the decline of the Indian peoples in general. This is a most difficult issue to assess adequately. Some writers, more cautious in evaluating the destructive effects of liquor, have suggested that missionaries and some travellers and administrators have allowed their biases to lead them to exaggerate. Others have pointed out that heavy drinking characterized both Indian and white, and that destruction of life and property was likely when either group drank a lot. A more certain case is that of disease epidemics, which are known to have wiped out large segments of various peoples, as we have seen. Epidemics repeatedly struck at populations which had no immunity; the source of these diseases was the European. It is also obvious that wars arising out of Indian involvement in European rivalries, and made more lethal by European weapons, were responsible for many deaths. The destructive effects of liquor are more problematical.

Through the middle of the eighteenth century the Ojibways, like the Ottawas, were for the most part friends, militarily and commercially, of the French. William Warren relates one of the traditions about the origins of the French-Ojibway linkage in the seventeenth century. The French officer appointed to secure their allegiance addressed the Ojibway leader, Ke-che-ne-zuh-yuah:

> Every morning you will look towards the rising of the sun and you shall see the fire of your French father reflecting towards you, to warm you and your people. If you are in trouble, you, the Crane, must arise in the skies and cry with your "far sounding" voice, and I will hear you. The fire of your French father shall last forever, and warm his children.[38]

Warren, who was himself part Ojibway, proudly indicates in his study, written in the mid-nineteenth century, that his major sources were the oral and traditional accounts which he personally was told by Ojibway people. He accepts, as do many others, the notion that there was something intrinsic in the French character which made them better suited to get along with the Indians than were the English and Americans.

The Ojibways, he says, "received the 'heart' of their French brethren and accepted their proposals of peace, amity, and mutual support and protection." They "learned to love the French people" because the French possessed "a character of great plasticity, easily assimilated themselves to the customs and mode of life of their red brethren." Religious rites and ceremonies, he asserts, were respected, and "no nation of whites have ever succeeded so well in gaining the love and confidence of the red man, as the Franks."[39] According to this view, the French came mostly for pleasure and enjoyment of this life, whereas the English and Americans came primarily for economic gain. So the latter two used the Indians for their mercenary ends while the French were just "living." The period of French domination was the "Augustan era" of the fur trade.[40] In any case, Warren's description gives us his interpretation of the Indian way of life and of a segment of French colonial society.

The Ojibways adhered to the French in the Seven Years War and played an important role. Their tactics under Chief Minavavana at Fort Michilimackinac were particularly imaginative and successful in capturing that fort. Alexander Henry, an English trader who was present at the event, described how the Indians played lacrosse outside the open gate of the fort. When the ball went through the gate, the players and onlookers ran after it. Upon entering the grounds, they attacked the garrison and seized the fort. Henry escaped because he was the sworn friend of Wawatam, one of the Ojibway leaders in the battle. A variant on this tactic was foiled at Detroit when an Indian girl revealed the plan to the post commander. The other chiefs who provided leadership of the Ojibway at this time were Ma-mong-e-se-da and his son, Waubojeeg. The latter visited Sir William Johnson in 1768 at Johnson's home in New York. Johnson later wrote of Waubojeeg:

> ...the Chief of the Chippewas, one of the most powerful nations, to the westward, arrived. As he is a man of much influence, and can bring some thousands into the field, I took particular notice of him, formerly at Niagara. [In 1764 a deputation of Ojibways met Johnson at Niagara for council which is reported to have had representatives from "twenty-two different tribes."[41]]; since which he has behaved well, and now came to be informed of my sentiments on the uneasy state of the Indians to the westward. He told me

his people would quietly wait his return before they took any resolutions; confirming all the accounts I received for the practices of the Spaniards and French.[42]

The threat of a French effort to make a comeback in North America, with the aid of the Spanish who had succeeded to the territory of Louisiana, was present. British policy was aimed at securing the adherence of these former French allies. The Indians seem to have realized that the British were the elements with whom they would have to get along.

At Fort Niagara in 1764 the first purchase of land was made from the Ojibways. By a treaty of May 9, 1781, Mississaugas and other Ojibways alienated a piece of land on the west side of the Niagara River. These were the first of a series of cessions by which Ojibways were reduced to reserves. Ironically some of the land ceded was granted to the loyalist Iroquois in 1784 in recompense for their losses in the American Revolution and in appreciation for their allegiance to the Crown. By this means the earlier lords of the area, the Iroquois, returned to their former hunting grounds as reserve Indians. A strip of land six miles wide on each side of the Grand River, from its source to its mouth, constituted their reserve. Led by their redoubtable chief, Captain Joseph Brant, refugees of the Six Nations (Mohawk, Cayuga, Oneida, Onondaga, Seneca, and Tuscarora) numbering about 1,600 came to settle their new domain. Everything was not settled, however, and it was to be several years before the exact boundaries of the territory were surveyed and clarified. A smaller group, led by Captain John Deseronto, settled at a reserve created on the Bay of Quinte. British authorities still looked upon the Iroquois as allies in future wars, and they did not miscalculate. The Iroquois were to be an important component of the resistance to American invasion in the War of 1812.

Brant saw in the Grand River Valley location broader prospects for the continued exercise of an important role by the Six Nations and he perhaps realized the strategic value of such a settlement in view of the British position in Canada and unsettled relations with the Americans. The British authorities wished to retain the allegiance of the Six Nations in case of future conflicts because not only was there the new entity, the United States, which was expansionist-oriented, but there was always the possibility that France, acting through the Spanish-held Louisiana Territory, might attempt to revive colonial activities from the Mississippi Valley. Brant was sagacious enough to realize the potential leverage which could be exercised with the British government in view of the fears, threats, and rumours which were prevalent in the decades after the American Revolution.

Although not an hereditary chief, Brant had been chosen for the position of Pinetree Chief, a title granted to men on the basis of merit and proven leadership qualities. In addition his family connections and education were important elements in establishing his position. He was the descendant of a chief who went to England in the early eighteenth century, in the reign of Queen Anne, in connection with some land speculation being promoted by business interests in England and in the Colonies. He was the brother of Molly Brant, who was the wife of Sir William Johnson, British Superintendent of Indian Affairs. Through Johnson's interest, Brant had received some formal education. Much fêted in later life during his travels abroad, he was early recognized by his teachers as a youth of considerable potential, even genius. Having distinguished himself as a wartime commander of Indian allies of the British, and holding a captain's commission, he was sophisticated in matters of state and seemed to his countrymen the man best able to serve on their behalf and most competent to deal with the British authorities.

The grant of land in the Grand River Valley was made in 1784. Known as the Haldimand Grant, it was named for Sir Frederick Haldimand, Governor of Canada from 1778 to 1786. No sooner had the grant been made than a debate arose over the interpretation of exactly what was meant by it. This imprecision had two aspects. First there was the question of what kind of title the Indians were being given. What was the extent of their power to hold and dispose of the land? Was it theirs to sell freely or was there some government restraint placed upon their full freedom of ownership? Did this grant amount to government recognition of a Six Nations state on the Grand River, an independent nation which was an ally of Britain? This was Brant's interpretation.

The second question, more mundane but also important, was that of how much land they had been granted. The terms of the grant had provided for six miles on each side of the Grand River from its source to its mouth. The proclamation of the grant, October 25, 1784, read:

> Whereas His Majesty having been pleased to direct that in consideration of the early attachment to His cause manifested by the Mohawk Indians, and of the Loss of their Settlement they thereby sustained that a convenient tract of Land under His Protection should be chosen as a Safe and Comfortable Retreat for them and others of the Six Nations who have either lost their Settlements within the Territory of the American States, or wish to retire from them to the British,—I have, at the earnest Desire of many of these His Majesty's Faithfull Allies purchased a tract of Land, from the Indians situated between Lakes Ontario, Erie and Huron and I do hereby in His Majesty's name authorize and permit the said Mohawk Nation, and such other of the Six Nation Indians as wish to settle in that Quarter to take possession of, and Settle upon the Banks of the River commonly called Ours (Ouse) or Grand River, running into Lake Erie, allotting to them for that Purpose Six Miles deep from each Side of the River beginning at Lake Erie, and extending in that Proportion to the Head of the said River, which them and their Posterity are to enjoy forever.[43]

The land had not been surveyed, however, and other and conflicting claims in the same territory had not been dealt with. This presented problems in view of Brant's policy of selling portions of the grant to raise money and get supplies necessary for the new settlers.

In the winter of 1784-85 more than 1,500 Indians moved into the area around Brant's Ford. Brant proceeded on the basis that the land belonged to the Six Nations and could be disposed of by them in whatever way and to whomever they pleased. The government did not accept this view. Brant perhaps realized that the Indians could not cultivate so much land and that its value for subsistence hunting was negligible. If the land was to be used primarily for agriculture anyway, then such a large grant was beyond their means to use fully and so it was to their advantage to sell some of it. Some of the people objected to the idea of selling land as if it were a commodity, but Brant received from the chiefs of the Six Nations the authority to sell land. All did not go well, and Brant found continual difficulty in getting the government to give clearance to the land sales being made. Threats of going over to the French were rumoured and suggestions were made that land be retained in New York State for the Indians, just in case.

Some whites in high places feared that, if Brant's sales were not approved by the government, he would lead the Indians in a rising against the settlement of York and the whites generally. They remembered the Pontiac rising. In February 1798, the land sales were officially registered. Of the original grant of approximately 570,000 acres, about 350,000 were sold by the time of the registry of sales in 1798. As the numbers of white settlers grew in the early nineteenth century, a problem developed with squatters on land claimed by the Six Nations. This issue was finally settled in 1841 when it was agreed that all land would be administered by the government under the Indian Affairs Office. The land involved included all the land then being cultivated by the Six Nations Indians and an additional area of 20,000 acres. Other land over and above that amount was to be sold and the money credited to the account of the Indians.

At the same time that these matters were concerning the Indians and the government, the Indians were also being introduced to a more intensified effort to change other aspects of their lives. In the early nineteenth century, Christianity, in the form of the Anglican Church, had long been adhered to by a segment of the Indians. Other church bodies sent in evangelists to win adherents. Methodists and Baptists were active, and both denominations had a degree of success.

An important element in the religious life of the Six Nations was the Longhouse religion which derived from the religious prophet and teacher, Handsome Lake (Ganiodayo). He had preached return to the worship of the past, a strong ethical code, and a reinterpretation of traditional ceremonies in the light of the experience of other people in the late eighteenth and early nineteenth centuries. The religion took its name from the houses of worship, the traditional long wooden buildings which in aboriginal times were the characteristic dwellings of the Iroquois. The new faith was evangelical and won adherents among the Iroquois in Canada and the United States. Among the earliest adherents in the Six Nations community at Brantford were the Cayugas, who today are still among the most devoted.

Efforts to introduce formal, Western-style education in the decades of the late eighteenth century and early nineteenth century resulted in a situation not unlike that found in other Indian communities. A school started before 1820 had an enrollment of thirty pupils by that year; five years later the figure had dropped to three. The teachers departed and the school ceased to function.

In the mid-nineteenth century apparently many of the Brantford Iroquois retained much of their indigenous way of life. Facilities for altering their culture were still not sufficiently well developed financially and organizationally by the whites to effect the changes which the latter expected to bring about. The bad example of whites was cited as the main reason for the failure so far to change the Indians, in the *Report on the Affairs of Indians in Canada, 1844:*

> The chief obstacle to their conversion is a joint determination on the part of certain of their Chiefs to persevere in their rejection of Christianity, and to induce all under their influence to follow their example. The glaring inconsistency, which they cannot fail to discover, between the profession and practice of many of the nominal Christians among the white people who have settled around them, and who are generally of very bad character, has furnished them with a plausible objection to the Christian religion.[44]

The Indian Commission report of 1858 found that "any hope of raising the Indians as a body to the social or political level of their white neighbours is yet but a glimmering and distant spark."[45]

This is a negative judgement. A positive observation, rarely made, might have been that the Indians preferred to retain as much as possible of their aboriginal culture because they were of the opinion that many of its values were preferable to those of the white man.

After 1800 only one more major war between the white men involved Indian allies on a large scale. Here again the Indians seem to have calculated their own advantages in choosing sides. Tecumseh and his followers had not yet given up hope that an Indian state could be created in the Ohio Valley and that the continuous stream of white settlers from across the mountains could be checked. Alliance with the British in the War of 1812 offered the opportunity that alliance with France had offered some of the same people in the time of Pontiac.

From the American or British point of view, the Indians were depicted as loyal to the former or to the latter. The British had good trading relations with the Indians. They had not been as scrupulous in looking to the Indians' interest at the end of the American War of Independence as the Indians had hoped and thought to be just; nevertheless, they offered an alliance which could be turned into an instrument for Indian survival. More than survival—the Indians, with British support, might yet build a native Indian state between the Appalachians and the Mississippi. Smaller states had existed among the Indians farther south.

Continual differences made harmony between Indian and non-Indian warriors difficult, if not impossible. The Indians retained many of their traditional fighting techniques, sometimes to the irritation of their white allies. Though they might be using European weapons they were not acculturated to seiges and sustained field operations. Their techniques were well suited to forest warfare, ambush, and the operation of raiding parties harassing enemy lines and forts. Their organization was such that forces of fighting men could disband themselves in a way inconsistent with regulations governing British and American troups. The loss of an outstanding leader might cause his followers to reconsider their participation and fade away. In addition the rivalries between the various Indian groups sometimes disrupted an alliance of native troops. Not all the Indian allies had the same stake in the conflict. Some might be enlisted for adventure or money, while others saw themselves as defending their land. Tecumseh and his allies were engaged in a desperate struggle.

In the case of the Indians who had been stalwart allies until the Battle of Moraviantown (October 5, 1813), the death of Tecumseh was followed by the virtual end of Indian confederates in that sector. Tecumseh was secretly buried by his men and his body never found. He had proved a more valiant warrior than had his British commander; General Brock had said of him: ". . .a more sagacious or a more gallant warrior does not, I believe, exist." G.F.G. Stanley, commenting on the last battle of Tecumseh's life, stated, ". . .when Proctor was finally shamed into making a stand at Moraviantown on October 5, 1813, it was Tecumseh and the Indians who did the fighting, not Proctor's red coats. Tecumseh gave his life; Proctor saved his by flight."[46]

The Six Nations also joined the war, as they were British allies of old and had left the United States as a result of their British alliance in the American Revolution. They were at first unwilling to be put in the position of possibly having to fight their kinsmen across the border. Another factor which influenced their initial response was that they wished to make clear that their relationship with the government differed from that of other Indians. They were independent allies. Also, they regarded some of the other tribes as cousins and juniors of themselves. They did join, however, and were particularly outstanding in the American defeat at Queenston Heights. At Beaver Dam in June, 1813, a force composed of men from the Caughnawaga, Lake of the Two Mountains and St. Regis reserves in Lower Canada, and Mohawks from Upper Canada, defeated an American force. Ottawa Indians under their chief, Blackbird, and Captain Matthew Elliott also fought in the Niagara peninsula campaign in 1813.[47]

Indians made an important contribution to the continuation of British control in Canada. Stanley has briefly summarized the Indians' accomplishment:

Both during the Revolutionary War and the War of 1812 the Indians fought on the British side. Some, like Burgoyne and Proctor might cast doubts upon their value as military auxiliaries, but few who read the story of both wars will question the contribution of men like Joseph Brant and John Deserontyon, Tecumseh and Blackbird.[48]

Whether the Indian had in any way improved his own situation is doubtful. The terms of the treaty were a rejection of an Indian state and a return to the *status quo ante bellum*. For the Indian this meant continued pressure and encroachment by the white settlers. The initiative was out of his hands, but he continued to manoeuvre where he could, bending when desirable or necessary, but always resilient.

In view of the military role into which Indians were cast, it is not surprising to find that in historical writing, when Indians are not discussed in military or fur trading terms, in both cases as adjuncts of European activities, they tend to drop out of the story of Canada altogether. When the Indians no longer engaged in military action, however, they were not removed from the considerations of the white society around them. By more peaceful means (perhaps), they were under an unremitting pressure of which they, or at least their leaders, were conscious. The process now became one of land alienation and treaties, settlement on reserves, and the three-fold efforts of administrators, missionaries, and teachers to change their culture.

In the first third of the nineteenth century, the geographical direction of European settlement in Upper Canada can, in a general way, be observed in the geographical pattern of Indian treaties signed. Thus by the mid-1830's, treaty-signing activities had progressed to the area of modern Bruce and Grey Counties. The incident described below is perhaps more dramatic than usual, but because it is so well documented, it provides us with insights into what the government was doing in relation to Indians, and the fluctuation of policy these actions involved.

The treaty of August 9, 1836, signing away Manitoulin Island, was linked to another treaty also signed in that month. By the terms of the second treaty the Saugeen Indians along the north-eastern shore of Lake Huron were to be relieved of their land and agree to relocate on Manitoulin Island. In order to implement this project, authorities had to secure the island first. By 1836 the Indians had already signed some two dozen treaties alienating land in Ontario. As we have already seen, most of these treaties were with various Ojibway peoples and involved land in southern Ontario.

In August 1836, the Ottawas and Ojibways of Manitoulin Island, at the prompting of Sir Francis Bond Head (then Lieutenant-Governor of Upper Canada) signed a treaty alienating the island. The pressure of the white immigration and an increasing demand for land was having its impact. Sir Francis told the assembled Indians that ". . .as an unavoidable increase of white population as well as the progress of cultivation have had the natural effect of impoverishing your hunting grounds it has become necessary that new arrangements should be entered into for the purpose of protecting you from the encroachments of the whites." He instructed them about the ways of the white man:

In all parts of the world farmers seek for uncultivated land as eagerly as you my red children, hunt in your forest for game. [Actually the Ottawas had practised agriculture for several hundred years.] If you would cultivate your land, it would then be considered your own property, in the same way as your dogs are considered among yourselves to belong to those who have reared them, but uncultivated land is like wild animals, and your Great Father who has hitherto protected you, has now great difficulty in securing it for you from the whites who are hunting to cultivate.[49]

The self-justification and veiled threat of the government representative in treaty-signing meetings is a recurring phenomenon which will be seen again at other gatherings of whites and Indians to affix names to treaties. The Europeans set the terms for what constituted a valid claim to the land, and the Indians were obliged to conform to them.

In 1837 Anna Jameson visited Ottawas residing on Manitoulin, their ancient home, and observed them hunting, fishing, and growing crops. Other Ottawas came to the island to receive their presents from the British government's Indian agent. The resident Indians had built their own church under the direction of Father Crue. "They have large plantations of corn and potatoes, and they have built log huts, a chapel for their religious services, and a house for their priest," she wrote.[50] She described the chapel as made of timbers still covered with bark, the floor strewn with green boughs and mats, and an altar and crucifix "at the end." "In front a bell is suspended between the forked branches of a pine. I have heard them sing mass here, with every demonstration of decency and piety."[51]

Mrs. Jameson's remarks regarding Indian women she applied to Indian society as a whole:

It seems to me a question whether the Europeans who, Heaven knows, have much to answer for in their intercourse with these people, have not, in some degree, injured the cause of the Indian woman: first, by corrupting them; secondly, by checking the improvement of all their own peculiar manufactures. . . . It is reasonable to presume that as these manufactures must have been progressively improved, there might have been further progression, had we not substituted for articles they could procure or fabricate, those which we fabricate; we have taken the work out of their hands, and all motive to work, while we have created wants which they cannot supply. We have clothed them in blankets—we have not taught them to weave blankets. We have substituted guns for the bow and arrows—but they cannot make guns; for the natural progress of arts and civilization springing from within, and from their own intelligence and resources, we have substituted a sort of civilization from without, foreign to their habits, manners, organization: we are making paupers of them; and this by a kind of terrible necessity.[52]

A gloomy view of the Indians' future was a common one in the nineteenth and early twentieth century and has not disappeared yet. Some Indians in the nineteenth century agreed with this prediction. The Ottawa chief, Blackbird, is reported to have remarked, "Yes, we are going it is true, and when we are gone our deeds will still fill pages in the white man's history."[53]

If we consider the first phase of Indian contact with whites to be one in which the Indian retained a high degree of autonomy, then the second phase must be that in which the Indians gradually lost this autonomy. As the Indians' dependence grew, then, they moved into what we have denominated as the second phase: this process tends to follow a westward course. As the frontier of white settlement moved west, a third phase, that of relegation to reserves, followed the second. However, it is important to remember that in those areas where white settlement was absent or was very thin, even when Indians had passed under treaties and reserves had been assigned, the intensity of the white man's impact was less than in areas where white settlement existed. In each case the policy of government administration—assimilating the Indian—was the same, but remoteness and consequent lack of immediate interest to the whites contributed to a differential impact. The policy was the same, from reserve to reserve, but in some cases the pressures of the reserve were augmented by the pressures of white settlers, and in some they were not. Not all the changes were the result of the immediate proximity of the white settlers, however, nor were they all the result of directed culture change. The very incisive observations of Mrs. Jameson, quoted above, clearly illustrate this fact.

FOOTNOTES:

[1] J. B. Brebner, *New England's Outpost, Acadia before the Conquest of Canada* (New York: 1927), p. 18.

[2] J. S. McLennan, *Louisbourg from Its Foundations to Its Fall, 1713-1758* (Sydney, N.S.: 1957), pp. 64-65.

[3] Brebner, *op. cit., p. 58.*

[4] Alfred G. Bailey, *The Conflict of European and Eastern Algonkian Cultures, 1504-1700* (St. John, N.B.: 1937), p. 22.

[5] W. S. MacNutt, *The Atlantic Provinces: the Emergence of Colonial Society, 1712-1857* (Toronto: 1965), p. 30.

[6] Brebner, *op. cit.,* p. 81.

[7] Quoted in R. O. MacFarlane, "British Indian Policy in Scotia to 1760," *Canadian Historical Review,* Vol. 19, (June, 1938), pp. 154-167.

[8] *Ibid.,* p. 166.

[9] *Ibid.,* p. 167.

[10] *Ibid.*

[11] *Ibid., p. 165.*

[12] Elizabeth Hutton, "Indian Affairs in Nova Scotia, 1760-1834," *Collections Nova Scotia Historical Society* (1963), p. 50.

[13] *Ibid.,* p. 46.

[14] *Ibid.,* p. 54.

[15] Wilson D. Wallis and Ruth Sawtell Wallis, *The Micmac Indians of Eastern Canada* (Minneapolis: 1955), pp. 210-211.

[16] Alfred G. Bailey, *The Conflict of European and Eastern Algonkian Cultures, 1504-1700: A Study in Canadian Civilization,* New Brunswick Museum Monographic Series #2 (St. John, N.B.: 1937).

[17] G. F. G. Stanley, "The First Indian 'Reserves' in Canada," *Revue d'Histoire de L'Amerique Francaise,* Vol. 4, No. 2, (September, 1950), pp. 178-210.

[18] For this section I have relied heavily upon two articles from *Revue d'Histoire de L'Amerique Francaise* by G. F. G. Stanley: "The first Indian 'Reserves' in Canada," (cited above), and "The Policy of 'Francisation' as applied to the Indians during the Ancien Regime," Vol. 3, No. 3, (December, 1949), pp. 333-348. Students should see also "Report on the Affairs of the Indians in Canada," *Journals,* Legislative Assembly, Canada (1844-5), Appendix E.E.E., Section 1, "History of the Relations between the Government and the Indians."

[19] Wilbur Jacobs, *Wilderness Politics and Indian Gifts: The Northern Colonial Frontier, 1748-1763* (Lincoln, Nebr.: 1966), pp. 161-162.

[20] *Ibid.,* pp. 183-184.

[21] *Ibid.,* p. 184.

[22] *Ibid.,* p. 185.

[23] William Hagan, *American Indians,* The Chicago History of American Civilization (Daniel J. Boorstin, ed.), (Chicago: 1961), p. 25.

[24] Francis Parkman, *The Conspiracy of Pontiac,* (New York: 1962), p. 169.

[25] *Ibid.,* p. 175. In a popular work by Alvin Josephy, Jr., *The Patriot Chiefs* (New York: 1969), Pontiac and Tecumseh are treated as Indian patriots. Similarly, individuals, organizations, and events are discussed as the "Background of Indian Nationalistic Thought" in Stuart Levine and Nancy O. Lurie (editors), *The American Indian Today* (Deland, Fla.: 1968). The background includes the League of the Iroquois (c. 15th C.), the Creek Confederacy (1600's), King Philip and his allies (1675), Pope and the Pueblo rising (1680), Pontiac (1763), Brant (1770's and 80's), Tecumseh (c. 1810-1812), Black Hawk (1830), and Wovoka (1880). Most of this "background" is in territorial United States, but some is in Canada, and some has implications for or parallels in Canada.

[26] See George I. Quimby, *Indian Culture and European Trade Goods* (Madison, Wisc.: 1966).

[27] George I. Quimby, *Indian Life in the Upper Great Lakes, 11,000 B.C. to A.D. 1800* (Chicago: 1960), p. 157. The term "Pan-Indian" is not used in this quotation in the same sense that it is used in earlier chapters of this study and in the references cited from other authors. The latter refer to a late nineteenth and/or twentieth century development in Canada and the United States, the growth of "Indian nationalism." For Quimby's definition of the term, see below.

[28] Harold Hickerson, "The Southwestern Chippewa," *American Anthropological Associations Memoirs 92,* Vol. 64, No. 3, Pt. 2, (1962), pp. 82-83.

[29] Harold Hickerson, "The Sociohistorical Significance of Two Chippewa Ceremonials," *American Anthropologist,* Vol. 65, No. 1, (1965), pp. 74-75.

[30] *Ibid.,* p. 80.

[31] *Ibid.,* p. 81.

[32] From Thomas Forsyth, *An Account of the Manners and Customs of the Sauks and Fox Nations*, p. 189, footnote 67, in E. H. Blair (ed.), *The Indian Tribes of the Upper Mississippi Valley and Region of the Great Lakes* (Cleveland, Ohio: 1911).

[33] William Warren, *History of the Ojibway Nation Based Upon Traditions and Oral Statements* (Minneapolis, Minn.: 1957), p. 372.

[34] Parkman, *op. cit.*, p. 57. See also D. Jenness, *Indians of Canada*, 6th ed., (Ottawa: 1963), p. 277: " ... the Lake Superior Ojibway, the Ottawa, and the Potawatomi, formed a loose confederacy or the Council of the Three Fires."

[35] J. L. Morris, *Indians of Ontario* (Toronto: 1943), p. 14.

[36] Harold Innis, *The Fur Trade in Canada*, Revised Edition prepared by S. D. Clark and W. T. Easterbrook, Foreward by Robin W. Winks (Toronto: 1962), p. 28: quoted from Father C. Le Clerq, *New Relations of Gaspesia*, ed. by W. F. Ganong, p. 277.

[37] Quimby (1960), *loc. cit.*

[38] Warren, *op. cit.*, pp. 131-132.

[39] *Ibid.*, p. 132.

[40] *Ibid.*, p. 133.

[41] *Ibid.*, p. 217.

[42] Edward D. Neill, *History of the Ojibways, and their Connection with Fur Traders, Based Upon Official and Other Records:* bound together with Warren, *op. cit.*, (Minneapolis, Minn.: 1957), pp. 444-445.

[43] Quoted from a letter in the Public Archives of Canada in Charles M. Johnston, *The Valley of the Six Nations: a Collection of Documents on the Indian Lands of the Grand River*, The Champlain Society for the Government of Ontario (University of Toronto Press: 1964), pp. 50-51.

[44] Report on the Affairs of the Indians in Canada" (1844), p. 310.

[45] *Ibid.*, p. XCVI

[46] G.F.G. Stanley, "The Indians in the War of 1812," *Canadian Historical Review*, Vol. 31, No. 2 (June, 1950), p. 154.

[47] Some of the Indian allies of the War of 1812 were among those who later came annually into Canada to receive British presents and eventually moved to Canada.

[48] George F. G. Stanley, "The Indian Background of Canadian History" *Canadian Historical Association Annual Report*, 1952 (Toronto: 1952), p. 18.

[49] J. L. Morris, *op. cit.*, pp. 27-28.

[50] Anna Burwell Jameson, *Winter Studies and Summer Rambles in Canada*, ed. by James J. Talman and Elsie McLeod Murray, Foreward by Fred Landon (Toronto: 1943), p. 251.

[51] *Ibid.*, p. 252.

[52] *Ibid.*, p. 254.

[53] James C. Hamilton, *The Georgian Bay—An Account of its Position, Inhabitants, Mineral Interests, Fish, Timber and other Resources* (Toronto: 1893), p. 96.

2. The Imperial Net Tightens:

From the Great Lakes
to the Rockies
into the reserve/treaty period.

In many cases, as we have seen, the impact of the new culture on the Indians had proceeded westward ahead of the actual physical presence of the white men. In the Eastern Woodlands, and along the edge of the Prairies, we have already noted the role of the Ojibways and Ottawas as transmitters of elements of the new influence. Still another people, to the north and west of them, had begun to experience this impact by the late seventeenth century. These were the Crees. The ramifications of white impact are perhaps nowhere better illustrated in Canada than in the case of the Crees. Their northern and western migrations, which eventually led to their occupancy of land from Ontario to the Rockies, saw them change into two groups—Woodland and Plains, brought them into sharper and fiercer conflict with their neighbours, the Blackfoot and the northern Athabascans, and through their contact with the white man led to the creation of a large Cree-white population of *Métis* which is so important to later events in the history of Canada.

The Crees are divided into two main subdivisions, the Woodland Crees and the Plains Crees, but in the seventeenth century they were not yet differentiated, and lived in the area south and southwest of Hudson Bay, in the Lake Nipigon area and along the Eastmain River, roughly the area occupied by the Woodland Crees in 1900. By the mid-seventeenth century some of the Crees were already involved in the fur trade. They rendezvoused in the summer with middlemen such as the Ottawas and the Nipissings. In their practice of coming to the shores of the lakes in the summer and returning to the interior in the winter, they followed a pattern like that of the eastern Algonkians and northern Athabascans, a pattern which was to continue for some Indians of northern Ontario until the twentieth century. The Crees were eager to get trade goods, and by 1670 some of them were dependent on traders for part of their food supply. The commodity desired and available at posts like the Sault was corn; it was nutritious and easily transported.

The coming of the Hudson's Bay Company in 1670 altered the situation of the Crees. Not only did they now have a choice of French or English goods, but they became middlemen as well. From having been on the extreme western edge of the trading relations they were, after 1670, in direct contact with their European source of goods. We have already seen how this development threatened the position of the Ottawa middlemen. The pattern of power and influence which had passed thus far across the continent with the acquisition of certain European trade items was now to work on the Crees. The Crees quickly became allies of the Hudson's Bay Company and entrenched as middlemen in the trade with more remote peoples. This position they guarded jealously, as had the Ottawas in their situation earlier and the Hurons and Algonkians before them. David Mandelbaum asserts that they readily adapted to new weapons, tools, and utensils, and the trading trip to the Hudson's Bay Company post became an important annual event.[1]

Armed with guns and seeking furs, they pushed out gradually into the Prairies, where they formed an alliance with their Assiniboine neighbours, a Sioux-speaking people, to fight against the Dakota Sioux. They also fought with their Athabascan neighbours, especially the Chipewyans, whom they tried to keep from first-hand contact with the Hudson's Bay Company. For a time they succeeded in pushing these northern neighbours farther northward, but by the end of the eighteenth century a general peace seems to have been established.[2]

The extension of French posts into the Prairies in the eighteenth century, especially due to the efforts of La Vérendrye, again provided the Crees with a bargaining position between French and English competitors. N. M. Crouse does not specify any particular Indians when he asserts that the French were preferred to the English; on the contrary, he states: "The English did not permit them to come within their fortifications, but held them at arm's length and selected what they wanted from their stock of furs, giving them in return what they thought was a fair price."[3] This looks like poor business practice on the part of the Hudson's Bay Company in a competitive situation. Another writer, however, concluded that on the basis of information gained from accounts of traders, no important difference existed between the English and the French in their tolerance, understanding, or rapport with the Indians. Nor is there evidence, according to Lewis Saum, that the French or English traders were themselves aware of any differences between themselves regarding their relations with Indians.[4]

The conflicts between Crees and other groups did not foster the best trading conditions and both French and English prevailed upon the Crees, with varying degrees of success, to end their hostilities with adjacent peoples. ⟨Fighting between the Plains Crees and their enemies was due mainly to raiding for horses rather than for territory or trade advantages.⟩ In addition to local trade, Crees served as guides for English exploration and also carried furs as far as Montreal.

David Mandelbaum, in his classic monograph on the Plains Crees, sums it up thusly:

> Within one hundred years after the arrival of the whites the Crees moved westward. The fur trade impelled the movement, the gun enabling them to push other people before them. They were brought to the fringes of the prairie country in their quest for fresh fur-trapping areas. Because of their function as

middlemen in the trade, they traveled into the plains to carry goods to distant tribes. Their superior armaments enabled them to gain a foothold in the plains.[5]

By the 1730's some of the Crees were permanently out on the Prairies. Their wealth and power due to the trade made them a popular people for others to adhere to. Thus, by the late eighteenth century, they seem to have attracted adherents from several other peoples, including Assiniboines, Ojibways, Dakotas, and Athabascans. The Crees probably first acquired horses in the 1770's, the more westerly bands getting them before those to the east. Their main sources were most likely the Blackfoot and Assiniboine.

An increase in population was drawing them westward. This is to be correlated with their deep involvement in the fur trade, exhaustion of nearby sources, and the desire to open up new areas or exploit more thoroughly existing sources which made expansion desirable and, indeed, a necessity. By the mid-eighteenth century they were in "economic subservience" to the European economy. Their livelihood was in the grip of European fashions for fur garments as a stylish item of apparel.[6] The pattern already noted for the more easterly Indians was being repeated. Their expansion served as a continued source of irritation to their neighbours, producing the threat of clashes already noted. Horse stealing and counting *coup* rather than territorial conquest seem to have been the motivations for clashes, as we have seen. In addition the Crees jealously guarded their position as middlemen.

Counting *coup* refers to the element of chivalry or honour in Indian warfare, by which a man gained prestige through acts of conspicuous bravery. Such an act might be to enter an enemy camp, touch a member of that group, and return safely. The death of the enemy thus touched might not even be involved, and where it was, the scalp collected served as a physical proof of contact more than of death as such. The French word, *coup*, refers to the blow struck, and *coups* counted meant great honour and public adulation at home. The horse became not only the most useful animal, but also the symbol and standard of wealth and prestige. Through the possession of horses a man could show his heroism and generosity. Stealing horses from enemy groups and sharing them with one's own group doubly established an individual's prominence. Social distinctions were made as a result. Horseless individuals or families attached themselves to those with horses, and together these formed a band. Young men whose fathers owned horses were not obliged to take part in the exciting but sometimes dangerous parties raiding for horses. Social mobility, however, did allow a young man of a poor family to rise in wealth and status as he acquired horses. These class differences are illustrated by the remarks of a Cree father to his son:

> Here, my son, dress yourself, this is no way to be. I never bid you go to the scenes I need not name; I love you too much. Poor men are they who go on the warpath. . .for they hope to steal horses, but you, your horse he is fleet of foot and you yourself are handsome; you are not poor. . . .[7]

Even the sons of the wealthy often went raiding, however, under social pressure from their fellows who might otherwise deride them as "women." Wealth and liberality, along with leadership ability in war, were necessary for chieftainship. Not only must the chief be willing to give away his greater wealth, he must also forego revenge and retaliation, which were part of the common man's right. The chief might be expected to give away his own property to heal a breach between two quarrelling parties.

We have been discussing the Plains Crees of the mid-eighteenth to mid-nineteenth centuries. An insight into their circumstances may be provided by an examination of a group of Woodland Crees in more recent times, who because their area of residence is remote from white contact, underwent less change in the early twentieth century, down to 1914. The following comments, quoted at length from J. W. Anderson about the Woodland Crees in the James Bay area, c. 1710-1914, present an idyllic view of Indian-white relations, but fit within the general framework of the early phase of white contact:

> There is an optimum period in the relationship of any primitive people in their dealings with the white man. This might be described as the period of time when the aborigines have sufficient of the white man's material civilization to ease the *burden* of life, but yet not enough to disrupt their *way* of life: muzzleloading nets and snares instead of tree and willow roots; canvas instead of birch-bark for canoes and wigwams; steel traps instead of deadfalls.[8]

Anderson continues:

> The Indian of the [optimum] period. . .was usefully employed at work he liked and was competent to do, for most of the year. His aboriginal way of life was not too greatly disturbed. He had very few contacts with the whites and then only with missionaries and traders and both of them were officials who had very definite responsibilities towards the Indians. He was still governed largely by his own tribal laws for there was little or nothing of the white man's "law and order" and, above all, the Indian had none of the long periods of summer idleness so common today.[9]

Thus, ". . .the optimum theory would apply not only to the Indians and Eskimos of our country, but perhaps to aboriginal peoples the world over."[10]

Anderson adds some concrete information on an era and situation often speculated upon and made the basis for illustration of various theses about the place and power of traders and missionaries in so-called "primitive" societies. He does not refer here to a hypothetical construction, apparently:

> Now a word about the relationship of the Indians with the white during this so-called "optimum period." The whites in question were the traders and the missionaries and their families, and the trader, more often than the missionary, because mission stations were not established at all trading posts. It is often thought that in earlier days the whites, traders or missionaries, more or less "bossed" the Indians around as they liked, nothing could be further from the truth. As already mentioned, the white man's "law and order" was

far distant. Indian tribal law and customs to a great extend prevailed. More-over, because of the "way of life" (e.g. their part in the fur trade as trappers, carriers, canoesmen, food supplier to factories, customers) the Indian, and particularly his chiefs and leaders, were men of importance in their respective communities. They were consulted on all important matters because both the missionary and the trader required the active co-operation of the Indians in their respective spheres. Such moral suasion or leadership exercised by these white men was by virtue of their character, and their ability to deal equitably with the Indians. It is unreasonable to suggest that one white man in a remote community, far removed in time and distance from other white men or the white man's law and surrounded by three or four hundred Indians, could exercise any unfair or domineering influence over the tribesmen. If he tried to, things would not go well with him. But if he treated his Indian neighbours with dignity and respect, he would find them for the most part reasonable and co-operative.[11]

An important qualification to this presentation must be the effects of epidemics and the increased deadliness of warfare. In addition, changes unobservable to many non-Indians were taking place in their social and political life.

The coming of the Hudson's Bay Company had its impact on Cree society in specific ways which altered its character. The role of the chief, for example, was likely to become more institutionalized to con-form to European attitudes as the Hudson's Bay Company traded through the chief and favoured chiefs who eschewed warfare. Cree expansion westward and northward in the nineteenth century was not stopped by a series of smallpox epidemics which struck them twice in the eighteenth century and again in the early nineteenth century. It is asserted that their numbers declined in the mid-nineteenth century from approximately 4,000 to about 1,000, though their territorial span remained unchanged. Mandelbaum thinks that these losses may not have been quite as destructive to the Crees as some assert. Numerous adhesions to the Crees from neighbouring peoples already referred to may have provided partial compensation.[12]

The decimation of the Assiniboines, due also to epidemics, may have aided Cree expansion into areas formerly occupied by the Assiniboines in southern Manitoba and Saskatchewan. A smallpox epidemic in 1836 is estimated to have killed 4,000 or more Assiniboines of Canada—a sharp decline of a people who had been resident in the southern Mani-toba area at least as early as the mid-fourteenth century.[13]

In the mid-nineteenth century the Plains Crees were still the most widespread Indian people in Canada. The coming of settlers and the decline of the buffalo, especially in the last third of the century, called for new adjustment capabilities. They were forced to come to grips with this challenge. It is worth remembering when we recount the changes of the Crees from a forest hunting people to a prairie-dwelling horse-nomad people (and a similar transition occurred in the history of other prairie and plains peoples, as well), that these sweeping changes which their culture underwent did not cause them to cease to be Indians. Many if not most of these changes were the product of the coming of the European's tools, weapons, domesticated animals, and diseases, as well as their economic patterns. These traits the Indian had woven together into patterns uniquely his own, but he had been able to do it in an atmosphere of greater remoteness from outside pressures for directed culture change than that which obtains for the Indian of today in most of Canada. Nevertheless, modern change, most writers seem to agree, has not led to a loss of a sense of Indian identity either, or completely ruptured the thread of continuity.

As the Crees were moving westward into the prairies, another Algonkian-speaking people, to the west of them, were also moving westward. These were the Blackfoot. Migrating north and west from the vicinity of southeastern Saskatchewan, by the second quarter of the eighteenth century they had acquired horses. Their territory of occupation by the nineteenth century extended from northern Montana to central Alberta. The most westerly and southerly portion of them were the Piegans, who extended down into Montana and were therefore in the most intimate contact with the Americans. They were also the "advance guard" of the westward expansion and found themselves clashing with Indian peoples to the west. Of these, they forced the Kutenais further westward into the Rockies, and the Shoshones to the south and west.

The acquisition of the gun in the early 1680's had been an important factor in setting the Crees in motion westward, which in turn had resulted in their pressure on the Blackfoot. Thus a kind of domino effect was created when the Blackfoot in their turn applied pressure on the Kutenais and Shoshones. As with the others in similar circumstances, these two peoples sought to acquire guns with which to resist the Blackfoot. By the opening of the nineteenth century, their desire had been realized when the Hudson's Bay Company built Rocky Mountain House in their territory. When the Hudson's Bay Company reached them at Rocky Mountain House (1799), Kutenai House (1807), and Kullyspell House (1809), the Indians of the Rockies were better able to equalize their relations with the Blackfoot.

But to return to the Blackfoot, the two other subdivisions of the Blackfoot peoples were the Bloods and the Siksika (sometimes called the Blackfoot proper). The Bloods and Siksika were located in Alberta in the nineteenth century and had less contact with the white man than did the Piegans.

The Siksika, the more easterly branch of the Blackfoot described above, found themselves in frequent conflict with the Crees. Apparently Blackfoot rivalry with the Crees, from whom they received their guns originally, was heightened in the nineteenth century as the competition for furs increased. The relative isolation from whites of the two northern segments of the Blackfoot is credited by some scholars with being the explanation of the far fewer numbers of Blackfoot *Métis* than Cree *Métis* by the nineteenth century. It is asserted that, although the Blackfoot had experienced considerable cultural influence and culture change as a result of their part in the fur trade, they were able to retain a greater degree of political and economic autonomy from the whites than were the Crees. This autonomy characterized their situation until the last quarter of the nineteenth century when the buffalo disappeared and they were obliged to sign treaties and go onto reserves.

The Blackfoot were frequently spoken of as constituting a confederacy to which were attached the Athabascan-speaking Sarcee Indians. Some scholars have questioned the accuracy of such a description. They point out that the three elements did not necessarily act together within the Blood-Siksika-Piegan combination, nor did they avoid internal fighting, as for example between the Piegans and the Bloods. As with the Crees, the basic unit of the Blackfoot was not the tribe, but the band, a body of up to a few hundred persons with a political leader whose authority derived from prestige, influence, and respect rather than from the powers of office as such.

The earliest description of the Blackfoot by European writers may be as early as the end of the seventeenth century. The peoples referred to in 1691 by the Hudson's Bay Company explorer Henry Kelsey were probably Blackfoot. In the first half of the eighteenth century the Blackfoot had acquired horses from more westerly and southerly Indians (the Shoshones are usually mentioned), and from the east (the Crees and Assiniboines) they were acquiring guns. The account written by Anthony Henday (1754-55) indicates that they were still armed primarily with bows and arrows at the time of his visit. Through the Crees and the Europeans they were drawn into the fur trade, and these various influences were to have wide-ranging effects on their life and culture in the eighteenth and nineteenth centuries.

However, the Blackfoot were never prominent in the beaver pelt trade as such. Instead they acted as suppliers of food, chiefly buffalo meat, and buffalo hides to the trading posts. They also sold horses to the traders. Rivalry with the North West Company and a desire to draw the Blackfoot more closely into the network of their trading system was responsible for the Hudson's Bay Company efforts of Anthony Henday (1754) and Matthew Cocking (1773) to attract them to the trading posts on Hudson Bay, Henday writes:

> I was invited to the Archithinue [Blackfoot] Leader's tent: where by an interpreter I told him what I was sent for, and desired of him to allow some of his young men to go down to the Fort with me, where they would be kindly received, and get guns, etc. But he answered, it was far off, and they could not live without Buffalo flesh; and that they could not leave their horse etc. and many other obstacles, though all might be got over if they were acquainted with a canoe, and could eat fish, which they never do. The chief further said they never wanted food as they followed the Buffalo and killed them with the bows and arrows; and he was informed the natives that frequented the settlements, were oftentimes starved on their journey. Such remarks I thought exceeding true.[14]

Henday also notes that the Blackfoot took a dim view of other Indians trapping in their territory.[15] Assiniboine Indians travelling with Henday traded the Blackfoot used axes and other tools for wolves' skins: "We are above 60 canoes and there are scarce a gun, kettle, hatchet or knife amongst us, having traded them with the Archithinue natives".[16] Henday managed to get in a lick at his rivals. He reports an incident with a French trader who adulterated his trade brandy to half brandy and half water and then, when the Indians with whom he was trading became intoxicated, used some "sharp practice" to get only the best furs of selected animals.[17]

Approximately twenty years later, Matthew Cocking went among the Blackfoot to try again to lure them down to Hudson's Bay Company posts. He, too, failed to convince them of the desirability of doing so, but his journal gives the first extensive account of the Blackfoot. He travelled as far as the vicinity of present-day Biggar, Saskatchewan. Like Henday he found the Blackfoot very hospitable and generous and regarded them as superior to the Indians who frequented the forts. (The "distance lends enchantment" theme is common in European comments on Indians. Local Indians are frequently described by writers as being less attractive or in some way or ways inferior to some more remote peoples.) This superiority he ascribes to their life unblemished by Western civilization: "I shall be sorry if I do not see the Equestrian Natives who are certainly a brave people, and far superior to any tribes that visit our Forts: they have dealings with no Europeans, but live in a state of nature. . ."[18]

The Blackfoot gave Cocking approximately the same reasons for not going to the Hudson's Bay Company forts as those given to Henday in 1754: ". . .at the same time by the mouth of my leader I endeavoured to persuade two of them to accompany me on my return to the Fort, where they would meet a hearty welcome and receive many presents: but they said that they would be starved and were unacquainted with canoes and mentioned the long distance: I am certain they never can be prevailed upon to undertake such journies."[19] Other writers bear out the contrast between the regular food supply available to the Prairies Indians in the form of buffalo meat, and the more precarious existence of woodland peoples. This contrast was exaggerated when they became more dependent upon European goods for their livelihood.

Both Henday and Cocking noted the practice among Prairies Indians of adopting into their numbers the captives of war. Some were held as slaves, but Oscar Lewis points out that among the Blackfoot in the nineteenth century girls and women captives became wives. This custom became more common after the first third of the nineteenth century, as there was an economic advantage to having several wives to prepare hides for sale.

Competition and the desire to draw the Blackfeet into the fur trade led to the construction of forts and trading posts on the edge of the Blackfoot area. Eventually too, as already noted, trading posts were created among the more westerly Indians who were enemies of the Blackfoot. Thus some redressing of the military imbalance had begun to take place by the early nineteenth century as the Indians of the Rocky Mountains came into more direct contact with the traders.

Economic motives for warfare increased. Horses, women, and trade were motivations for raiding parties. Women performed an important economic function among the Blackfoot, in that they prepared the pemmican and buffalo hides used in trade. Oscar Lewis finds that the coming of the horse and gun changed the character of warfare among the Blackfoot. The raiding parties become smaller, they were more loosely organized, the war chief became less important, but the numbers killed in raids increased. The small war party became the characteristic form of warfare among the Blackfoot.[20]

The coming of the fur trade and the acquisition of the horse and gun are directly correlated with an increase in wealth, the use of the circle camp to keep horses safely enclosed, an increased number of wives, larger tipis, a drop in the marriage age for girls and a rise in the marriage age for men, an increase in inter-tribal relations which led to cultural borrowing, including the adoption of age-grade societies and religious bundles, and in general a greater degree of cultural uniformity among the Indians of the Prairies than had previously been the case. It also created larger units of population living together.

Age-grade societies are societies in which social status level is marked by age. Lewis calls them "an ideal mechanism for expressing and channelizing the vertical mobility which came with the increase in wealth."[21] Harold Driver comments on the impact of the fur trade on the Prairies Indians in the following terms: "Even religion was effected ...the wealth brought by the fur trade encouraged men to buy, as an investment, medicine bundles which might later be sold at a profit or kept as symbols of prestige. Bundles changed hands often, became more numerous, and sold for higher prices."[22] The medicine or religious bundle is a collection of objects, which might include any of the following—herbs, arrows, tobacco, feathers, skins, roots, rocks, stone pipes— within a rawhide bag. Each "article had a definite significance and called for a special song whenever its owner exposed it to the light," Diamond Jenness states. "They were thought to bring prosperity and good fortune and so there was much rivalry for their ownership." Jenness continues: "The formal transfer was a solemn ceremony that generally extended over many days and even weeks; for the new purchaser had to learn not only the significance of all the objects in the bundle, but the full details of the visions to which they traditionally owed their origin, and the songs, in a large bundle numbering perhaps half a hundred, that established their validity."[23]

Lewis observes that ". . .the accumulation of wealth, the manipulation of property, spending, buying, and selling, dominated Blackfoot life. Social position depended upon the liberal use of wealth, ostentatious displays, and other forms of social investment. . . . The ownership of horses therefore became a major index of social status."[24] Horses were a form of capital which when loaned earned interest for the lender. By this means those with a plentiful supply of horses could acquire more and thereby live off the "interest" of their investments to the younger men who were trying to establish themselves in the society. Class differences were demonstrated in the case of raiding parties, for example. A rich man would not follow a poor man on a raid. Very likely a man of greater status would not be asked to follow a man of lesser status. The poor man had more to gain by horse raiding than did the man already wealthy in horses.

The Blackfoot gained a reputation for being good businessmen, drivers of hard bargains who could take advantage of the rivalries between the European traders. Whites accused them of creating artificial scarcities to raise prices of buffalo meat and hides. This they did, it was said, by chasing buffalo away from trading post areas.

Not all relations on the Prairies were characterized by warfare. There is evidence that in the late eighteenth century and in the early nineteenth century some Blackfoot, Crees, and Assiniboines (the latter two are traditionally enemies of the former) were at peace with one another, hunting together and sometimes intermarrying. European influences both encouraged and discouraged warfare. Missionaries and traders and later administrators urged an end to fighting, but the economic arrangements created and the pressure for trade items led to a continuation of rivalries. In the nineteenth century Cree chiefs Poundmaker and Maskepitoon and Blackfoot Chief Crowfoot sought to end the inter-tribal warfare which supplemented epidemics as the main cause for the marked decrease in the Prairie Indian numbers.

In the 1870's the white treaty commissioners came to the Blackfoot on the United States side of the border. The Indians saw the dangers of the influx of American traders dealing in alcohol and the trade rivalries introduced by the withdrawal of the Hudson's Bay Company monopoly in their area after 1870 when the territory was ceded to Canada. The introduction of the R.C.M.P. established the sway of Canadian law in the territory in the early 1870's and on September 22, 1877, the Blackfoot and their Sarcee allies signed Treaty 7.

The permanent residence of the Sioux in Canada took place in the 1860's. These people, more specifically the two Sioux peoples, Santee and Teton, are culturally and linguistically related to the Assiniboines. The Assiniboines were allies of the Crees and along with some of the Ojibway groups warred against the Sioux. The tradition of warfare between Sioux and Ojibway is incorporated into the prayer made by the young Ojibway man while on his quest for a guardian spirit. He prayed: "Help me, Supernaturals, against hunger, sickness, poverty, and the Sioux." British-French rivalries played their part in these clashes as they had further east. The great French explorer La Vérendrye lost a son as a result of the conflicts.

During the American Revolution at least some of the Sioux were allied to the British under Chief Wapashaw, and during the War of 1812 American efforts to create internal fighting among the several Sioux peoples were partially successful. In the mid-nineteenth century, Dakota Sioux bought guns from the *Métis* at the Red River settlement. At the same time the Sioux were ceding large areas to the United States. Some felt they were being cheated in the dealings. The American Civil War brought economy measures, and obligations to the Indians were neglected by the government. United States troops on the settled frontier were minimal, and the Sioux decided to strike against the encroaching newcomers. Led by Little Crow, the Santee Sioux attacked settlements in Minnesota and were initially successful in their attack. Counter-attacks by American forces led the first Santee refugees to enter what is now Canada in December, 1862. They camped near Fort Garry. Their situation was desperate. Some offered to sell some of their children in order to secure assistance for the remaining members of the family. Although it was feared by settlers that the refugees might be a source of difficulty in Canada, such did not prove to be the case. They remained in Canada despite American efforts to get them to return to the United States.

The next major influx of Sioux came in late 1876 and early 1877 when the Teton Sioux Chief Sitting Bull and Medicine Bear (of the Yankton) fled to Canada for refuge with his followers. In May 1875, he and Crazy Horse led the Sioux and, accompanied by Cheyenne and other allies, defeated Colonel George Custer at Little Big Horn. United States Army forces struck back, and Indian efforts to resist the encroachments of the whites and ramifications of white presence were ultimately unsuccessful. *Forty Years in Canada*, by S. B. Steele, describes an incident in the events. United States Army General Terry came into Canada to consult with Sitting Bull and the others to convince them to return. Sitting Bull replied:

> For sixty-four years you have kept me and my people and treated us badly. What have we done that you should want us to stop? We have done nothing. It is the people on your side who have started us to do these depredations. We could not go anywhere else, so we took refuge in this country. It was on this side of the country that we learnt to shoot, and that was the reason I came back to it again. I should like to know why you came here. In the first place I did not give you the country, but you followed me from one place to another, so that I had to leave and come over to this country. I was born and raised in this country with the Red River half-breeds, and I intend to stay with them ...You have got ears and you have got eyes to see with, and to see how I live with these people. You see me, here I am. If you think I am a fool, you are a bigger fool than I am....You came here to tell us lies, but we do not want to hear them. I do not wish any such language used to me, that is, to tell me such lies in my Great Mother's house....[25]

The speech was punctuated by shaking hands with the senior R.C.M.P. officers present at the interview.

As in the case of the earlier Sioux they were happy to find a refuge, and the anticipated "trouble" with them in Canada did not occur. Sir John A. Macdonald wrote in 1878 "That it is only just to them to say, that they have behaved remarkably well ever since they crossed into

Canada." Two years later, however, Alexander Morris expressed the view that if the Canadian government were to get assurance of their safety from the United States government, they could and would then go back. Despite efforts by the Americans and the Canadian officials, many of the Sioux stayed, though in 1881 Sitting Bull returned to the United States with most of his followers. In the meantime a group of Nez Percé, Chief Joseph's people, also fled to Canada and joined the Sioux.

In 1874 the earliest Sioux refugees had been granted two reserves, where they followed their traditional way of life, hunting the buffalo while it lasted. However, efforts to alter their life style began immediately with the creation of the reserves; other reserves were created later. The Sioux in Canada have no treaty rights, but in other respects they are administered as other Indians. Father Gontran La Violette concludes his book, *The Sioux in Canada:* "Thus the Sioux refugees are true Canadians; they are protected by the Great Father, and they will live forever in their land of adoption, loyal to their King and to the country where in time of strife and danger they found sanctuary."[26]

The most northerly Indians of Canada are the Athabascan-speaking peoples, who occupy the Northwest Territories and the northern portions of British Columbia and the Prairie Provinces. These people— Chipewyan, Sekani, Beaver, Slave, Dogrib, Yellowknife, Tahltan, Nahani, Sarcee, Chilcotin, Hare, Kutchin, and Carrier—generally lived south of the northern tree line, though they might go into the open country or "barren lands" in search of food or if under pressure from the expanding Cree. Like their Algonkian-speaking neighbours to the south and east, they lived in small groups with what Western observers regard as a very informal political structure. Within a largely egalitarian society, the leader exercised "authority" through his superior knowledge, wisdom, and generosity, and his ability to make it possible for them to survive.

These peoples are thought to have dispersed from the Peace River area; spreading out in various directions, they borrowed cultural elements from the peoples who were their neighbours. Diamond Jenness illustrates this characteristic by the example of the Sarcees, who moved southward and associated themselves with the Blackfoot, and took over a Prairies-style culture. Others borrowed elements of Eskimo and West Coast Indian culture. Most are still to be found in the valleys of the Yukon and Mackenzie Rivers.

The largest group of these peoples were the Chipewyans, who occupied the largest territory at the time they were first observed by the incoming Europeans. As the most easterly group, they early came up against the Crees, who in the later seventeenth century were expanding west and northwest, as we have seen. At first disadvantaged because they lacked the European tools and especially weapons which the Crees possessed, the Chipewyans retreated northward. The situation began to alter after 1717, when the Hudson's Bay Company built a post at what became Churchill, Manitoba, and the Chipewyans could deal directly with them. After this they armed themselves. With their newly acquired power they were able to push northward against the Eskimos, who had no firearms, and west and northwestward against their fellow Athabascans, the Dogrib and Yellowknife, for whom they acted as middlemen at a good profit to themselves and whom they jealously prevented from direct contact with the white supply source. As with other peoples earlier they were drawn into the fur trade, and their situation in relationship to adjacent groups became dependent on the new wealth and power they had gained.

J. A. Mason summarizes this sequence of events in his *Notes on the Indians of the Great Slave Lake Area:*

> Naturally the coming of the whites provoked a radical change in the habitat, as did the establishment of trading posts in the method of life. The groups which first secured firearms upset the balance of power and drove the weaker ones further away. Consequently at this late date even a perusal of all available literature would not satisfactorily establish the details of former habitat, for much of the change occurred before white occupation. The Cree were the cause of most of the change in habitat as they were able, after obtaining firearms, to pursue their raids for scalps far up into the region of Great Slave Lake, driving the less courageous and ill-armed Athapaskans north to the poorer lands.[27]

In 1715 peace was declared between Chipewyans and Crees, but apparently this peace was a delicate thing. Intermittent fighting continued until 1760, with the Chipewyans assisting the Beaver and Slave Indians against the Crees. By the 1770's the situation seems to have relaxed somewhat and the Chipewyans were able to extend their migrations southward due to a relaxation of pressure from the Crees.

How much of this was due to the Hudson's Bay Company efforts to promote trade by reducing war and how much was due to the massive destruction of population as a result of the European introduction of disease and more deadly war and the alteration of the life of the people is not clear. The explorer, Samuel Hearne, estimated that the smallpox epidemic of 1781 caused the death of 90 per cent of the Chipewyans. Many Crees, as well as others, also died.

As the opportunities for fur trading increased, the Indians divided their hunting between subsistence and commercial. The yearly cycle of migration now included regular visits to the most accessible trading post. Weapons, tools, clothes, and food from the post came to be included in the material culture of the Indians. Sometimes a family had a regular residence at the post and hunted and trapped in an area convenient to this location. In this way residence patterns of the Indians were also changed. Missionaries and administrators favoured a pattern of settled residence as a more efficient way to regulate and instruct the Indian. The Indians seem to have been as pragmatic about their activities as they were able to be, given the growing restraints and complexities into which they were willingly and unwillingly moving.

A frequent residential pattern, both among these northern Athabascans and the eastern Algonkians, was that of settlement at the nearby fort or trading post through the year and seasonable movements out from this residence to hunt, trap, and fish.

In the north as in the south, the Indians came into contact with the white man earlier in the east than in the west. The eastern Chipewyan were the first, as already noted. The contact around Great Slave Lake occurred in the mid-eighteenth century. Farther west among the Fort Nelson Slave Indians the earliest contact seems to have occurred in the early 1780's as fur traders sought new sources and set up permanent posts to tap the wealth. Then came the missionaries in the 1860's and finally the Indian administration. Under the direction of the administrators, the Indians elected a chief and headman, and these men then signed the treaty by which their land was alienated. The legal necessities of the administering authority imposed a foreign political apparatus onto the Slave Indians in order to facilitate their entrance into a whole complex of foreign culture.

J. J. Honigmann has found that despite the changes which had taken place and the extent to which the Slave Indians had accepted the technology and food of the white man, nevertheless ". . .white values and white sanctions find only slight reception in Fort Nelson Slave culture when they are unrelated to survival goals."[28] This he asserts while noting that the Indians have largely accepted Christianity. Elsewhere in his study he states: ". . .new ideas and behaviours. . .may. . .be adopted and fitted into the existent configuration without any major change occurring in the orientation of the total culture."[29]

Cornelius Osgood studied the Kutchin Athabascans in 1932. Of these people and their culture change he observed:

> In reviewing the evidence, it is clear that a great difference exists between the present-day Kutchin and those whose culture flourished at the time of the first historic contact. It is also clear that it is the more objective elements of the society which have suffered the greatest change, and that underneath the sometimes distasteful appearance of undigested borrowings lie innumerable unsuspected remnants of ancient thought which are responsible for the behavior and point of view so alien to a European mind.[30]

In contrast to this point of view, some authorities, observing the poverty, sickness, and unemployment on reserves in the north, have postulated a cultural phenomenon they call "deculturation." This means that a people have, through contact with Western civilization, lost elements of their traditional culture without gaining new elements to fill their place. That is, they have neither borrowed new elements from the white man's culture nor invented alternatives of their own. The result is a cultural loss and impoverishment.

This form of cultural change is described as essentially destructive. In this condition the Indian people are totally dependent on the government or other outside sources for meeting whatever needs the lost elements met, or else they are condemned to go without. For example, the loss of political or organizational life has meant that the only source for such has become governmental personnel. Another example is in the area of social and moral training; with the collapse of the indigenous social and moral culture, the active element in the important spheres of daily life is an outside force, the European religion and church. The resultant form which the Indian communities tend to take in this situation of directed culture change by outside agencies is one of a uniformity which cuts across aboriginal cultural differences. Ethnic differences are eliminated in this deculturative situation, and all the peoples experiencing this form of tie-in with the Canadian culture are all alike. This concept has been applied elsewhere in Canada and the United States; perhaps this is the kind of thing Robert A. Manners has in mind also when he refers to Indian communities having a ". . .badly watered-down old way of life between two worlds."[31]

The concept of deculturation as discussed here is a controversial one, and it may be doubted whether it is quite consistent with the evidence submitted for the Athabascans or any other Indians.

FOOTNOTES:

[1] David G. Mandelbaum, *The Plains Cree*, Anthropological Papers of the American Museum of Natural History, Vol. XXVII, Pt. II (New York: 1940), p. 172 and 180.

[2] Walter M. Hlady, "Indian Migrations in Manitoba and the West," *Historical and Scientific Society of Manitoba, Papers*, Series III, No. 17 (1960-1961), p. 42. This article contains a useful map of migrations for each of the peoples discussed.

[3] N. M. Crouse, *La Verendrye, Fur Trader and Explorer*, (Toronto: 1956), p. 65.

[4] Lewis O. Saum, *The Fur Trader and the Indian* (Seattle: 1965), pp. 67-71.

[5] Mandelbaum, *op. cit.*, p. 178.

[6] *Ibid.*, p. 176.

[7] *Ibid.*, pp. 295-296.

[8] J. W. Anderson, "Eastern Cree Indians," *Historical and Scientific Society of Manitoba, Papers*, Series III, No. II (1956), p. 31.

[9] *Ibid.*, p. 37.

[10] *Ibid.*

[11] *Ibid.*, pp. 37-38.

[12] Mandelbaum, *op. cit.*, p. 180.

[13] Hlady, *op. cit.*, p. 35.

[14] "York Factory to the Blackfeet country; the journal of Anthony Hendry, [sic], 1754-55," (Ed. by Lawrence J. Burpee), *Transactions of the Royal Society of Canada*, Sec. II, 3rd Series, Vol. I (1907), p. 338.

The Canadian Indian

[15] *Ibid.*, p. 334.

[16] *Ibid.*, p. 351.

[17] *Ibid.*, p. 352.

[18] "The Journal of Matthew Cocking, 1772-73," (ed. by Lawrence J. Burpee), *Transactions of the Royal Society of Canada,* Sec. II (1908), p. 110.

[19] *Ibid.*, p. 111.

[20] Oscar Lewis, *The Effects of White Contact Upon Blackfoot Culture with Special Reference to the Role of the Fur Trade,* Monographs of the American Ethnological Society (Ed. by A. Irving Hollowell), (Seattle: 1942, Second Printing 1966), pp. 46-59.

[21] *Ibid.*, p. 42.

[22] Harold E. Driver, Indians of North America (2nd Ed.), (Chicago: 1969), p. 216.

[23] Jenness, *Indians of Canada*, pp. 323-324.

[24] Lewis, (1942).

[25] S. B. Steele, *Forty Years in Canada* (Toronto: 1915), p. 128.

[26] Fr. Gontran La Violette, *The Sioux in Canada* (Regina, Sask.: 1944), p. 131.

[27] J. A. Mason, *Notes on the Indians of the Great Slave Lake Area* (New Haven: 1946), p. 12.

[28] J. J. Honigmann, *Ethnography and Acculturation of the Fort Nelson Slave* (New Haven: 1946), p. 147.

[29] *Ibid.*, p. 15.

[30] Cornelius Osgood, *Contributions to the Ethnography of the Kutchin* (New Haven: 1936), p. 174.

[31] Robert A. Manners, "Pluralism and the American Indian," *The North American Indians, A Sourcebook* (New York: 1967), p. 678. (Reprinted from *America Indigena*, 22, 25-38, 1962.)

3. Under Colonial Administration:

Indian resistance to assimilation and the reserve period.

The era of the Hudson's Bay Company, when the nature of the fur trade made it desirable to disturb as little as possible the Indians' culture and life style, gave way to the era of the settler and the eventual removal of the Indians to reserves, frequently under threat of direr consequences if peaceful submission and prompt willingness to accept the white man's "treaty" were not forthcoming. A reading of Alexander Morris's volume on the treaty-making in the Prairies reveals this intimidation and offers the evidence for G. F. G. Stanley's comments on the nature of these "treaties"—that is, that they were not really negotiated treaties between two more or less equal parties. Nevertheless, the fact that "treaties" were signed is a remnant of the older relationship and the recognition of the Indians' political independence and a kind of equality as between nations which characterized the earlier contact. Not until the 1870's did the United States government cease to use the word "treaty" for the documents which validated the disposal of Indians in the United States and its territories. The last "treaty" signed in Canada was in 1923.

Diseases, inter-tribal warfare, and social disintegration played their parts in the numerical decline and cultural changes among the Indians of the Prairies and northern territories, as we have seen. Indians and whites alike came to see that, unless steps were taken, more peoples might be destroyed. Out of this situation was shaped the system which produced the "reservation period" of our scheme. The creation of reserves, though not new to the 1870's—they had been in existence in Ontario for a number of decades by this time and in Quebec since the seventeenth century—was extended to the Prairies to dispose of the Indians of that vast area. However, not only did this period see the extension of the system of reserves to the Prairies, but it also witnessed the organization of federal responsibility for Indian affairs. Indians of Ontario and the East, as well as Indians of the Prairies and British Columbia, were now brought under one central administration.

The era thus begun extended until the post-World War II period, about 1951. For the Indian it was the period of his irrelevance to Canadian life. He came under national government administration and the systemization of directed culture change. This was the completion of the conquest of his territory. The government crystallized the administrative rules and machinery by which they would now control those who were already under their authority and those who were soon to come under it. During this period individuals assimilated, groups dwindled. Many experts thought that Indians as social groups would die out. Some allowed that they might survive, but only as assimilated, Christianized communities. Lord Dufferin's prediction that the *Métis* would form an important link between whites and Indians in the future of the Prairies proved to be meaningless, when by 1900 both Indians and *Métis* were swallowed up by the influx of hundreds and thousands of Europeans. This is the period when missionaries sought to convert the western Indians to Christianity as they had already undertaken to do in the East, and to preserve them by making them over into Christians (that is, Westernized red men).

This period is a relatively unexplored part of Indian history, and it seems reasonable to suppose that were it to be more carefully studied much light would be shed on the current events of Indian affairs in Canada. Examination of this history might also illustrate and clarify the ways in which Canadian colonialism was being practised on the Indians and how the Indians were meeting this "manifest destiny" brand of imperialism. To call this the period of irrelevance is not to lose sight of the earlier assertion that Indian history must keep the Indian at the centre. Although much work remains to be done, existing studies suggest that it was at this time that the Indians were attempting to come to grips with the new realities of their position vis-à-vis the dominant white man, particularly the administrator and the missionary, the two main representatives, after the fur trader, of Western civilization. This was the era when the Indian was having more intensively urged upon him the agricultural economy and the education of the dominant society. This was the period when a stereotype grew—what the Indian is and what he can and cannot, will and will not, do and be. These stereotypes have continued down to the present time, and they form part of the context in which contemporary Indian leadership must operate. The real and imagined aspects of the picture of the Indian held by whites today and of the whites held by the Indians—many of these were created in this period, a time of synthesis for the Indian.

It has already been noted that the first reserves in Canada were created in French Canada in the seventeenth century. The purpose of these reserves was primarily that of changing the Indians' culture. A British policy in this regard began to show itself most clearly and consistently by the beginning of the nineteenth century. By this time Indians in southern Ontario had begun to sign treaties releasing large tracts of land and to take up residence on reserves. This concentration of populations freed the land for white occupancy as immigrants came into the territory following the American Revolution. It was argued that Indians on reserves would also be protected from the more harmful and destructive aspects of contact with white men. By means of a controlled environment, the Indian was to be led gradually into a new way of life and a new view of life.

It is clear that the beginning of the era of reserve life was not the same across Canada; obviously it came sooner in eastern Canada than in the West. In more remote northern areas of eastern Canada, in Ontario for example, the reduction of the Indian lands has taken place as recently as the first quarter of the twentieth century. In addition, as Euro-Canadian occupancy of public land did not immediately follow the alienation of the land from Indians, it was still possible for Indians to hunt and fish on the land they had surrendered. Their way of life, though modified by contact with traders, missionaries, medical people, administrators, and teachers, was still less altered than that of Indians in southern Canada, where Indian-white contacts were more intensive.

As we have seen, this is the period when the Indians were undergoing tutelage which was supposed to assimilate them into Western culture. As the intended result has not been achieved, it would be instructive to examine in closer detail what did occur, in order to gain some answers to the question of why Indians have not assimilated or why they are not assimilating more rapidly.

Since the first half of the nineteenth century, at least, records and reports by administrators and missionaries have been made of various Indian communities. Observations on their acceptance of Western culture have been incorporated into official and non-official summaries and documents. On the basis of dress, housing, church attendance, technology, and occupations, observers have attempted to describe and estimate the degree to which the old culture was dying out and the new, Western culture was being accepted. These observers tended to regard the Indian culture in its various forms as essentially static. Changes in dress or technology manifested by the Indians were therefore less likely to be interpreted as adaptive changes or cultural synthesizing than they were to be regarded as steps along the one-way street to assimilation.

The depth and intensity of the indigenous culture was either not understood or grossly underestimated. It could hardly have been understood by those who regarded the Indian as a child who needed only to be raised to adulthood or as a blank sheet of paper, culturally speaking, who was to be written upon with European culture. Indians for their part did not indiscriminately accept the superiority of all the new over the old. They did not see an either/or choice; they both adapted and incorporated. Furthermore the differences between the white and Indian cultures created barriers which separated the latter from the former even when resistance was neither conscious nor deliberate. All of these factors assisted Indians in retaining their identities as communities.

Their selectivity extended to attendance at school and church. For example, children might attend school during one school session and then be away during another, according to the seasonal patterns of the

Indian group's activities. Or they might attend school for a few days when not needed at home or when there was no hunting or fishing trip to go on and then be absent when these activities were pursued. The net effect was that the systematic process of culture change was interrupted, delayed, bogged down.

Other factors were also operating. The mode of instruction, the physical circumstances of instruction—desks, classrooms, regulations, required dress, the necessity of haircuts, language of instruction—were likely to be factors which reduced the total impact intended by the teachers. Indian children were used to a learning process linked to their daily round of activity, learning by doing from early childhood. They were taught by parents, grandparents, and other relatives in circumstances that were not always informal, but which were rooted in patterns consistent with the first five or seven years of their lives. The new education had grown out of a different cultural experience and was being grafted on imperfectly, so that it did not "take" as had been intended. Even so, the education made available was perhaps of a kind easy to incorporate into the pre-existing pattern without clear-cut alteration. It was to a considerable extent technical and manual. Thus social relationships and responsibilities and community ties were frequently left unchanged by its introduction.

More significant for cultural change were the alterations in economic base which various Indian groups were obliged to undergo. The effort to shift the Indian from hunting, fishing, and gathering to agriculture was the main emphasis of efforts to change his way of making a living. A settled life, perhaps in larger units, with the changing character of Indian leadership, presented challenges to the Indians. Chiefs sometimes became instruments of the Indian administration's apparatus of government. The community lost its economic and political autonomy. The ability of the chief to perform functions such as distribution of goods, and to provide leadership in the informal way which characterized many Canadian Indian societies, was threatened by the power and wealth which was at the disposal of the Indian agent. Energetic young men could attract the support and assistance of the white personnel who dominated the Indians' contact with the outside world and controlled decision-making about reserve business. Sometimes chiefs who were appointed by government did not qualify for their role by traditional practice. Rivalries and conflicts within the community might develop. To the outsider the Indian divided into "progressives" and "conservatives."

Such developments did contribute to changes in the political and social arrangements by which the Indians lived. Polygamy was not allowed. The potlatch, a feast where property was distributed and/or destroyed, was forbidden, as were ceremonial dances—the Tamanawas, or shamanist dance—under pain of imprisonment. Some of these activities went underground. Some were altered in their form. Gift-giving was done at weddings, birthdays, and anniversaries in the new circumstances. Annual "pow-wows" became the occasions for performing some of the dances. Traditional societies and fraternities sometimes disappeared, but in other cases, they were transformed into some altered form to meet a need created by the new circumstances. *f*

Often the Indians took only very slowly to agriculture. Indian Affairs records and missionary reports show that years and years passed in which the acreage of cultivated land increased slowly, if at all. Descriptions of the reserves spaced over decades and even scores of years seemed to be very similar. Their communities continued to exist. Population trends had gradually turned upward by the early twentieth century. In many communities the native language persisted.

In 1844 a report on Indians on reserves in Upper and Lower Canada was made on the basis of investigations carried on two years previously. Many of the topics dealt with were to recur in later discussions and debates concerning Indians. We can see in this document, which is not the earliest of its kind, the embryo of the type of findings which formed the annual reports of the Indian Affairs Department of later years.

The survey indicated that the Indian population on reserves in Upper and Lower Canada was rising. The health of the settled Indians was asserted to be better than that of the hunting Indians. Health was linked to economic well-being, which was in turn linked to acceptance of agriculture and of Christianity.

The report shows the evaluation by the commissioners of the extent of Westernization already achieved by the Indians, measured in terms of economic changes, religious changes, schools, and adoption of European dress, housing, and language. The outward signs of "progress" toward assimilation are chronicled with the implication of the willingness and explicitly asserted aptitude of the Indian for change. The categories chosen to illustrate these developments lent themselves to quantification—for example, increased acreage under cultivation, increased live stock raised, statistics on houses, school attendance, church attendance, etc.

Generally the Indians of Lower Canada were described as having taken on some of the ways of Western civilization but not all those made available to them. Aboriginal religious customs and ceremonies had been abandoned, and in their place the Christian rites of the Roman Catholic Church were practised. Their fondness for hunting was abating even among the Algonquins, Nipissings, and Abenakis.

On the other hand, religious rivalry between Roman Catholics and Protestants had contributed to the absence of schools on some of the reserves reported upon. Schools had had to close down. While the Iroquois and Huron were to some extent engaged in agriculture, they had since aboriginal times been agriculturalists. Thus the aboriginal agriculturalists were responding to efforts to encourage them to farm, whereas the peoples who were aboriginally hunters still preferred hunting and resisted taking up cultivation. On two reserves the Abenakis were reported to be making no progress in agriculture. The same was reported for a Micmac reserve. Other traditional hunting peoples were described as "the least civilized" in Lower Canada. In some cases these reports refer to reserves which had been in existence since the second half of the seventeenth century.⊦

The economic security of a settled life may have contributed to the larger families noted by the commissioners, five to six children for the sedentary peoples compared to only two to three children for the hunters: the settled people have a lower infant mortality rate. The extent to which the sedentary groups were settled and the hunters were nomadic is not altogether clear. The report describes sedentary peoples in Upper Canada for whom hunting occupied between two weeks and three months of the year. Aboriginally in these same cultures, the men had hunted and simultaneously the women had practised agriculture.

On the other hand, the hunting peoples were located on reserves in villages and did some cultivation. The description seems to suggest degrees of cultivation and hunting, with some groups more toward the agricultural end of an agricultural-hunting continuum, and other groups more to the hunting alternative. The Indian languages were found to be spoken in all the communities. The dichotomy of male and female occupations may have been reflected in the observation that men didn't work, or not very much. Most of the work was done by women (this in Lower Canada). Traditional wigwam structures were still a common form of housing.

In Upper Canada the commissioners found that agriculture was more likely to be practised by the Christianized Indians. The Indians were categorized as resident Indians (their population was rising), wandering Indians, and visiting Indians from the United States. These latter were former British allies who came to Canada annually to receive presents. Indian residents in the United States ceased to receive presents after 1843. This led to a migration of Indians to Canada.

The total population included in this survey was slightly under 9,000 people. This figure included Six Nations Indians, Ojibways, Potawatomis, Delawares, Munseys, and Hurons. The commissioners found that the Six Nations Indians were the most Christianized and most agricultural. The Ojibway were less so, though some did practise agriculture and have schools. Methodist missionaires were very active among many of the Ojibways; one of their most illustrious converts was the Welsh-Mississauga, the Rev. Peter Jones. The Potawatomis were the least changed and were prominent among those Indians who had recently come to live in Canada. Allies of the British in earlier wars, they were sufficiently unacculturated to elicit the descriptions "wild" and "turbulent." The "pecking order" of the commissioners' approval seems to have been as follows: Iroquois and Huron, Ojibway and Ottawa, and finally Potawatomi.

The settlement of Wekwemikong on Manitoulin Island was reported upon in some detail. Here a community of Indians were said to be taking to agriculture and settlement more rapidly than were the Ojib-ways. Again, Christianization, agriculture, Westernization were linked to the notion of the "progress" of the Indians toward assimilation. The commissioners seem to have been unaware that, like the Iroquois and the Hurons in aboriginal times, the Ottawas too, though perhaps to a lesser extent than the other two, had practised agriculture. The settlement of Wekwemikong was composed of Ottawas who, again resembling the Iroquois and Huron, had experienced the efforts of mission-aries since the seventeenth century.

The commissioners found that Indians regarded the Proclamation of 1763 as an Indian charter of rights, and referred to it several times in their representations to the government. Some Indians who were en-countered in the investigations had kept a copy of the proclamation. The particular topic referred to in this historic document was that having to do with the purchase of land from the Indians. This responsibility was restricted to an authorized government officer only, and it was legal only when accomplished at a public assembly of Indians concerned.

The report asserts that as settlers' demands for land grew or the Indians were regarded as undesirable by the whites, agreements for surrender of land were made. In answer to challenges of the good faith of the whites in drawing up terms of purchase, the commissioners con-tended that the only alternative would have been white takeover by force; Alexander Morris included this thought in his conversations with Indians signing treaties in the Prairies in the 1870's.

A number of topics, proposals, and situations which were to charac-terize Indian affairs appear in the report. There is, for example, men-tion of a proposal by Governor Sydenham in 1841 that all Indians who practised agriculture be released from government supervision and be treated like any other citizens. Variations on this approach have con-tinued to form a part of official thinking on government responsibility and obligation to Indians. An expression of the opinion that govern-ment "tutelage" is bad for the Indian is a corollary of the previous view and was also noted.

Emeric de Vattel, the Swiss jurist, is cited for justification of Euro-pean takeover of land. The argument used then and since is that the earth belongs to mankind generally and to those who can most effec-tively utilize it. Thus agricultural people are justified in displacing hunting people, since the farmer can utilize the land more intensively than can the hunter. The question of whether isolation from or near-ness to white settlement is best for assisting desirable culture changes was aired.

The report is a clear-cut statement asserting the Indians' capability for absorbing Western civilization and is designed to document this conclusion. It is a pointed refutation of the themes expressed by Sir Francis Bond Head (discussed elsewhere in this book). As such it was a reinforcement of government's intention and contributed to the atmos-phere in which the Indian lived. The conclusions reached helped to shape the Indians' environment. Commenting on Sir Francis's views, the commissioners found that they differed from "the most competent authorities and do not appear to be supported by experience."[1] This debate is described in more detail below.

In this context a reference should be made to the Coldwater Indian Reserve. Started in 1830, it had been extinct for several years by the time of the commissioners' investigations in 1842. The "Coldwater Experiment," as it was called, was designed to change the way of life of a group of Ojibways, who were placed in a community located at the southeast corner of Georgian Bay. Here the government in collaboration with missionaries was to carry out a systematic effort. The failure of this "experiment" had contributed to Sir Francis's conclusions that Indians were incapable of changing. Now further evidence was mounted to disagree. Thus the findings of the Commissioners were in essential agreement with the conclusions of the Methodist missionaries and the Aborigines' Protection Society, and the arguments used were similar. Nevertheless, while Sir Francis was certainly mistaken, the conclusion reached by the others were not entirely accurate either.

The experience of Coldwater reveals numerous situations and conditions which were recurrent in the history of Indian reserves. Methodist and Roman Catholic missionaries competed for adherents and thereby created social conflicts. Missionaries and government personnel clashed over policies and practices, incompetent administrative staff made some efforts ineffectual, inferior equipment was supplied and frustrated Indians and whites who used it, adequate financial support for programs was not forthcoming. Ignorance of Indian culture and values, however, must rank as one of the main factors on the side of the whites' failure.

Whether the "experiment" can be regarded as a failure from the Indian side is another matter. The project was based on the desire to change Indian culture to something which the Indians apparently didn't want. Men regarded agricultural work as demeaning. Hunting and fishing were occupations more consistent with their traditions, and were certainly preferred to school attendance. Jobs such as road building were not meaningful in the context of their culture. They were willing to convert to Christianity in some cases, but this didn't mean a wholesale acceptance of European civilization. Many whites regarded Christianity and Western culture as synonymous, as we have seen, though missionaries and administrators considered certain elements of the white man's life style as undesirable for Indians and whites alike.

The extent to which the Indians used disagreements among the white religious and administrative personnel to gain leverage in Indian-white dealings is not clear. The Indians may have thought of Coldwater as an obligation the white had to the Indian, a recompense for land taken away. The white man had created a situation of hardships for him, and Coldwater provided some alleviation. In any event, white settlers encroached on Indian lands and pressure on the Indians increased. The government did not give them adequate protection from the white settlers. The very ends of the various "experiments" like that at Coldwater were often subverted by the government's own agents; far from protecting Indians from white settlers, reserves provided land for white squatters and an opportunity for exploitation of Indians by administrators—the farm instructors who gave no instruction, the Provisioners who supplied ungrowable seed and cattle too old to bear young.

At the same time that investigations were taking place in the Canadas, Upper and Lower, the Maritime Provinces were carrying on their own examinations of the Indian's situation. Pressures from London and internal concern were at work here, too. Lord Glenelg was seeking information on the "progress" of the Indian toward "civilization." Internally some sense of concern as well as calculation about more intensive use of land impelled the local authorities to look into matters. Here and there they looked over their shoulders at the Canadas and thought they saw a satisfactory model for arranging their own Indian affairs. In both New Brunswick and Nova Scotia the reports issued in the early 1840's described a people who, though in long contact with the white man, had retained many elements of their material and non-material culture and had certainly retained a separate identity.

The Perley Report for New Brunswick shows Indians in that province, Malecite and Micmac, reluctant to take up agriculture. Few lived in frame houses, preferring the traditional houses. Fishing and hunting were still practised, though logging had become a seasonal occupation. The Indian languages were still spoken, though French and/or English might also be used. Some communities were found to be harder hit than others by the demoralizing effects of contact with European culture. Population was on the decline, and in general the Indian population was worse off since British takeover than they had been previously under their Jesuit mentors.

The report proposes the kinds of solutions already described in connection with the Canadas. Agriculture, the settled life, and schools would be the main mechanisms by which the desired cultural change would take place. Positive and negative inducements would be created to get parents to send children to school. Financial aid would be made available to those who co-operated. Schools should be integrated with whites, and Indian settlements should be near white communities to accelerate change. The Micmacs are said to have been making greater strides toward Westernization than the Malecites. Much stress is placed upon the widespread acceptance of an abstinence pledge among the Micmacs. It was a topic much discussed in the nineteenth century and very much an issue within white society itself at that time.

The report shows that Indians left their European-style economic occupations to go off to hunt and fish. References are made to the wandering habits of the Indians. Chiefs are described as holding government warrants to be chiefs, though there is no indication that the men were not chosen by traditional means as well. An example is cited of a chief, recognized by government, taking upon himself the rights to sell and lease reserve land and pocketing the money; this man was deposed by his own people and a new chief installed. The commissioners noted one group that followed seasonal work patterns and persisted in "ancient habits, forms and ceremonies" more than any other Micmacs. Schools were non-existent or not functioning. There is little or no comment on their religious life or social organization.

The general impression from the report is that the Malecite and Micmac Indians of New Brunswick, though in long contact with Europeans and much influenced by this contact, had retained much of the old culture. Adaptation to new occupations—lumbering, for example—had taken place. Western-style dress was widespread. They had become selective in their response to the West. Biologically, they had acquired some white admixture, though comments in the report about their resemblance to Malays suggests that that this was not universal.

The report also suggests a people beleaguered by white encroachment. Although reserves had been allocated, they were frequently unsurveyed and without regular government administration. The existence of reserves (or more particularly, Indian communities) assisted in the retention of the Indian culture, though adapted, but the absence of clearly demarcated boundaries made the reserves subject to continual white encroachment. Squatters and timber raiders were problems. Indians who attempted to resist the loss of their land and resources were threatened with violence. With this information it is not surprising, then, to find that well into the nineteenth century little systematic government effort had been made to alter the Indian culture, though alteration had occurred.

In Nova Scotia much the same situation existed in the 1840's. Readily available information for a period of two decades indicates that from the early 1840's to the mid-1860's, despite an increasingly active program by the provincial government, the Micmac Indians of Nova Scotia resisted the plans for cultural change which had been designed for them. Joseph Howe, newly-appointed Indian commissioner for Nova Scotia in 1843, called attention to the French and German settlers in that colony. These, he observed, though living among the British for a hundred years, still were essentially French and German. It was not surprising, he asserted, that the Indians would take time to change.

Although reserves had been created and Indian policy had begun to emerge by this time, Howe found the reserves inadequate, isolated (no roads), and encroached upon by whites, as well as some counties which had no reserves. Population decline would, he believed, make the Indians extinct in forty or fifty years if the rate remained unchanged. Most of the Indians lived in their traditional housing, the wigwam; they ate seed potatoes instead of planting them[1]. The Micmacs resisted instruction in any language but Micmac. What schools had been started were irregularly attended due to the persistence of patterns of seasonal migration; Indians regularly left their summer sites and went to winter sites. However, the commissioners did not doubt the intellectual capability of the Indians. In the middle-1840's, natural disasters contributed to the difficulties of adaptation. For several years potato crops were ruined by a blight, and the famine was compounded by an accompanying wheat blight.

Through the next two decades, two themes recur in the commissioners' reports: the gradual acceptance of Western civilization by the Micmacs and their refusal to accept Western civilization. Indications of acceptance of settled agricultural life gave optimism to the Indian agents that the Micmacs would gradually change. On the other hand, examples of seasonal movements, failure to attend to agricultural pursuits, and the attendant difficulties of dealing with a "wandering" people led to a continuing note of frustration and pessimism.

Hunting, fishing, basket-making (for the white market), logging, some lumbering, and some farming are repeatedly described as the means of economic existence. Efforts to encourage the Indians to cultivate were further disrupted by white encroachment, lack of adequate surveys, and continual threat of loss of reserve land. Dams built illegally on Indian land in conjunction with mills also built illegally on Indian land flooded the Indian land, thereby hindering agricultural as well as regular hunting and fishing activities.

In 1847 the Micmacs were referred to as "semi-barbarous" and also as an apparently "doomed race." The Indian commissioner found that they had not "improved" their condition since the mid-eighteenth century. The Indians were still keenly aware of the treaty terms agreed to in the eighteenth century. Grants due them under the treaties were not regarded as cause for humiliation or "hand-outs," but as testimonies of the British respect for them and accepted as such with pride.

Various diseases, including tuberculosis, were a serious debilitating factor among the Indians, the reports show. The loss of traditional food sources threatened the continued existence of these people. Logging operations, for example, drove off game; livestock destroyed edible indigenous roots; and herds of swine destroyed beds of shellfish.

Apparently the conversion of the Micmacs by the Jesuits did not lead to a general acceptance of a Western style of life. The failure of the Jesuits to insist upon Western culture along with Christianity was regarded by the government administrative officer as a major factor in Indian lack of "improvement." A recurring theme in most European sources on Indians over the centuries is the notion that the Indian has become morally and culturally worsened by indiscriminate contact with European culture. This idea frequently appears in the observations of the officers of Indian administration in mid-nineteenth century Nova Scotia.

Indians continued to follow seasonal patterns of occupation and residence, going into the woods in winter to hunt and trap, and drawn to the water's edge in summer to fish. As we have seen, reserves were gradually chipped away as squatters were granted the right to purchase reserve lands. Immigrants from Scotland are particularly cited. White immigrants to New Brunswick and Nova Scotia promised the possibility of increased production on the land, and economic development. They were to be encouraged to settle by making land available. Surveying reserves and studying their agricultural potential was as much a part of the interest of the government (or perhaps more?) as was the welfare of the Indian. As the reports show, Indian welfare was interpreted in terms which were the same as those for the non-Indian populace. The acceptance of the life style and value system of Western civilization had as a major aspect the more intensive exploitation of the land and natural resources. Writing in 1861 the Indian commissioner noted that the Micmacs were "Disinclined to do farm labour on their *vast reserve land*" (italics added). They seemed "destined to live a roving life," and he added, "almost wholly dependent on charity."

The Indians' views and suggestions on their condition and what to do about it seemed to Indian commissioner Samuel Fairbanks, in 1863, to offer nothing that was better than the existing policies. The Indians were, he believed, under a policy which provided land enough for farms, a liberal provision for the sick and needy, and growing funds from the sale of lands. It wouldn't be the fault of the government if the Indians weren't better off in the future, he concluded. The report doesn't make clear the context in which Indian opinion was solicited, and no specific evidence from Indians is included with the report. Perhaps casual conversation is being referred to.

In Inverness County, in 1862, government land policy was found to run counter to Indian custom, when the government tried to divide land into parcels of 150 to 160 acres for family farms. It proved to be a delicate task. The Indians were reported to hold "everything in common." What came of this request is not recorded in the report. In Queen's County in the same year it was suggested that, as the existence of reserves held up white settlement, Indians should be given grants of land and then allowed to do with them as they saw fit. The anticipated response seems to have been that the Indians would sell all or much of the land to whites and then the Indian land would be disposed of. As late as 1866 the annual report of the commissioner stated that the Indians preferred "wandering about." During the two decades examined in these reports of the mid-nineteenth century, little or nothing was said about the work of schools or missionaries.

During the end of the third quarter of the nineteenth century the Indian way of life in Nova Scotia, though altered and impaired in some ways, was not destroyed. Indian communities, by retaining continuity in their social and ideological traditions, had survived three centuries, perhaps four, of contact with and impact by Western civilization. Those who adopted agriculture did not necessarily lose the core of their culture or whatever irreducible minimum made them culturally distinct.

They managed to hold onto a basis for new adaptations and syntheses. In the last third of the nineteenth century the process of culture change accelerated as the Indians came more effectively under the impact of planned change.

Philip Bock in his anthropological study of the Micmac community at Restigouche found that there was an acceleration of cultural change in the second quarter of the nineteenth century. In 1868 an observer noted that while the Micmacs wore Western-style clothing and lived in houses of logs and planks laid out in streets, they were still not convinced agriculturalists. The majority worked as lumbermen, hunters and fishermen. The women kept gardens and made baskets. The Roman Catholic Church was an important spiritual as well as social and economic centre, and the priest also ran a store on weekdays. A school was opened in 1856, but had a slight attendance because many families were still not settled year-around on the reserve.

Only with the years at the turn of the century did "fundamental" changes occur in the political, economic, and educational aspects of the Restigouche Micmacs. In the political sphere chiefs ceased to be created on the customary basis of common understanding and agreement. Election of chiefs and councillors every three years became the usual procedure. The construction of a sawmill in the community brought in more whites and thus increased contacts with whites. It also introduced more job opportunities.

Another factor contributing to change was the opening of a new school under the auspices of an order of Roman Catholic nuns. Nevertheless, irregular attendance limited the impact of the school. Regular attendance was one-fifth of those registered, and "good" attendance did not come until the Family Allowance Act in 1946-47. The Micmac language continued to be used, and from 1903 to 1921 a monthly newspaper was published in Micmac. The picture given of Restigouche seems consistent with the larger description gathered from government reports and outside observers: while factors for cultural change were at work, so were those for cultural continuity.

In Ontario and in Eastern Canada in general, the period of irrelevancy came earlier than it did on the Prairies or in British Columbia. Sir Francis Bond Head urged a separation of Indians from whites to allow the Indians to survive, and as we have seen, Manitoulin Island was designated for this purpose in the late 1830's. Sir Francis used the argument that Indians were deteriorating in contact with whites to justify his unsuccessful effort to carry out Indian removal in Upper Canada. As Sir Francis put it:

> The fate of the red inhabitants of America, the real proprietors of its soil, is, without any exception, the most sinful story recorded in the history of the human race.[2]

After cataloging some of these injustices, he concluded that Indians were a dying race:

> What is the reason of all this—Why the simple virtues of the red aborigines. . .
> should, under all circumstances, fade before the vices and cruelty of the old
> world, is a problem which no one among us is competent to solve: the dispen-
> sation is as mysterious as its object is inscrutable.[3]

Sir Francis was convinced that the Indians had not become and would
not become farmers. The solution therefore was to clear them from
cultivable land and send them to a place where they could fish and hunt
as they preferred to do anyway.

The Aborigines' Protection Society, with its Wesleyan Methodist
contacts in Upper Canada, quickly went into opposition to Sir Francis'
scheme. They called attention to the fact that Indians were being Christianized and Westernized:

> Another witness to the fact that Indians are capable of being civilized, Mrs.
> Jameson, is the more trustworthy, inasmuch as her narrative directly contra-
> dicts the theory as to their uncapacity of civilization, which she unwisely
> admits, notwithstanding that her own experiences of the recent date of 1836
> and 1837, amply confirms the proof long and abundantly accumulated in their
> favour. The charming family scenes among *improved* Indians mingled with the
> whites, introduced to the English reader by this clever writer, give an earnest
> of what the mass of them would soon become if their good tendencies were
> duly fostered.[4]

They introduced other evidence from Canada as well:

> *The Christian Guardian*. . .which may be called a missionary journal, is not at
> present the only Canadian newspaper that embraces the Indian cause. *The*
> *Palladium*, published also in Toronto, designates the removal treaty of Sir
> F. B. Head, a "perfidious trickery," and his bargain for the land as "in-
> famous:" and even so long ago as in 1821, when Dr. Morse went to Canada
> upon a mission from the government of the United States to form plans for
> benefitting the Indians, and he found warm cooperators on [sic] the Province.
> The importance of forming a correct estimate of the real disposition of the
> colonists towards the aborigines, is obvious; and it may, we think, be safely
> conjectured that if the Government were compelled to be just and considerate,
> and active as in their favour, a powerful support from the well-disposed might
> be relied upon, whilst the errors, the lukewarmness, and false views of the
> Government have the pernicious effect of even increasing the influence of
> their enemies.[5]

What the Society regarded as a successful effort at acculturation had
been taking place in Upper Canada in the early 1830's. The program,
they reported, involved a system of encouragement to agriculture,
which presumably is to be associated with the work of men like the
Rev. Peter Jones and his brother, of Welsh-Mississauga extraction. This
"progress" was then interrupted by the Removal Plan of Sir Francis in
the late 1830's. The Society's correspondent declared:

> Long and extensive experience has been had of removals of Indians by the
> influence of government, and it is difficult to decide whether its impolicy be
> the more reprehensible or its injustices the more to be reprobated.[6]

In a letter to Lord Glenelg, Colonial Secretary, written August 20,
1836, the Aborigines' Protection Society correspondents accused Sir

Francis of being motivated by a desire to get the Indians out of the way, as they were impeding "the progress of civilization." Some of the point of the Society's criticism that the land was not fertile is blunted when we note that Sir Francis did not actually intend the Indians to practise agriculture on Manitoulin Island. Nevertheless, a footnote to this should be made from Mrs. Jameson's comment that in fact the main island was fertile, though the smaller ones, as the Society charges, were largely rock. As it happened, the Indians did make some efforts at cultivation there. On April 3, 1839, the Society memorialized Lord Durham, recently appointed to go to Canada to deal with larger constitutional issues, to the following effect:

> But in the policy of Sir Francis Head, we observe, notwithstanding the tone of benevolence which he assumes, the avowed intention forthwith to deprive them at one fell swoop, of all their remaining reservations, taking a million and a half acres of the richest land in all Canada from one tribe, six square miles of fertile land from another, a like quantity from a third, besides various other pastimes. Nor is this land wholly neglected and unoccupied by the Indians, or such as they have held as hunting-grounds, but it includes so many infant settlements, in which, with much labour, and after repeated disappointments, the germs of Christianity and civilization have at length taken root with fair promise of fruitfulness. It includes cultivated lands appropriated by individuals, as well as houses, schools, and churches. At the very time at which the affairs of the Aborigines within the Province seem to have reached the point of their lowest decline, when the contraction of their borders and the extinction of their game appear to have brought the absolute necessity of a new mode of subsistence, to second the gentle persuasions of the Missionaries, alluring them to the industrious and peaceful habits of civilized life, they are called upon to abandon the advantages which they are just beginning to enjoy, and are to be banished to the 23,000 rocks of granite, dignified by the name of Manitoulin Islands. On these islands, from ancient motives of veneration, calculated to render permanent their native superstitions, but perfectly useless, as Sir Francis admits, for every purpose of civilized life, the Indians, flattered with the prospect of retaining their national character, and of finding the enjoyments which their forefathers possessed, when they had the range of the whole country, are doomed to live on berries yielded by the few shrubs which can take root between the crevices of the rocks, and on the fish which frequent the shallow waters. It is obvious that they must invade the territories of other tribes, and engage in wars, serving the purpose of depopualting the country in readiness for the next advance of the whites.[7]

Deputy Superintendent of Indian Affairs, Duncan Campbell Scott, for many years the senior civil servant for Indian administration, summed up with chilling wit this case of attempted removal of Indians to one big reserve to rid the land of them:

> One Governor of Upper Canada, seeing them so wretched, resolved to send them back to Nature for healing, and to remove them to hunting grounds where they might recuperate or die away unseen. But better councils prevailed.[8]

Sir Francis's proposal ran counter to the new trend in Indian administration for directed culture change, or at least tangential to it, and so brought upon him the opposition displayed above. The policy of "the Bible and the plough" continued to be that of the Indian Affairs Branch into the mid-twentieth century, though the Bible has perhaps become less important, and urban occupations are suitable alternatives to the plough.

Corresponding efforts by government to alter the life of the Indians in the other British provinces of North America were under way. These efforts led to the creation of commissions and investigations to gather information as a basis for action. The 1840's and 1850's witnessed a number of such projects, as we have seen. Their reports generally called for greater efforts to Christianize and Westernize the Indians, agriculture being regarded as a major component in his physical survival, since hunting for food or trade purposes was no longer deemed adequate. The Indians' cultural survival was neither desired nor expected. The Reports seemed to corroborate Sir Francis's conclusions about the net effect of European civilization on Indians. They found the living conditions desperate and deprived by European standards. Counter-evidence was offered to show that optimism was not without basis, however, if some new scheme were only to be tried to induce the Indians to change.

That the situation among many of the Indians was slow in being altered is apparent from the reports of major physical change over periods of thirty and forty years in the middle and late nineteenth century. Viewed another way the Indian resistance to the new way of life is clear. The evidence of positive resistance is less apparent, however, in government reports than is the negative evidence of unachieved schemes and programs.

In the summer of 1845, Paul Kane visited some of the Indian settlements on Manitoulin, where he heard a musical recital of "simple and plaintive notes" on an instrument like the flageolet.[9] The government's policy of assimilation was underway. At one village Kane observed that the man he paid to be translator had little English but considerable influence among his fellow Indians. At this village he noted the presence of a government-financed staff consisting of pastor, doctor, Indian Agent, and blacksmith. In addition the Indians were housed in forty or fifty log houses built by the provincial government. At another village the missionary was a Roman Catholic, and under his direction some agriculture had been undertaken. As we have seen, together with the theme of ultimate acculturation and "progress" toward it, there runs a refrain of concern for the destructive influence of at least some aspects of an exposure to Western culture or to Westerners themselves in the form of settlers. In more recent years this idea has evolved to the point where the administrators, missionaries, and teachers themselves are seen as a destructive influence.

The report of the Commission on Indians, issued in January 1844, asserted that civilization was ruining the Indian,—that social, economic, moral, and physical deterioration were the result of the contact. Few schools were available to aid the process of Westernization, and teachers were needed to check and correct the debilitating aspects of Indian-white relations. When the settlers came into lands occupied by Canadian Indians, "The road became too long for them [the Indians] to traverse: the great majority lost heart and fell by the wayside, despite the help they received from a government that honestly sought their welfare."[10] Honest the government may have been, but they were also ignorant of the complex nature of their task of assimilation, and inadequate to effect it in any case. In the summer of 1970, Prime Minister P. E. Trudeau responded with feeling to the bitter accusations of Indian Association of Alberta delegates. The government might be called ignorant and stupid, he averred, but they should not be accused of acting in bad faith.

During the period of reserves on the Prairies, many of the same themes outlined above recurred. The ancient economy of the Indian of the Prairies was dissipated; by the mid-1880's the buffalo had virtually disappeared, and could no longer provide food, clothing, fuel, shelter, materials for tools, and goods for trade. The Indian was put under pressure to grow grain in his prairie homelands. Some were drawn to new cities and towns to work on the periphery of the economic life of the nation. The population figures for Indians plummeted and not until after the turn of the century was the Indian population clearly on the rise again, though it was to be many years before this fact became generally known. European dress and many aspects of European material culture replaced concomitant parts of the indigenous culture. The Indian side of this era awaits intensive study.

It has been almost a century since the first Indian Act (1876) set up the framework for Canada's administration of its aborigines. The Indians had been gradually brought under European influence and then control as European occupation moved westward. In 1867 the British North America Act gave the federal government responsibility for the management of the Indians. Since that time significant changes have taken place in the way of life in Canada for Indians and non-Indians alike, and these changes are presently manifesting themselves in the need for changed methods and perhaps changed philosophies in the relationship between the government and its "wards."

In the second half of the nineteenth century, however, Canada was essentially an agricultural country and new areas were being opened up for agricultural development. The Indians had to be removed peacefully. A series of treaties were "negotiated" to settle them into restricted portions of their former territories. In eastern Canada reserves had been created in the pre-Confederation era. In the Prairies and parts of British Columbia, the Indians were dealt with by commissioners who secured treaties and/or land on the basis of precedents from eastern Canada.

After the treaties were made with Prairie Indians, the main aim of the government in the 1870's and 1880's was that Indians should accept the culture of the white Canadian society and by eventual enfranchisement become merged with the general society. The term "enfranchisement" as used here was a technical one, meaning the legal and voluntary surrender of Indian status by an individual; acquisition of the vote was a part of the new status thus achieved. Enfranchisement included surrender of an individual's rights to Indian lands and other privileges and prerogatives which went with Indian status. To the white man who framed the law, to encourage the procedure of enfranchisement, the gain—full citizenship—seemed more than to outweigh the loss. The Indian's response to this opportunity can best be judged by the minute number who have willingly accepted it over almost one hundred years. It should be remembered that Indian women who married non-Indian men were involuntarily enfranchised. Since 1960 Indians have had the federal vote without loss of Indian status, and some, still fearing to jeopardize their Indian status, refuse to vote.

While the desired and expected acculturation was taking place, the reserves were to serve as a protective device and a training ground, according to government plans. A basic ingredient was the role of agriculture as their prime economic activity, just as it was the major economic activity of other Canadians of the period. The buffalo was largely exterminated by intensive trade-motivated hunting, and along with it other game either fled before the influx of settlers or was killed off in an era before conservation was practised. Thus agriculture was seen by the benefactors of the Indians, official and unofficial, as the only means of survival as well as the acceptable form of livelihood.

In the Prairies, as elsewhere, the clergy-directed village of Indians became the instrument for providing the transition from the days of hunting to a period when the whites would be hemming in the Indians. This at least was the dream of the Christian missionaries. With the building of the railroad in the 1870's began the influx of white settlers. The missionaries anticipated their coming and the threat they posed to the Indians. They hoped to protect "their" Indians and at the same time implement the agricultural life which was considered not only the civilized way to live, but the only hope for survival. Accounts of the discussions between Indians and white treaty commissioners further illustrate this point. Indians were threatened vaguely at the time of Treaty No. 3 talks: "If we do not succeed to-day I shall go away feeling sorry for you and your children that they could not see what was good for you and for them."[11]

In November 1871, the officer who had been sent to Fort Garry to settle treaty misunderstandings there, wrote to his superiors in Ottawa: "We told them that whether they wished it or not, immigrants would come in and fill up the country; that every year from this one twice as many in number as their whole people there assembled would pour into the Province, and in a little while would spread all over it, and that now was the time for them to come to an arrangement that would secure homes and amenities for themselves and their children."[1]

The work of the missionary in the task of getting Indians and *Métis* to settle down to agriculture is portrayed by a biographer of Father Lacombe: "simple-hearted", "affectionate children of the forest" gathered about the priest for instruction, unwilling to work with shovel and hoe. Contemporary travellers visited a little settlement which they later described as "presided over by a Roman priest." Lacombe is credited with directing the efforts at a number of successive missions, moving on to new areas as younger or new men were installed to continue the work he began. Katherine Hughes recounts:

> With all the ardours of his warm nature Father Lacombe burned to reach every tribe on the plains—group after group, to gather these poor nomads in fresh colonies to live there in pastoral contentment and certainty of food. As each settlement was formed it would be his aim to turn it over to some of his younger brethren, while he pushed on again into the wilds with his Red Cross flag and his plough to bring into Christian submission still other bands of savages.[12]

The Christian Indian Utopia was also to be established among the *Métis*. Bishop Neill says of John Eliot's (1604-1690) work with Indians and specifically of the first baptisms in 1651:

> Finding that it was almost impossible for the converted Indian to live a Christian life, if he remained within his tribe, Eliot took a leaf out of the Roman Catholic book, and began to form "Praying Farms" of which Natick was the first. By 1671 he had gathered about 3,600 Christian Indians into fourteen settlements, and had begun the training of Indian preachers, who numbered twenty-four at the time of his death. Indians who came to dwell in the settlements made a covenant in the following terms: "The grave of Christ helping us, we do give ourselves and our children to God to be his people. He shall rule over us in all our affairs, not only in our religion and the affairs of the Church, but also in all our works and affairs of the world."[13]

Protestant missionaries too foresaw the demise of the buffalo and urged the Indians to turn to agriculture. Early Wesleyan missionaries such as R. T. Rundle and Henry Steinhaur, the latter an Indian from Ontario, saw that the Indians would be forced to change their way of life and so taught them to cultivate the land. The Rev. George McDougall predicted the end of the buffalo and the consequent need for agricultural training. Like their counterparts in other denominations, the Wesleyan missionaries enjoyed considerable power in the communities with which they were associated. The Rev. John McDougall has been described as ". . .judge and arbiter over old quarrels, domestic and tribal; physician and surgeon; preacher and teacher."[14]

The efforts of the missionary to save the Indian from the predictable catastrophe of the extermination of the buffalo did not meet with immediate success. Some Indians took up agriculture under clerical leadership and direction; others found such a course too incongruous with the past and a dull prospect for the future. The cultural change required was too abrupt to be encompassed easily. Often the missionaries did not understand, and they interpreted the reluctance or resistance of the Indians in much the same way that they viewed other cultural chasms that proved unbridgeable or difficult and slow to cross.

Indians were most usually thought of as childlike or "savagely backward." Missionaries were, however, generally not guilty of the grosser forms of racialism implied in the debates in which Las Casas defended the Indians of Central America against Sepulveda's Aristotelian arguments.[15] Aristotle had made the argument that there were two classes of men, one by nature meant to be free, and one by nature suited for slavery. Las Casas in his defence of the Indians of Mexico and in his insistence upon fair treatment for them argued not that Aristotle's categories were false, evil or inapplicable, but that Indians fitted the first category, while Sepulveda argued that they belonged to the second. The Indian "inferiority" was culturally derived, the missionaries thought, and could therefore be remedied. The motto of the Aborigines' Protective Society, for example, was *"Ab Uno Sanguinis."* The phrase comes from *Acts* 17:26: "[God] hath made of one blood all nations of men for to dwell on all the face of the earth." Appropriately, the quote is derived from the first history of Christian missions, and is an account of a sermon delived in Athens by the greatest of all Christian missionaries, Paul of Tarsus. Many settlers on the Canadian Prairies thought less highly of the aborigines, describing them as vermin and two-legged animals.

The missionary from time to time had an opportunity to cultivate his respect for Indian culture despite its strangeness. Ryerson Young, a nineteenth century Methodist missionary among the Crees, describes his own experience:

> We were surprised at times by seeing companies of pagan Indians stalk into the Church during the services, not always acting in a way becoming to the house or day. At first it was a matter of surprise to me that our Christian Indians put up with some of these irregularities. I was very much astounded one day by the entrance of an old Indian called Tapastanum, who, rattling his ornaments, and crying "Ho! Ho!" came into the church in a sort of trot, and gravely kissed several of the men and women. As my Christian Indians seemed to stand the interruption, I felt that I could. Soon he sat down, at the invitation of Big Tom, and listened to me. . .to aid himself in listening, he lit his big pipe and smoked through the rest of the service. When I spoke to the people afterwards about the conduct of this man, so opposite to their quiet, respectful demeanour in the house of God, their expressive and charitable answer was: "Such were we once. . .let us have patience with him. . .let him come; he will get quiet when he gets the light.[16]

Young recounts another incident illustrating the Indians' quick realization of the implications of what the missionary taught:

> After prayer I requested them all to again seat themselves on the ground, as I wished them to hear about these great truths. . .many responded to my request, and, with the exception of an old conjuror or two, who feared for their occupation, [Young could appreciate professional rivalry] all spoke in the same strain as did the head chief: "It is just what I have been expecting to hear

about the Great Spirit." The last to speak was an old man with grizzly hair, and wild, excited movements. His hair was braided and reached to his knees. . . .

"You say, 'Notawenan ("our Father")': He is your Father?"

"Yes, he is my Father."

Then he said. . ."Does it mean He is my Father. . .?"

"Yes, O yes!" I exclaimed. "He is your Father too."

"Your Father—missionary's Father, and Indian's Father, too?" he repeated.

"Yes, that is true," I answered.

"Then we are brothers?" he almost shouted out.

"Yes, we are brothers," I replied.[17]

The complications of being a white man who was expanding into the Indians' lands and the problem of the missionary acting formally or informally as an instrument of white expansion, and at the same time being a brother of the Indian, are illustrated by an exchange with some Saulteaux (Ojibway) Indians which Young narrates. That the Indians saw the potential usefulness of the missionary to their own interests also emerges from the account.

After the pipe ceremony was over, the chief began his address of welcome. He said a good many kind things, and told me of their anxieties as to their future and that of their children. The fire-canoe (steamboat) was rushing through the waters, destroying their fisheries. The white hunters, with their fire guns and steel traps, were fast killing off the game. The surveyor was driving his lines of stakes into the ground, and the white people, more numerous than mosquitoes, were crowding in on the prairies. They had nothing but peace in their hearts, but still he could not help thinking that a treaty ought to be made with them before the fire-canoe or the surveyor came. They were powerless themselves to speak before the Queen's representative, the Governor. They had heard of the missionary's love for the Indian, and so they had sent across the great Winnipeg for him, and their hearts were glad that he had come. With their right hands they had fired off their guns, which all said, "welcome!" With his left hand he had handed the pipe of peace, which also from the heart again said, "welcome!" Their hearts were all glad that with their eyes they saw the missionary among them. Their ears were now open to hear what he had to say about their future, and what he thought the Queen's men would do for them.

But before the missionary would speak of this he must, he told them, speak of something even more important, more important than treaties and land. "What has he got to talk about that is more important than the treaty?" was the Indian response. A sermon was preached and a hymn sung, translated into Saulteaux. The missionary preached while the Indians set up a heavy cloud of smoke from their pipes. Then tea and fish, and then a return to the concern expressed earlier. "We went over the business of the approaching treaty, and I told them all I knew about the matter, and assured them that they need have no fear or alarm. The Dominion Government would treat them honourably and fairly."

The Indians may have concluded that the imminent flood of white men meant ideological as well as physical disruption of their lives. Their culture had been adapting to new circumstances for centuries and the process was not about to end.

At first many of the Pariries Indians did not go to their reserves, and only the threat of starvation forced them eventually to move reluctantly to them. This occurred during the famine crisis of 1879-1880. To receive food from the government agents the Indian consented to go to their reserves, but to take up agriculture meant a considerable alteration in their whole way of life, since unlike the Indians of the Upper Saint Lawrence Valley region they had not practised agriculture in pre-contact times, and in their sense of value. One means of bringing about the desired cultural change was tried in the form of residential schools, which were used to get the children away from the "retrograde" influence of their parents. The schools did not prove to be as successful as was hoped for, though they were not without effect upon the culture and the course of Indian history.

Another effort to expedite the acculturation was the governmental system created for the administration of the reserves, a sort of "indirect rule." These band council governments also had hard going in the early years. They represented a form at variance with Indian practice. The following quotation is from notes and unfinished manuscripts of the Rev. Canon Edward Ahanekew (1885-1961), a Cree:

> The Old Men of Reserves are an institution. The fact that there used to be no written language among the Indians forced them to depend entirely on the memory for things of the far past, as well as for those of more recent date. Because of this, the accuracy of the memory of the old men of the race is surprising. The minutest details regarding events that took place in childhood he remembered, and it is most interesting to hear two or more old men comparing notes as to the surface markings and points of a horse which may have lived some forty or fifty years before.
>
> The Old Man had a responsible and important position to fill in the band. In a sense, he supplied our moral code, he took the place of legal advisor, and of written history. His also was the task of firing the spirits of the young men with stories of daring deeds done in the times past.
>
> . . .It was the old men who were the influence for good.
>
> . . .By moral suasion alone they sought to right wrongs and to settle disputes.[19]

This shows the means by which continuity with the past was preserved in Indian society through the role of the chiefs.

In effect, direct rule by the Indian Agent now became the reality:

> Resistance on the part of the old conservative chiefs was resented by the Government and denounced as noxious and heathenish. Moreover, the fact that the Government has assumed the power to depose chiefs by refusing them recognition as such under the treaties, militated against any attempt to exercise the traditional influence which alone attached to their position. The chiefs and headmen became mere names, archaeological expressions.[20]

Friendly and co-operative leaders such as Crowfoot won the admiration of the white Canadian and have continued to enjoy a good reputation among historians as well as popular writers. By the mid-twentieth century much of this has passed into legend. There has been a greater emphasis by historians upon explication of the cultural conflict in which the Indians found themselves, and a less judgemental treatment.

The news that the treaties were going to be written, the Methodist missionary E. R. Young reported, brought great excitement in the minds of the Indians and an awareness that their relationship to the white man was about to undergo an important change. The government, in order to carry out its responsibilities now that it had taken over the area of the Hudson's Bay Company, and in order to make these treaties, had to have people representing the Indian side. "The word came out to us, at Rossville Mission House, that the Government wished the Indians to elect one of their number as chief, with whom they could make a treaty and whom they could confer with if difficulties arose in the future."[21] They wished the people to select ". . .a wise, judicious man, in whom all confidence could be placed."[22] In other words, the government was asking the Indians to undergo a culture change—selecting a "chief" to represent them in negotiations with the government—in order to assist the government in effecting further changes. The "chief" was to play a role beyond that of the usual one played by a chief in the past (where, as we have seen above, he embodied general consent, and worked by means of personal influence). The government planned to use the new "chief" as the instrument of its own plans, that is, to sign a treaty putting himself and his fellows on a reserve.

In some cases it was the younger men who had to be restrained by the farsighted chiefs, who saw the handwriting on the wall and collaborated with the government agents. The Blackfoot in particular were noted for their refusal to join anti-white movements, with their friends the Assiniboines. The reaction of the Blackfoot is to be explained, at least in part, by the character of their indigenous culture: "Warfare had become a matter of individual aggrandizement," Oscar Lewis writes, "and there appeared to be no motive which would unite the tribes or the bands. In addition to these factors in their social organization and warfare, there was the further disruption of their intertribal unity by the fur trade. . . ."[23] Lewis continues:

> Of no less importance, was the conciliatory role played by the chiefs and headmen, who very often did not consider it to their personal interests to resist the influence of the whites. The early missionaries first commented upon this when they recorded the support they received from the chiefs in their efforts to suppress intertribal warfare and horse stealing. Father Point states: "Among the Blackfoot, the rich people who undertake to rebuke the wicked who possess nothing, have naught to gain and all to lose." Indeed, peace would insure the security of those who had large herds.[24]

Some chiefs succeeded in restraining the younger men. "Crowfoot," Lewis states, "who was largely responsible for the maintenance of peace, was motivated by personal, and to some extent tribal, interests."[25] He was one of those who foresaw the future and planned accordingly. As we shall see, the 1885 Riel uprising failed to engage the Blackfoot.

It was to be the last time that Indians figured significantly in "Canadian history," and was so because, as in so many earlier cases, they were associated with military events. Efforts were made by the Cree Chief Big Bear to unite the Indians in a common front against whites to demand better treaty terms. He was not successful, though some groups, mostly drawn from the Crees, though by no means all of these, did later rise when the *Métis* rose under Riel in 1885. Rivalries and differing aims prevented the fullest co-operation among the groups that did in fact take up arms. In the meantime the government tended to belittle the seriousness of the situation. After the fighting the Indians slipped into obscurity. Land and the whole pattern of cross-cultural misunderstanding due to differing values and life styles had contributed to the course of events. The Indians were shoved aside, as they had been in earlier situations, and so tended to become "out of sight, out of mind."

As this is the last military activity by which the Indians have been included in "Canadian history," some understanding of the Indian role in events is called for. After the treaties were signed, the Indians of the Prairies began to go onto reserves thus created. At first the pressure of settlers was not very great, and though the buffalo were declining they could still be hunted. Indian administration and the missionaries were putting pressure on Indians to settle down to agriculture; as we have seen, they were reluctant to do this, as other Indians had been before them, because such a change from their traditional way of life was considerable and it was not a desirable one in the view of many Indians. Among those who were resistant to the idea of agriculture was the man who came to be the central figure of that resistance, Big Bear. He had not been eager to sign a treaty and he was not eager to go onto a reserve. Others of the same mind joined him, and his band grew rapidly in the years immediately before 1885, aided by the mobility from band to band which characterized the political structure of the Prairie Indians. Young men, dissatisfied with the course of action of the chiefs of their own bands, came to Big Bear. If the white men were closing in, Big Bear might still, by manoeuvring, get a better resolution of the Indians' situation than they had so far received. Another chief, Poundmaker, had turned to agriculture in an effort to set an example and if possible secure from this new way of life the necessary subsistence for his followers. Red Pheasant, Starblanket, Mistawasis, and others were leading their people to agriculture as well.

By the mid-1880's, however, the situation of the Prairie Indians had considerably worsened. Crops had not come in, due to natural and man-made conditions. Bad crops and no crops created disillusionment among the Indians. The buffalo had now virtually disappeared so that hunting on a serious scale was out of the question. The nation was in a depression and economies meant less assistance for the Indian. The white settlers frequently treated the Indian with scorn, ridicule, and contempt. They invaded his reserves, took timber off his lands, and grazed their cattle there, cutting fences to do so. Indian resentment grew, and hunger—even starvation—increased. The implications of the treaty signing and the creation of the reserves became grimly apparent.

Big Bear seems to have hoped that the Crees, acting together, would by their unity be able peacefully to achieve redress for their grievances and solutions to the problems which they were then facing. The participation in the second Riel uprising of Big Bear and Poundmaker was not hasty, nor were they without caution and restraint. When, however, they were approached by the *Métis* to join in rising against the encroaching white men, their dissatisfaction and disillusionment led them (albeit cautiously) to agree. Only once did the situation get out of hand, at Frog Lake, where Big Bear's advice and influence were ignored and contravened. This incident was not a military action, but began with an argument between Wandering Spirit and his brother-in-law, the Indian Agent, which escalated into the murder of six people. Most authorities assert that in the case of this incident Big Bear was innocent of both the action and the intentions.

Most of the military clashes which occurred did not involve Indian participation, and the efforts of the Indians and *Métis* to alter the course of events by force failed. The unsuccessful *Métis* and their Indian allies fell together before the overwhelming power of the white newcomers. Big Bear and Poundmaker were jailed. William Fraser says of these events:

> Big Bear foresaw the humiliating subjugation of his people and made a tremendous effort to prevent it. History made his failure almost inevitable, but left him no honourable alternative other than the course he took. The name belongs with those Canadians who have resisted tyranny and opposed injustice.[26]

Other groups hoped that the government had learned a lesson from this occurrence. Bands that had not risen pointed to the extremity of their situations and urged that swift government action to relieve their conditions could avert the spread of disaffection. In the meantime the government conceived a plan by which Indians were to be impressed with the character of the forces with which they were now dealing. Starblanket and other Cree chiefs who had not joined the rising were given a tour of eastern Canada so that they might become better informed of the size and scope of the new white man's society.

Among the Blackfoot there were also rumblings. Though less intermixed with the white men by marriage and interbreeding than were the Crees, the Blackfoot had been deeply dependent on the buffalo for their livelihood. Now this source of food, clothing, housing, and fuel was gone. They could, however, still sell horses to the white men and did so. Led by the sagacious Crowfoot, the Blackfoot were now carefully courted and received a more openhanded treatment from the government to prevent their joining the rebellion. It was hoped that Blackfoot loyalty might even extend to fighting against their traditional rivals, the Crees. Sir John A. Macdonald proposed to Edgar Dewdney, the Indian Commissioner in the Territory, that the Blackfoot be enlisted and armed to make war. Dewdney advised that if such a proposal were implemented, peace might be even more difficult to restore, and the idea was dropped. The tension felt by the whites is illustrated in the comments of John McLean. His book, *The Indians: Their Manners and Customs*, was published in 1889 not long after the events. He wrote: "When the air was filled with reports of battles, and strange Indians visited the reserves to converse with *our Indians*, we felt very anxious to know whether they had accepted the bonds of union or not [italics added]."[27] In the end the Blackfoot did not join. Crowfoot "...played upon the fear of the whites to get a promise of larger rations in the future," but he had seen that resistance was hopeless. Several years earlier, he had voiced his concern for the future of the Indian:

> We all see that the day is coming when the buffalo will all be killed, and we shall have nothing more to live on and then you will come into our camp and see the poor Blackfoot starving. I know the heart of the white soldier will be sorry for us, and that they will tell the Great Mother who will not let her children die.[28]

An Indian view of the origins of Indian participation in the second Riel rising and more particularly in the Frog Lake massacre was given in 1931 at the unveiling of a memorial to those killed. The speaker at this occasion was himself a Cree Indian, the Rev. Edward Ahenakew. Ahenakew, awarded the degree of Doctor of Divinity in 1949, was a kinsman of Ah-tah-ka-koop (Starblanket), Poundmaker, Mistawasis (Big Child), Ermine Skin, and Kamekosit Peyao (Red Pheasant). All of these men were prominent Cree leaders in the last quarter of the nineteenth century. Alexander Morris refers to Starblanket repeatedly in his account of the signing of Treaty # 6, the Fort Carlton Treaty. He and Mistawasis are referred to as the "recognized leading chiefs" and "the two head chiefs of the Carlton Crees." This was the treaty which Poundmaker and Red Pheasant also signed. Poundmaker was a leader within the band of Red Pheasant. The Sandy Lake band, into which Edward Ahenakew was born in 1885, was led by Starblanket. This band was one of those which did not join the Riel rising. Because of his background and his insights into Western culture it is useful to our understanding to quote Ahenakew at length:

> Imagine a people, who had lived and roamed over this great Northwestern land, breathing in the freedom of the prairie at every breath, their will never called into question, kept within bounds only by the teaching and exhortations of the old men of the nation, knowing most exactingly the ways of the country, skillful in all things pertaining to the making of a livelihood, conquering the necessarily hard conditions under which they lived, feeling man-

hood that coursed through their physical bodies; such a people must love freedom as their God-given animal, the noble bison, did. They must resent anything that tended to bring that freedom to naught, or even to restrict it—it were unnatural if it were not so.[29]

For such a people to settle down and take up agriculture was a "complete reversal" of their former way of life. "They did not realize that there was henceforth to be a definite systematized code of laws which would act like a fence around their spirits. . . ." and "As years went by they felt this evertightening hold. . .and as the government kept pulling in the reigns of control, the Indians began to realize many things not anticipated when the treaty was made."[30] The day would dawn when they ". . .would be ignored altogether." "Had the white men exercised more tact in their dealings with the Indians," Ahenakew continues, ". . .the Indians would have been friendly and the deed might never have taken place. The cumulative force of everything that came in touch with the Indians at this time seemed to have worked towards some such thing."[31]

The most famous of Siksika Blackfoot chiefs was Crowfoot. His friendship with Father Lacombe undoubtedly gave him knowledge and understanding of the white man which increased his skill in dealing with the newcomers over and above that of other Blackfoot chiefs. His role in the signing of Treaty #7 reflected and enhanced this position. He promoted peace with the Crees, even adopting the Cree Chief Pound-maker as his son and influencing his people to reduce tensions with the Crees by returning stolen horses. Crowfoot apparently felt that general-ly the white man's advice to him had been sound and he was prepared to sign. He hoped that by signing the treaty he would insure the aid and protection of the government for his people. He seems to have had particularly in mind protection from the rapacity of the white men, especially traders.

Once on the reserve, the Blackfoot entered into the "new" life which brought changes. "New men" began to emerge whose adaptation to the white man's ways gave them material rewards. Though their character had not been tested in horse-stealing raids or war, they gained some prestige and they had wealth to offer their kinsmen. At first, money earned was turned over to the chief for his redistribution, but gradually this practice was replaced as individuals retained their own earnings. By the end of the nineteenth century the local Indian Agent reported that the Indians didn't share their savings with others as they had done formerly.

The chiefs who were successfully making the change didn't have the wealth that some of the new agriculturalists were gaining. Those who switched most readily gained the approval and public recognition of the Indian Agent and missionary. The place of the chief was disturbed as several types of chiefs emerged. There were those who were regarded as chiefs by the Indian (the Blackfoot traditionally had no "head" chiefs), there were those regarded as chiefs by the Indian and the white man, and there were those who were regarded as chiefs by the whites only. These were sometimes known as "white" chiefs.

Rivalries and disagreements among these various figures, Lucien and Jane Hanks suggest, may have contributed to the "proliferation" of bands shortly after the Blackfoot settled on reserves. This splitting up increased the amount of cultivated land. The factor of defence was no longer a consideration. In later years this hiving off became more difficult as the Indians became involved with land claims, band funds, annuities, and the complications of Indian administrative bureaucracy.

The Indians were not always willing to have their children in school. Education of the kind used by the newcomers was sharply at variance with the learning-by-doing and elder-to-junior relationship which was the form of so much of the teaching technique of the Indian. Missionaries advocated restrictions on rations granted to families who didn't see to it that their children were in school. Severe punishments for those who left school, and police aid to retrieve them, were urged.

Residential schools were created, for the Indian children. There, efforts were made to erase the effects of their infancy and childhood experiences. They were sometimes under considerable pressure, including physical punishment, to give up their customs and religion, and to stop speaking their mother tongue. In some cases corporal punishment was the penalty for being heard to speak their own language. The quality of the instruction was not high and the level of their schooling was "well below" what it would have been after the same number of years of schooling in a school for white children.

The older generation continued to be the repository of knowledge about traditions and customs which in some cases were being repressed due to the efforts of administration and missionaries. Nevertheless not all the customs were lost, though some have undergone alteration. Although the young men might lose interest in these customs, the pattern was for men who were in their forties to return to an interest in these things. Viewed in the context of Canadian Indians generally, the experience of this community of Blackfoot, though it has distinctive aspects, also illustrates the extent to which recurring patterns of Indian experience can be observed across the country.[32]

One ubiquitous phenomenon in the narrative so far is the existence of and activities of the "friends of the Indians." These were people who were not involved in Indian administration or police work, but who as missionaries or laymen concerned themselves with Indian welfare and attempted by a variety of means to influence both government policy and practice regarding Indians. Missionaries and religious bodies were those best situated to effect their desired ends. As men on the scene they were accepted by the white society as experts until anthropologists displaced them in this capacity in the twentieth century. Furthermore their experience and personal knowledge made them suitable intermediaries for dealing with the Indians. They were frequently asked for assistance and advice.

Several of these figures who were associated with the important changes in the Indian life in the Prairies from the 1850's to the 1880's have already been noted. Father Lacombe of the Oblates of Mary Immaculate, and the Rev. George McDougall and his son, the Rev. John McDougall, both of the Wesleyan Missionary Society, are among the best known. Much of the direction of events of this era is credited to them. By this means the Indians' initiative in determining their own actions is minimized. Lacombe and the elder McDougall are, for example, credited with influencing Crowfoot to remain at peace in the second Riel uprising. The effect of this kind of analysis may be that the history of the Indian is again subordinated to that of the European, and this emphasis diminishes the stimulation of research interest in Indian history.

The Hudson's Bay Company worked through the missionary for the same reasons that the government did, in order to control and manipulate the Indians for the ends they desired. McDougall ". . .saw that in an era of transition he was called to protect and assist the 'aboriginal proprietors' of the land, and to do what he could to save them from poverty, neglect, and possibly extinction."[33] Or again, Lacombe is said to have been able to read on the faces of the Indian the sense of bewilderment, displacement, and loss of pride which they had, in his view, undergone by the 1880's: "Their old motives of race pride were gone. Their faces and forms had taken on a cast of subjection and servility. They were a dark fringe on the ranks of humanity."[34] He ". . .could see the Indian of the morrow disregarded, uncared for, unwelcome, thrust back further and further from his old territory. His heart brooded over it all, and he felt himself called to give the remainder of his life to their protection—as he had once given his years to their evangelization."[35]

Trips to Ottawa, consultations with government officials, letters to persons of prominence, and other forms of representation and the exercise of influence were the means by which the "friends of the Indians" worked on the dominant white society. In dealing with the Indians they relied on the Indians' confidence in them to act effectively upon the impinging white world. The role of the Indians in these affairs is now being reassessed by modern Indian writers, and by scholars as well. It is hard to know exactly what the Indians thought, but in the indigenous society the chief had been the man who could get things done and his leadership derived from his practicality in dealing with problems faced by the community. When white men came forward, promising to aid the Indian in solving various problems, which had arisen as a result of situations created by the white man, the Indian did not necessarily reject this assistance. Over a period of time as the ineffectiveness of these people became apparent, and as the Indian came to feel that these people were themselves diminishing his initiative in his own affairs, the missionary, the administrator, and even, more recently, the anthropologist, have suffered a diminution in Indian eyes.

In the period of the reserves the Indians had lost their political and economic autonomy and initiative. The government policy of assimilation aimed at removing their remaining social and religious identity as well. In this they succeeded less well than in the other two categories. Their analytical techniques were too imprecise to discern what were the crucial elements necessary for the Indians to retain their community and cultural identity. In some cases Indian social and religious life had to go underground and it was frequently modified in any case. But it was not destroyed, and because it wasn't, the Indians did not lose their identities. Social and religious elements have a large place in the efforts now being made by Indians, especially the younger leaders, to define and delineate the nature of their Indianness.

In 1876 the Indian Act was passed. This piece of legislation was a new step in the regulation of Indian life. It provided the framework, built on earlier precedents, for the controls, prohibitions, and restrictions under which hundreds of thousands of people were going to live from that time to our own. The origins of both its terms and its purpose were not new. As a number of students of Indian administration have pointed out, the purposes and aims of the administration have been stated many times from the mid-nineteenth century to the mid-twentieth century in approximately the same terms, "protection" and "advancement."

A commission was created in 1857 "to inquire into and report upon the best means of securing the progress and civilization of the Indian tribes in Canada, and on the best mode of so managing the Indian property as to secure its full benefit to the Indians without impeding the settlement of the country." In 1931 the Deputy-Superintendent General of Indian Affairs (and one of Canada's leading poets), Duncan Campbell Scott, wrote that "...the duties of the Department [of Indian Affairs] are to administer and protect the estate of the Indians and to carry out the policy of the Government for their advancement towards civilization."[36] Stating the ideal and the underlying policy of the administrator more paternalistically and revealingly, Scott wrote in 1913 that: "Protection from vices which were not his own, and instruction in peaceful occupations, foreign to his natural bent, were to be substituted for necessary generosity."[37]

T.R.L. MacInnes, a senior civil servant in the Indian Affairs Branch, in a paper presented to the Canadian Political Science Association in May, 1946, repeated Scott. He states: "...two aims have guided Canadian Indian administration—protection and advancement," and went on: "In the earlier and transitional period, the emphasis has been on protection and advancement. Progress admittedly has been slow."[38] Commenting on the Indian Act at that time, he stated:

> Indian administration is conducted under authority of the Indian Act, a Dominion statute which contains nearly all the Canadian law dealing expressly with Indians. Probably there is no other legislation which deals with so many and varied subjects in a single act. It may be said indeed to deal with the whole life of a people.[39]

The two "basic units" of administration are people and land. J. E. Hodgetts traces policy regarding these back into the late 1820's. Commenting on a project in the mid-1830's he observes: ". . .the curious paradox seems never to have struck the white administrators: the Indian must obviously be forced to embrace the superior culture of the white man and yet contact with that culture and with the bearers of that culture seemed to render the plight of the natives even worse. Consequently, the programme of isolated reserves was designed to protect natives against the worse features of that civilization which it was also the policy to foist on the Indians."[40]

The history of Indian administration in Canada goes back to the seventeenth century and British relations with Indians in North America, as we have seen. The first management of Indian affairs fell to the officers commanding the various posts where they were in contact with Indians. In 1696, for example, the government of the Colony of New York appointed Commissioners for Indian management and control. In the mid-1750's two officers were placed in charge of Indian affairs, one for the northern colonies and another for the southern colonies. The choice for the northern colonies was Sir William Johnson. Johnson held that office until his death in 1774 and seems to have lived up to the ideal that officers appointed to deal with Indians be especially suited to the job by temperament and experience; this meant that they must be able to win the loyalty and affection of the Indians. The result of such a happy coincidence of disposition was that the English settlements were to be made safe, trade would flourish, and the expenses of colonial administration generally would be kept down.

The Indians were to be won to a British alliance by a "policy of necessity." One historian of Indian administration refers to this as keeping the Indians "at bay by friendship." The policy was activated by the principles of profound distrust while cementing treaties, healing each treachery with the salve of presents, and being ready with "ample rewards for negative services."[41] The military phase of Indian administration is usually said to have lasted until about 1830.

The Proclamation of 1763 attests to the importance of the Indians in the eighteenth century. They had fought with the British in the recently concluded Seven Years War. Many had risen with Pontiac at the threat of white encroachment and what they regarded as the indifference of the British toward the western Indians. The Proclamation was in part a response to this event; by the terms of the Proclamation a vast Indian territory was to be created from which whites were debarred. In addition, in those areas where whites were allowed to settle, land purchase could be made by the government only. This Proclamation has frequently been called the Charter of Indian Rights, the Magna Carta of the Indians of Canada.

Commissioners in the mid-nineteenth century record the Indians as speaking in these glowing terms about the Proclamation. The document's importance lay in its assuring the existence of an Indian property right, of an aboriginal title to the land.[42] In 1830 administrative changes took place in Indian affairs which may be said to have symbolized the changing position of the Indians in relation to the white settlers and the changed purposes of Indian administration. The necessity for Indian allies lessened or ceased as the War of 1812 receded into the past. The continual influx of settlers clearly set the numerical balance in favour of the whites. Already in the late eighteenth century treaties were being signed by which Indians were parted from their land. This we have already observed. In the early nineteenth century the pace quickened. The recurring treaties meant recurring land cessions. By the mid-nineteenth century the route of treaty-signing led north and west along the north shore of Georgian Bay and Lake Superior. The next leap westward awaited the 1870's.

In the meantime a new idea had begun to take over the thinking of those concerned with Indian affairs. The gist of this idea was that a systematic effort be directed towards changing the Indian culture by means of the combined activities of administrators, missionaries, and educators. Indian populations had been hard hit by intensive contact with whites. Disease, social disruption, abuse from the introduction of alcohol—all these elements plus squatting on Indian lands, sharp dealing (not to say dishonesty) by whites with Indians, had, it was said, shown the Indian the worst side of the white man. Now it was hoped that the best side would be made available. In practice, of course, this meant that the Indian was to be pressured into giving up his way of life in exchange for a new way which the white man insisted was superior and inevitably going to take over anyway. The Indians were told, and some of them accepted this prediction, that they would die out as a biological entity if they did not change their way of life. Agriculture and the sedentary Western life-style were the only solution.

Most "authorities" asserted that the Indian could and would make the change if given the time and training. We have already seen that the Indians did not necessarily accept this prospect with enthusiasm. They seem to have preferred to pick and choose. The kinds of gifts given to Indian allies illustrate the shift in official thinking. Arguments were put forth that the usual gifts eventually found their way to white merchants and the Indians got little recompense for them. Instead, goods useful for a settled, agricultural life should be given.

The new policy was already emerging in the late 1820's and corresponds to developments in other British colonies. The consistency of the policy, which continued into the mid-twentieth century and beyond, has frequently been noted by writers. The rightness of the policy in the minds of white administrators and observers is seen in various reports and studies both by Canadians and others from the nineteenth century to the present.

Freeman Blake, United States consul at Hamilton, Ontario, asserted this in 1870 in his *History of the Indians in British North America showing their condition and management, being a Report to the Honourable the Secretary of State.* Blake wrote:

> Whatever may be the ultimate result, those who have aided in this honourable effort may safely be assured that their country will be known in history as having strived to do justice to the aborigines, whom the white man found in possession of it, and that they have so far founded their empire or dominion upon the principles of humanity and true civilization.[43]

Other Americans, perhaps appalled by the history of Indians in the United States, have tended to agree with Blake's judgement. Allen Harper and John Collier have, for example, expressed the opinion that Canadian policy is essentially just. Most of those writing on the topic have accepted the desirability of the policy of assimilation. Published reports of the opinions of Canadian Indians on this subject in the nineteenth century are mostly taken from Indians at least partially assimilated. Contrary opinions do not become prominent until the mid-twentieth century. Thus about 1830 the policy of military administration in what is today eastern Canada was ending and a new phase of administration was beginning. "Protection" and assimilation were the themes thereafter.

In 1828 Sir John Colborne was appointed Lieutenant-Governor of Upper Canada. He advised a change in policy from the pre-existing militarily based approach now made meaningless by peace and white settlement; instead, there would be an organized effort to assimilate. His approach corresponds to the new phase of "cultural imperialism" beginning to be applied elsewhere in the British Empire at this time through the influence of the humanitarians and evangelicals. In Upper Canada over the next decade or so, several settled Indian communities were created, and it was hoped they would be the scenes of successful new policy. Among the Mississaugas at the Credit River, the Rev. Peter Jones was an active figure in helping to implement these intentions. At Coldwater and at the Narrows, near Lake Simcoe, similar experiments were tried and judged unsuccessful by officialdom. Elsewhere, too, European-style houses were built, schools established, farm instructors appointed to train the Indians in European agricultural techniques. All of this was paid for out of monies formerly given in the form of presents and/or coming from land surrender payments. Much emphasis was placed on the dress, behaviour, and appearance of the Indians in judging the degree of "progress" in assimilation, as we have seen earlier.

An interruption occurred when Sir Francis Bond Head, Lieutenant Governor of Upper Canada (1836-38) decided that the experiments were unsuccessful, that the Indian could never be changed, and that it would be best to send them off to remote areas, "safe" from white influence, where they could live their old life. The policy of assimilation had been challenged. Not more than about ten years old, it was faced with a sharp reversal. Missionaries and others committed to changing the Indian rallied and brought to bear their lobbying power in

London. Sir Francis's "retrograde" effort was thwarted and the assimilation policy entrenched.

Reports of government commissioners in Canada and the Maritimes seemed to show that Indians were changing. By the mid-nineteenth century the policy of assimilation was incorporated into the Indian administration in the Maritimes as well as in the Province of Canada. In 1860 the Province of Canada received responsibility for Indian administration; the office of the senior official in Indian administration, the Chief Superintendent of Indian Affairs, was joined to that of Commissioner of Crown Lands. The commissioner's job included the management of sales of surrendered Indian land. The combination of these offices was part of the centralization of Indian administration under one government department. This "clientele" form of administration grows out of the findings of the Indian commissioners of 1857 and the realization that a more efficient administration was required to achieve the assimilation sought.

In his book, *Pioneer Public Service,* J. E. Hodgetts indicates the ambivalences which have developed within this "solution":

> Certainly under the new management of a centralized department the interests of the Indians received better attention. But one might query the adequacy of the budget thus made available. Further, one might ask whether placing the costs of managing Indian affairs directly on the taxpayer might not have aroused a more general critical interest in their administration. As it was, the Department operated mainly in a quiet backwater, isolated from parliamentary interest and by the same token unable to stir up any interest in expanding the services to the Indians. Periodically, the white man feels the weight of the albatross (Indian affairs administration) and institutes a full-scale inquiry, amends the Indian Act, and sits back again, his conscience partially salved. This being the situation perhaps it has been for the best that the Indians had a single Department wholeheartedly concerned with their affairs, if not always able to attract the funds or efficient personnel required for its work.[44]

There is in these observations food for thought for those who support and those who oppose the Indian Affairs Branch, as well as those who would have no federal department. The "mandarins" are not very elite, in Hodgetts' opinion.

Various acts were passed in the Province of Canada which formed the background and basis for the federal Indian Act of 1876. In June, 1857, royal assent was given to "an act to encourage the gradual civilization of the Indian tribes in this province." This act grew out of the findings of the Indian Commission of 1857. The report called for compact reserves and separation from the white men without isolation from white influences. It was hoped by this means to prevent squatters and encroachment on Indian land, protect Indians from other undesired (by the administrators and missionaries) contacts with whites, and still give them the presumed advantage of European example as embodied in the administrators and missionaries.

The Act of 1857 defined an Indian within the meaning of the act. It made the assimilation goal clear and looked for the eventual elimination of all legal distinctions between Indians and other Canadians. The act also set out a procedure for "enfranchisement," the legal process by which an Indian could cease to be an Indian. An Act of 1859 replaced the Act of 1857 but incorporated the main provisions of the earlier act.

The British North America Act, Section 91, Subsection 24, gave to Parliament exclusive authority to legislate for Indians and land reserved for Indians. The federal government took over this responsibility from the provinces of Canada, New Brunswick, and Nova Scotia. A new act, a federal act, consolidated previous acts and brought together what were regarded as the best features of the legislation of these provincial administrations. This piece of legislation became the first federal Indian Act (1876). A branch of government was created dealing specifically with Indians. The Indian Act with some modifications has continued to govern the affairs of Indians of Canada down to the present time.

One of the most important elements in the Act was that it defined who could be legally considered an Indian. Those who did not meet these requirements are, as far as the government is concerned, not Indians. They have no part in the treaties, annuities, rights to land, fishing, hunting, and government assistance and regulation applicable to legal Indians. Only about one half of those who are Indians under the law are also under treaties. The number of people who today are legally Indians stands at about a quarter of a million. At least another quarter of a million or more people are of Indian or partial Indian descent biologically or socially, but are not legally Indians. Such important definitions as membership in bands—all legal Indians (sometimes the term "registered Indians" is used) must be members of a band—and powers of the band councils are set forth in the Indian Act. Other matters governing Indian land holdings, band funds, inheritance, election of chiefs and band councils, taxation and legal status generally are set out.

With the signing of the Prairies treaties in the 1870's, the necessity for a more carefully formulated regulation was thought to have been introduced. Like the Indian Act, these treaties were altered to incorporate the inclusion of new Indian groups under government administration. The last treaty was signed in 1923 in northern Ontario.

G.F.G. Stanley's comment on the treaties and their significance is worth quoting at length. Other writers have used different language to say much the same thing.

In the first place they were not really "negotiated" treaties in the proper sense of the word. The concessions granted to the Indians were never made in deference to the demands or wishes of the Indians. Discussion was confined to an explanation of the terms. The Indian could not change these terms: they were given only one power of acceptance or refusal. The fact is that the Indians never understood what was happening. They did not understand the legal concept of individual ownership of land. They appreciated the principle of *usufruct*; and many of the chiefs thought that they were yielding to the whites only the right to use the land, not the right of exclusive private ownership. It was this misunderstanding which lay behind Canada's only Indian uprising which occurred in 1885 when several of the Indian bands of the Saskatchewan valley joined the armed protest of the metis.[45]

In *Native Rights in Canada,* Douglas Sanders and others find Stanley's conclusion unsatisfactory. They attempt to find a middle ground between Stanley's assertions and the historical implications of the treaty-making for contemporary Indian affairs. The symbolic value of the treaties is, in the eyes of the Indians, very great. The rights and powers of the Indians were recognized by the government in the fact that treaties were signed. "The view of the contemporary Indian leadership, that treaty rights are of basic importance, may arise in part out of the wish to respect the political power and astuteness of the Indian leaders who negotiated the treaties."[46]

Indians may feel that somehow the chiefs who signed the treaties are being denigrated if the treaties are criticized. Sanders *et al* conclude that they were "real negotiations," that the treaties were not forced though gifts were made before and after treaty signing. On the other hand it was clear that white settlement would come whether the Indians consented or not, and "...the Indians were essentially giving consent to what was inevitable." They reconcile these differences by concluding that it is this fact—that is, that the Indians were "giving consent to the inevitable"—which "gives the sense of unreality to the treaty-making procedure more, really, than the culturally weaker position of the Indians in negotiating legal documents."[47]

Their position, then, is not entirely opposed to Stanley's, but only partially so. The Indians were told something like "take it, or it is your lookout." Ottawa instructed its commissioners to raise the gifts or annuities a little if necessary, and the treaties do vary in part, perhaps corresponding to the resistance of the Indians.

By the treaties the Indians received annual money payments, trade goods, guns and ammunition, tools, implements and seeds, medical assistance, and instruction in farming. They had given up their land, though this was not always immediately apparent. Their new neighbours had not yet arrived. They were thereby removed from the path of westward expansion of men and vehicles. The railroad across the Prairies to British Columbia accelerated their displacement.

The inclusion of the Indians of the Prairies under administration required the creation of the broader and more sweeping terms of reference for regulating the lives of people already administered in eastern Canada and the new people to be administered in western Canada. The further application of the Indian Act was to be applied to peoples yet to come under its sway by treaties which continued to be signed until the last one in 1923. The challenge of more Indians within Canada had resulted in the response—the Indian Act—and an expanded Indian administration department.

FOOTNOTES:

[1] "Report on the Affairs of the Indians in Canada" (1844), p. 11.

[2] Sir Francis Bond Head, *A Narrative* (London: 1839), Appendix A, p. 3.

[3] *Ibid.*

[4] *Report of the Aborigines' Protection Society on the Canadian Indians* (London: 1839), p. 44.

[5] *Ibid.,* p. 47.

[6] *Ibid.,* p. 17.

[7] *Ibid., pp. 25-26*

[8] Duncan C. Scott, *The Administration of Indian Affairs in Canada* (Toronto: 1931), p. 2.

[9] Paul Kane, *Wanderings of an Artist among the Indians of North America, From Canada to Vancouver's Island and Oregon through the Hudson's Bay Company's Territory and Back Again* (Toronto: 1925), p. 10.

[10] Mellor, *op. cit.,* p. 410. Quoted from *Cambridge History of the British Empire,* Vol. VI, p. 16.

[11] Alexander Morris, *The Treaties of Canada with the Indians of Manitoba and the Northwest Territories* (Toronto: 1880), p. 61.

[12] Katherine Hughes, *Father Lacombe, The Black-Robe Voyageur* (Toronto: 1920), p. 106.

[13] Stephen Neill, *A History of Christian Missions,* Penguin Books (London, Eng.: 1964), p. 225.

[14] James E. Nix, *Mission Among the Buffalo: The Labours of the Reverends George M. and John C. McDougall in the Canadian Northwest,* 1860-1876 (Toronto: 1960), p. 37.

[15] See Lewis Hanke, *Aristotle and the American Indian* (London: 1959).

[16] Edgerton Ryerson Young, *By Canoe and Dog Train* (London: 1894), p. 62.

[17] *Ibid.,* pp. 118-121.

[18] *Ibid.,* pp. 243-246.

[19] Ruth M. Buck, "The Story of the Ahenakews," *Saskatchewan History,* Vol. 17, No. 1 (Winter, 1964), p. 22.

[20] G.F.G. Stanley, *The Birth of Western Canada, A History of the Riel Rebellions* (Toronto: 1960), p. 241.

[21] Young, *op. cit.,* p. 249.

[22] *Ibid.*

[23] Oscar Lewis (1942), pp. 68-69.

[24] *Ibid.,* p. 69.

[25] *Ibid.*

[26] William Fraser, "Big Bear, Indian Patriot," *Alberta Historical Review* (Spring, 1966), p. 15.

[27] John McLean, *The Indians: Their Manners and Customs* (Toronto: 1889), p. 56.

[28] Oscar Lewis (1942), p. 69.

[29] Edward Ahenakew, "An Opinion of the Frog Lake Massacre," *Alberta Historical Review*, Vol. VIII, No. 3 (Calgary: 1960), pp. 10-11.

[30] *Ibid.*, p. 11.

[31] *Ibid.*, p. 15.

[32] Lucien M. Hanks Jr. and Jane R. Hanks, *Tribe Under Trust—a Study of the Blackfoot Reserve of Alberta* (Toronto: 1950), *passim.*

[33] Nix, *op. cit., p. 13.*

[34] Hughes, *op. cit.*, pp. 263-264.

[35] *Ibid.*, p. 264.

[36] Scott (1931), p. 5.

[37] Duncan Campbell Scott, "Indian Affairs, 1840-1867" in *Canada and Its Provinces* (Adam Shortt and A. G. Doughty, Eds.), Vol. V (Toronto: 1913), quoted from J. E. Hodgetts, *Pioneer Public Service* (Toronto: 1955), pp. 210-211.

[38] T.R.L. MacInnes, "History of Indian Administration in Canada," *Canadian Journal of Economics and Political Science*, Vol. 12 (1946), p. 393.

[39] *Ibid.*, p. 388.

[40] Hodgetts, *op. cit.*, p. 209.

[41] Duncan Campbell Scott, *Canada and Its Provinces* (Adam Shortt and A. G. Doughty, Eds.), Vol. IV (Toronto: 1913), p. 699.

[42] Douglas Sanders and others, *Native Rights in Canada* (Toronto: 1970), p. 37. This survey of land and treaty questions in Canada was published by the Indian-Eskimo Association of Canada: for a set of extracts, see *Bulletin 202*, published by the Anglican Church of Canada (May, 1970).

[43] Freeman Blake, *History of the Indians in British North America showing their condition and management, being a Report to the Honourable the Secretary of State* (Washington, D.C.: 1870), pp. 32-33.

[44] Hodgetts, *op. cit.*, p. 225.

[45] Stanley (1952), p. 20. As noted elsewhere, many Indians of Canada are not under treaty agreements with the government but they are registered or legal Indians and are members of Indian bands. This is particularly true in the provinces of British Columbia, Quebec, and parts of the Maritimes as well as in the Northern territories. Indians of the territories and Eskimos do not have reserves set aside for them.

[46] Sanders *et al, op. cit.*, p. 109.

[47] *Ibid.*, p. 110.

4. Indian Resurgence:

The development of land protest in British Columbia, the search for identity, and organization for survival.

In previous chapters we have seen how important land was to the Indian. We have observed the writing of treaties by which the Indians lost their land, the encroachment of squatters and poachers, the gradual diminution of reserves as additional land was sold after the treaties, and we have seen how for the Indian the land still represented primarily a place to fish and hunt and move about following his seasonal pattern. It has been observed that the Indians sometimes fought to defend their land and to defend themselves from European encroachment.

In British Columbia land again became the crux of native protest. The settlement of British Columbia, as in the Prairies, proceeded at a pace whereby both whites and Indians in the early decades of European occupation had plenty of land. Following the completion of the railway to Vancouver, the Indians began to feel the subsequent northward movement of settlers by the end of the nineteenth century. In the first decade of the twentieth century, one Indian leader, Squamish Chief Joe Capilano, took the Indian land protest to England in hopes that he might receive redress from the King. Within a few years the protest had crystallized into a movement which extended into the north almost to the Yukon Territory.

The protest and resistance took a peaceful form, unlike that in the Prairies in 1885. Originally, treaties had been signed in British Columbia under Governor Sir James Douglas. However, financial difficulties soon led to a suspension of this practice. Under later governors, the province completely reversed its previous practice and not only refused to sign treaties and pay money, but even rejected the idea that Indians had any claim to the land. Instead, reserves were laid out for particular groups as pressure arose from the increased presence of white settlers in the area of the Indian group concerned. The resulting arguments, claims, and counter-claims by Indians, white settlers, and provincial government were considerable. This was the situation which pertained when British Columbia entered Confederation in 1871. This event began a series of protests, land commission investigations, recriminations between the federal and provincial governments, surveying commissions, federal-provincial consultations, and other such activity which lasted until 1927.

Unlike the situation in Saskatchewan, the early era saw the threat of violence but escaped the thing itself. Incidents which were feared to presage risings proved to be minor exceptions or single acts of violence. The continued influx of settlers, especially in the first two decades of the twentieth century, increased the concern of the Indians in areas until then fairly remote and hitherto of limited interest to potential settlers.

The influx of whites, however, when it did occur, precipitated the organization of the Indians for protest against the loss of their land. The reality of the loss became clear when the land was actually being occupied and was no longer available to them. Thus a long history of complaint to federal and provincial authorities crystallized in the early twentieth century into a formal and systematic protest and petition. Indians, supported by "friends of the Indians" such as the Rev. A. E. O'Meara, James Teit, and the Rev. L. N. Tucker, gained experience in parliamentary protest through this resistence, and even though the immediate effect of more than a decade of agitation ended in 1927 in what must have seemed failure to the Indians, the collaboration of a number of tribes expanded the range of Indian protest to a new level of province-wide cooperation.

The Indians who acted as spokesmen for the protest did not forget the issue, even after the government rejected the Nishga Petition and the Allied Tribes' land claims in 1927, and twenty years later in the late 1940's the land question was raised again, along with other grievances, by some of the same individuals, as well as by another generation becoming even more skilful in the techniques of protest. The granting of the vote to Indians in British Columbia permitted the protest to be carried into the Legislative Assembly and gave it a wider audience. In the 1960's the protest was renewed under the leadership of a Nishga Indian who is the only Indian in the provincial legislature of British Columbia, Frank Calder. In British Columbia the land protest can be documented as a continuing concern of the Indians over a period beginning at least as early as 1850—some one hundred and twenty years. The protest as a movement can also be demonstrated to have a high degree of continuity in personalities and organization over much of this time.

The intensive documentation of this movement provides an insight into the history of the mid-twentieth century Indian self-awareness and militancy for one area. It is reasonable to assume that a careful study of the sources in British Columbia would reveal more data, and that similar studies in the Prairie provinces might provide material for the establishment of continuity of leadership and issues in those areas as well. This would in no way mitigate the assertion of "new self-awareness," and "new militancy," but it would seem rather to reinforce the significance of these phenomena by indicating the context and the extent and nature of the new phase into which the Indians are now frequently said to have emerge. In doing so it would provide information for the era we have called the period of "irrelevance," the period of gestation for the current activities. By putting them into perspective it should make more meaningful both the early history and the present events and provide more useful tools for analysis of the history of Indians in Canada.

Among the Indians, especially in the Prairies and in much of Ontario and British Columbia, at the beginning of this period, at least, the native leadership was unskilled in methods which would be effective in dealing with administration. Furthermore, the Indians did not have the vote and were a diminishing segment of the population. Their ability to wield any sort of political power was therefore small. The political and governmental systems which they had previously used were of little or no aid in mastering the techniques of government and politics by which whites conducted their public life. Some of the circumstances in which the Indian Act was written and the Indian administration was shaped have already been presented. Agriculture, declining numbers, and continuing wardship with its implication of political and cultural immaturity, were to be the elements of the Indians' needs for the indefinite future, from the point of view of the administrators.

As we have seen, land figures as a prominent feature of Indian concern. Protest and anxiety as to the future of their land, as outlined above, were manifested in various parts of Canada as the settlers moved westward and the pressure on Indian land accompanied them. From Nova Scotia, where the Indians allied themselves with the French as the lesser of evils in threatening physical occupation of the land, to British Columbia, where land protest has a continuity to the present day, there is at least this common thread of native response. In British Columbia this issue provided an important factor, if not the only important factor, in the resurgence of the Indians in the most recent phase of Indian history. How did this come about? For a description of these developments in coastal British Columbia, it is necessary to go back to earliest Indian-white relations.

The Indians of coastal British Columbia had a culture which was unique. Unlike most of the Indians of Canada they lived in more or less permanent residences despite the fact that they were not agriculturalists. This unusual feature of their life was due to the large quantities of seafood and wildlife available. Skilled at woodworking and with a settled existence they were able to make and accumulate a much more elaborate collection of material possessions than non-agricultural people usually do. The pattern of one group, for example—the Tsimshian—was to spend the winter months in their villages, where they carried on a rich ceremonial life. In the spring they moved to locations on the coast.

The Nass River mouth was one of the most renowned. Here they fished and prepared the fish and oils for storage. Later in the summer they gathered edible wild roots, plants, and berries, and by October they were back in their villages. Some of the products of this annual activity formed items in the trade between the coastal peoples and the interior peoples. Other coastal and inland people traded with those Indians who had the customary claim to work these fisheries. Sometimes, of course, rivalries developed as groups competed for a coveted spot. Conflicts might result in coastal raids of revenge.

Although the culture of the Indians of coastal British Columbia is described as of a single type, scholars subdivide their culture by linguistic elements as well as by traits of social organization, art styles, and political and religious distinctions. The various peoples who make up the Northwest Coast culture, from the Tsimshian, Haida, and Kwakiutl in the north to the Salish-speaking peoples of the southern coast, the Comox, Squamish, Sechelt, Musqueam, and others, were affected sooner or later by the coming of the Europeans.

The earliest continuous contact dates from the 1770's. The voyage of Captain Cook in 1778 initiated British contact with the area four years after the Spaniard Perez first touched there. Spanish navigators vied with English in these early years for the privilege of being the first Europeans to map the area. By the end of the decade American ships were active along the coast, and a rivalry between British and American traders characterized the commercial life. During the several decades from the 1770's to the 1830's the main item of trade sought by the outsiders was sea otters. The Chinese had responded to sea otter pelts in a manner comparable to the enthusiasm of the European continent for beaver pelts. From this interest developed an extensive trade which quickly exhausted, commercially speaking, the maritime sources of furs. At the same time, Indians were absorbing into their own culture elements of the new culture, especially tools and weapons.

Because written sources before the late eighteenth century are few or non-existent, it is not easy to establish how much change occurred. Material changes occurred as a result of the introduction of iron and steel tools. With the increased wealth and the elaboration of material culture, other aspects of the West Coast Indian life also experienced an alteration and florescence. We are reminded here of the impact of the horse on the Prairie peoples such as the Cree and the Blackfoot. The highly developed form and content of the art of these peoples when first observed systematically cannot have been the product of a short term of artistic tradition. It is more likely that it is a flowering of the scale and quantity of a previously developed range of objects and of the artistic adornment of these objects. Woodworking is a good example of this flowering, and "totem" poles in particular are thought to have undergone a marked florescence as a result of new tools. The term "totem pole" is applied to a variety of forms—the display of family crests in an heraldic pole, the preservation of a great man's body in a mortuary pole, and the decoration of house posts and entrance, poles— which consist of animal, human, and mythological images carved in deep relief on the hollow shaft of a cedar bole. The scale, elaboration, and formal subtelty of this major sculptural style are probably the result of the introduction of new iron tools into a pre-existing wood-working tradition with a mature symbolic system and a ready source of materials on an heroic scale. This set of circumstances produced a rich and monumental artistic style.

It has been noted that the social impact of the European culture on the Northwest coast society was primarily influenced by the nature and effects of trade. By and large the new goods were incorporated into the old patterns and could be viewed simply as extensions of already existing cultural directions. What on the surface appeared to be acceptance of the new, on closer examination indicated a thorough-going conservatism against these innovations.[1] Supporting this conclusion is the finding that productive efficiency rose through the introduction of superior tools and weapons. Increased markets brought more income. Organization of production, however, remained unchanged. Hunting the sea otter already formed part of the aboriginal culture, and the increase in numbers hunted and wealth acquired from the hunt were part of the flowering which occurred.

The distribution of new wealth, however, continued to be in the hands of the chiefs, and while the general wealth of all probably rose, the status relationships—and the West Coast Indians were very status conscious—remained the same. Although at a later date "new men," those who had achieved new wealth and status as a result of disruptions and changes attendant on more intense contacts, did occur, this came later. Later, too, epidemic diseases threw the mechanisms of normal accession to chieftancy into imbalance. Men and women then competed more vigorously, even fiercely, to establish their positions. Population movement began to occur, and peoples settled around the source of the new tools, weapons, foods, and clothing, the new objects of wealth. Then they engaged in rivalries to establish and regularize their new relationships. But this aspect of change was just beginning in the third decade of the nineteenth century. One leading authority points out that the new wealth "strengthened the existing social and economic systems."

The society of the coastal Indians had traditionally emphasized the accumulation and distribution of wealth, and the new trade was incorporated into that tradition and into pre-existing trading patterns. Chiefs grew richer and material display became more splendid. Trade routes and commercial ascendancy were guarded jealously by those who had it. While social organization remained intact and the new trade was incorporated into existing values, other elements of West Coast life were changing. Those groups who possessed the new weapons had the upper hand over those not yet in possession of them. Conflicts developed and traditional rivalries and feuds were sometimes exacerbated. We have observed similar developments in the East.

Besides guns, ammunition, and tools, the Indians took blankets, molasses, bread, rice, alcohol, tobacco, and domestic utensils, such as needles and scissors, in exchange for their furs. When they felt cheated or otherwise misused, Indians attacked their exploiters. For this they frequently gained the reputation of being warlike and difficult to deal with. In the interior in the 1850's Indians defended themselves against the influx of gold miners. (The peoples of the interior of British Columbia, mostly Salishan-speakers, will be discussed in more detail later.) The Indians were bothered by the sudden inundation of the land by prospectors, and learning of the value placed on gold by the white men, were unwilling to see their land and the gold in it taken without their receiving adequate consultation or recompense.

Accounts from captains and crews of ships trading on the coast tell of attacks by Indians. In the earliest days of trading Indians were not ordinarily permitted on the ships. However, this practice broke down as competing captains vied for the pelts brought by the Indians. Nevertheless, Europeans tended to be suspicious of Indian behaviour and interpreted their conduct accordingly. The desperate measures used by the Europeans to gain furs included kidnapping and holding the chief or chiefs for ransom. Indians retaliated when and where they could. Large gatherings of Indians ceased to be thought of as a happy sign of many pelts to be acquired and came to be a cause for alarm lest a raid on the ship was impending. Mutual distrust came to exert its influence. The Indians suspected imprisonment if they boarded the ships unprotected. They feared the theft of their furs or the bombardment of their villages. On the other hand they might be seeking revenge for an injury perpetrated on them by previous Europeans or some others whose aggression had not yet been avenged.[2]

The more northerly Indians had been the first to be drawn into the maritime fur trade. Accordingly they—the Haidas, the Tsimshian, the Kwakiutl, as well as the Tlingit of Alaska—were the first to experience intensely the impact of the European. The most southerly peoples, for example the Coast Salish Indians, were not much touched by white contact until almost the middle of the nineteenth century, when the Hudson's Bay Company headquarters moved to the site of Victoria on Vancouver Island. Homer Barnett ascribes this relative lack of contact to the absence of a substantial quantity of otters.

The Nootkas of Vancouver Island are an exception to these comments about the southern Indians. They had the doubtful privilege of being the first Indians to be reached by the Spanish navigator Juan Perez in 1774 and by Cook four years later. After a lapse of several years more ships came. The pelts acquired by some of Cook's men turned out to be very much in demand in China, and the fur trade began. It was under these circumstances that Indian culture was to feel the impact of the Europeans and began a new era of adaptation and change. The resulting widespread movement of at least a few people in the very earliest years of the trade is illustrated by the crew of Captain John Meares's ship, the *North West America,* which in 1788 brought Chinese labourers, and some Hawaiians, to Nootka. However, the traffic was not all one way. In the same year Meares had met in Canton a Nootka man, Comekela, brother of the Nootka chief Maquilla.

Meares's description shows his condescension toward the Indians. It also illustrates the selective borrowing of Comekela in his choice of copper utensils with which to decorate himself. Copper was a metal greatly valued by the West Coast Indians, and its possession meant wealth.

> His scarlet (regimental) coat was decorated with such quantities of brass buttons and copper additions of one kind or another as could not fail of procuring him the most profound respect of his countrymen, and render him an object of the first desire among the Nootka damsels. At least half a sheet of copper formed his breast-plate; from his ears copper ornaments were suspended, and he contrived to hang from his hair, which was dressed en queue, so many handles of copper saucepans, that his head was kept back by the weight of them, in such a stiff and upright position, as very much to heighten the singularity of his appearance. For various articles of his present pride Comekela had been in a state of continual hostility with the cook, from whom he had contrived to purloin them; but their last and principal struggle was for an enormous spit, which the American had seized as a spear, to swell the circumstances of the magnificence with which he was on the moment of dazzling the eyes of his countrymen—and situated as we were, this important article of culinary service could not be denied him. In such a state of accoutrement, and feeling as much delight as ever fed the pride of the most splendid thrones of Europe or the East, we set out with him for the shore, when a general shout and cry from the village assured him of the universal joy which was felt on his return.
>
> The whole body of inhabitants moved towards the beach, and with a most unpleasant howl, welcomed him on shore. . . . After the first ceremonies of welcome were over the whole company proceeded to the king's house, into which persons of rank were alone permitted to enter, and where a magnificent feast of whale blubber and oil was prepared.[3]

The above quotation is a reminder that the Nootka hunted the whale, going out into the Pacific in enormous sea-going canoes. Meares's plans for Comekela were not entirely realized, as the latter soon returned to the life of his own people and neglected the interests of the European.

> Comekela was, at first, very active in forwarding our commercial arrangement; but he had become very deficient in his native tongue, and he now spoke such a jargon of Chinese, English, and Nootkan languages, as to be by no means a ready interpreter between us and the natives;—besides, in returning to the manners of his country, he began to prefer the interests of his countrymen, and, amidst the renewed luxuries of whale flesh, blubber, and oil, to forget the very great kindnesses we had bestowed upon him.[4]

Another island people, the Haida Indians of the Queen Charlotte Islands, were also among the earliest to develop trade contacts with the incoming Europeans. They, together with the Nootkas in the south (Vancouver Island) and the Tlingits in Alaska became the middlemen in trading goods to the Indians more remote from European trade. Copper was an important trade item prior to the coming of the European; it was beaten into the desired shape without being heated. Now iron became important. White traders who visited the Northwest Coast have commented on the interest shown by the Indians in the metalwork on board the ships.

The trade in seal and otter skins continued to be the main economic link between Indians and whites until about 1830. By that time the maritime mammals had been reduced to a point where they were no longer as commercially important as they had been, and new fur sources were being sought. Traders hoped to tap the resources of the mainland. In addition to the coastal mainland, however, they also sought to reach into the resources of the interior by establishing routes up the river valleys. Trading through these river routes predates the coming of the European and represents an adaptation from indigenous patterns, as had been the case of the Huron and Ottawa trading patterns. Copper, fish, and fish oil were only a few of the items which had formed the basis of the native Indian trade.

British and American traders approached the area of the mouths of the Nass and Skeena Rivers. To forestall American activities in the area, the Hudson's Bay Company under the direction of Dr. John McLoughlin decided to establish a post at the mouth of the Nass River in 1831. Three years later the post was removed south to the mouth of the Skeena River. The lower reaches of these two rivers and the coastal area between them was inhabited by the Tsimshian people. Divided into three subgroups, but speaking a mutually intelligible set of dialects of the Tsimshian language, they are among the most brilliant of totem-pole carvers. Formerly they had been in touch with European traders only indirectly through Indian middlemen; with the creation of a post in their own midst the cultural impact was intensified. There was a florescence of their material culture, e.g., totem poles, masks, headdresses, feasts and ceremonies. New wealth made possible greater potlatches. Nishga (the Nass River branch of the Tsimshian) artists became renowned for their work as carvers. In the 1830's, along with these developments, came the first serious smallpox epidemic among them.

Indian life became more affected by the pressure and importance of the white traders. Trading posts had been created in the interior of British Columbia. Efforts were being made to tap fur sources from the interior side as well, that is from Canada and Hudson Bay. The new post, Fort Simpson, not only served to link the Hudson's Bay Company with the coastal people, it also reinforced Tsimshian trading patterns with the interior. Tsimshian Indians settled around the post (near present-day Prince Rupert), and some learned to read and write and were employed as interpreters.

In these early days, as we have already observed, the control of the trade remained in the hands of the chiefs, and adaptations were made within the context of existing social and cultural patterns. Some chiefs, through advantages of location, priority of contact, or because of an early realization of the new potentialities, established trading monopolies. Chief Legaic and his Tsimshian people held a monopoly of trade for thirty years along the Skeena River. By the mid-nineteenth century the Tsimshian had a flowering culture in many ways, despite the inroads made by epidemics. They were linked by trade with coastal and interior peoples, and the new wealth helped to create what has been called the "zenith of their splendor and opulence."[5]

A new phase in their history began when the missionary influence was introduced. The first missionary among them was a layman, William Duncan, sent out by the Church of England. One of his first tasks was to learn the Tsimshian language. This in itself represented an important step, because prior to this time most dealings between Indians and whites along the west coast were in Chinook jargon. This trade language was a mixture of words from both Indian and European languages, and Duncan quickly saw its limitations for the purposes he had in mind. The result of Indian acceptance of Christianity was to create cultural cleavages among themselves. Duncan began his mission work among the Tsimshian of Fort Simpson, by this time moved from the mouth of the Nass to the mouth of the Skeena. Several years later, in order to strengthen his group of converts and aid them in resisting both traditional influences and undesirable European influences, he and they removed to a village site abandoned years before when Fort Simpson had become a popular place for settlement. The place was called Metlakatla, and here Indians came to experiment with a new way of life, being moulded under the guiding hand and watchful eye of Duncan.

At Metlakatla he began an experiment in systematic culture change that was to bring him awe and respect in many quarters. The task he set for himself was to change the culture of the Indians who settled in the village of Metlakatla. Working through existing chiefs who joined him and through an Indian council created under his authority, he introduced his Indian adherents to Western technology, Western life styles (housing, clothing, daily routines, jobs), and Christianity.

For the next twenty years Indians did come to Metlakatla and they did undergo varying degrees of culture change. This theocratic type of community placed a great emphasis on changing the outward material life of the Indians as an important aspect of changing the inward spiritual life. Because Duncan thought they could absorb the religious concepts of the West more slowly than the material aspects, and because of his own preferences in matters of religion, he refrained from teaching them the Anglican variety of Christianity which would have seemed likely, given his employer. Instead he tried to create a kind of generalized, evangelical protestantism geared to what he believed the Indians could absorb. To some extent he seems to have been attempting to work out his own variant on the idea emerging within the Church

Missionary Society of creating indigenous Christian churches which synthesized elements of traditional culture with Christianity.

At Metlakatla not only did Indians begin to learn something of Western technology and Christianity, they also acquired some experience in Western styles of leadership. David Leask in particular emerges as a figure who was a product of these new experiences. He played an active role as spokesman for the Indian advocates of Duncan when the latter became involved in controversies with Church and state in the 1880's.

From Metlakatla the cultural impact of the missionaries, for many years primarily Duncan and men sent out to work with him (a difficult assignment which several could not fulfill), spread out to adjacent Tsimshian communities. Some of the most important linkages were with the Nishga Indians of the Nass River valley. Here a daughter mission of Metlakatla was created at Kincolith with a hospital which served to draw people in. The Indian patients and their relatives were then evangelized. In the 1870's Methodist missionaries arrived on the scene to win adherents and create rivalry with Duncan and with the Anglican missionaries.

Remote from the main areas of white settlement, the Tsimshian could observe developments farther south and on Vancouver Island. They visited Victoria to taste of the Western civilization. Because of their relative remoteness, especially those on the Nass River, and the slow penetration northward by the white man, they had time to work out an adaptation for dealing with the newcomers.

One of the main elements in their resistance was the issue of land. They saw Indians to the south struggling to retain their land and they feared the same for themselves. They took advantage of the new command some of them had of the English language, which was introduced by mission schools, and by the fishing industries and the fur traders, to make their case. They also drew support from sympathetic whites, especially certain missionaries. Because of their protests they were obliged to give testimony, interviews, hold conferences, be visited by commissions, and undergo investigations. All of this has produced a gold mine of primary research material for the historian seeking to learn more about their affairs in the late nineteenth and early twentieth centuries. It is perhaps no coincidence that the first native Canadian elected to the provincial legislature in British Columbia is a Nishga Indian from the Nass River valley.

Not until the mid-1880's did many of the northern Indians of British Columbia come under effective control of the Indian Affairs department. They, like other Indians in the province, sometimes found themselves "in the middle" in the controversies between province and Dominion. They struggled to retain as much land as possible. They challenged the work of land commissioners, investigators, and surveyors whose activities dragged on for decades.

Another important element in their culture was the potlatch. This, too, was threatened and then outlawed. Potlatching was a central feature of the Indians' social organization and cultural life. When it was prohibited it went underground. After being outlawed for approximately seventy years it was again legalized and came to the surface. The potlatch is particularly identified with the Kwakiutl people, because of the widely read interpretive study of Indian culture by Ruth Benedict in *Patterns of Culture.*

The Kwakiutl were located on the coast just south of the Tsimshian. Like other Northwest Coast peoples they lived in villages, and the village formed the political unit of their society. In the middle nineteenth century, through the impact of white contact, the Kwakiutl underwent some important changes. Disease and relocation had reduced the population and led to the reconstitution of Kwakiutl communities. This was the beginning of what Helen Codere has called the "Potlatch period" (1849-1921) in Kwakiutl history. One major centre of settlement emerged at Fort Rupert. This Hudson's Bay Company post became the scene of regroupings of people into new social units following the effects of epidemics and of population removal to a new area. Their efforts to re-establish their social positions led to the elaborate potlatches which early writers described and which have come to form a popular stereotype of the character of these ceremonies. Potlatching among the Kwakiutl was to some extent a substitute for warfare which had been suppressed as European control in the territory grew.

Trade articles were being introduced into the daily life of the Indians and handicrafts were dying out as manufactured goods gained the ascendancy. The Fort Rupert Kwakiutl in particular became middlemen and acted as interpreters for the Hudson's Bay Company. The basic values of the Indian society continued despite these alterations. Among these people, too, there was an elaboration of material culture while social institutions remained fundamentally unchanged through the nineteenth century. This situation continued into the twentieth century, despite the fact that by the 1880's Anglican missionaries were evangelizing among the Kwakiutl and the people had come under the administration of the Indian Affairs branch. Helen Codere finds that the Kwakiutl culture has retained its central integrating interests over a period from the late eighteenth century down to the mid-twentieth century. These interests are a "concern" with social status and the "maximization" of social status.

The Kwakiutl have orally transmitted the stories and the legends of their kinship groups or lineages, which extend back in time for as many as twenty generations. These accounts are thought to contain a high degree of accuracy for calculating chronological sequences and even exact dating. By this means historians may be able to reconstruct the past of the Kawkiutl or some elements of them in the pre-contact time. Of these remembered family histories, Helen Codere says:

> They are probably accurate precisely because the Kwakiutl were preoccupied with the great tradition of social positions, positions which had come down in an unbroken line of succession from their remote ancestors and had been honorably maintained by the potlatches of each successive generation. . . . Considering that the Kwakiutl concept of greatness in potlatching was greatness in the quantity of property distributed, it is unlikely that a Kwakiutl would ever minimize a potlatch given by one of his own ancestors, since in doing so he would be minimizing the greatness of his own potlatch position and name. Therefore, the historical reconstruction which shows relatively small potlatches for early times is no doubt factually correct.[6]

Codere has shown that European-manufactured trade blankets were taken up as the standard unit for trading and after 1840 quickly displaced most other items. She has further shown that the number of blankets used in potlatches expanded greatly, from 9,000 in the years 1849-1869 to 18,000 between 1890-1909, and up to 33,000 between 1930-1949 (years after the prohibition). In the meantime, slaves ceased to be given away in potlatches, and warfare between the Kwakiutl and their neighbours stopped due to the pressures of European customs. A shift took place in which potlatching replaced physical violence. There was an increase in the number of potlatches and the amount of wealth invoked in the individual events. Helen Codere asserts that ". . .they chose to potlatch with the proceeds of their new economic achievements and that, as a result, potlatches became grander and . . .more extensive."[7]

Population declined sharply from the 1830's due to the spread of disease, and this fact probably encouraged the potlatching activities. A reduced population might avoid warfare; more titles and honours were vacated due to a high death rate, and population movement increased the desirability of re-establishing lines of prestige and status. Helen Codere concurs with F. E. LaViolette in the view that "Certain attitudes and practices characteristic of Kwakiutl economic life from the time of the earliest records, and presumably in pre-contact times, facili-tated this adjustment." They were ". . .extremely able and industrious," and ". . .their. . .industrial procedures and food-getting techniques were varied, specialized and concerned with production far inexcess of mere need. . . . From the time of their earliest contacts with Europeans in business and trade, they were uniformly and continuously energetic and astute. These qualities and traditional habits were extraordinary assets in meeting the new economic conditions and in taking advantage of their expanded opportunities. . .the habituation to standardized and pluralized manufactured objects was carried over into the new economic situation in their acquisition of European manufactures." Potlatches were encouraged by the manufactured goods which could be used for them. Codere concludes that the cheap goods made available by the industrial revolution encouraged the potlatch.

A form of adaptation and blending of old and new took place. As a result, "developments in the occupational field were an unusual combination of sustaining traditional occupations, entering commercialized

versions of old occupations, or entering new ones which possessed traditional and congenial features. . . .Already familiar with the natural resources of their land and trained in their exploitation, they were able to
take an indispensable place in the commercialized fishing and lumbering
industries of British Columbia."[8]

The term "tribe" may be misleading in talking about the Indians of
Canada, because generally speaking there was no effective political unit
of a "tribal" scope. The units of government which characterized most
Indian peoples were small units, sometimes bands or even families.
Among the settled peoples of the West Coast there was no tribal political unity, either. The Kwakiutl, for example, lived in villages more or
less autonomous from other Kwakiutl villages. After the mid-nineteenth
century, however, and with the creation of Fort Rupert, many
Kwakiutl settled around this fort and created for the first time a community which was substantially larger and more important than all the
other remaining Kwakiutl communities. At Fort Rupert they formed
what has been called the Kwakiutl confederacy. They enjoyed an economic and material advantage over other Kwakiutl, because they had
immediate access to the new goods now being introduced. It was here
that some of the most dramatic and impressive potlatches took place.
The "Fort Ruperts," as these Kawkiutl came to be called, acted as
middlemen and interpreters in dealing with their fellow Kwakiutl and
others, many of whom came to the fort or were otherwise traded with.

The culture change which was taking place under these circumstances was not of a directed or systematic kind. Helene Codere writes
of this relationship:

> Kwakiutl contacts with the Hudson's Bay traders at Fort Rupert seem to have
> been harmonious and profitable for all concerned. It is difficult to assess the
> effect that the small settlement of Hudson's Bay men had upon the culture.
> Company policy had long been to conduct business with Indians as they were,
> not to revolutionize their way of life, and this seems to have held at Fort
> Rupert.[9]

The Indian did not come under the regular administration of the Indian
Affairs department until 1881, when an agency was created at Alert
Bay. In that year also an Anglican missionary became resident there as
well. The missionary, the Rev. A. Hull, became a prime element in
efforts to crush the potlatch.

It was hoped that the "Christian communities" of Indians would be
a means to end the practice. Having abandoned other elements of their
culture such as warfare and the winter dance ceremonies, many clung to
the potlatch as a major element in the system of establishing of and
recognition of social ranks. Prior to 1900 the Indians had both the
missionaries and the Indian agents against them on the issue of the
potlatch. Some Chrisitanized Indians—the Methodist seem to have been
the most enthusiastic—wished to see a more vigorous implementation
of the new prohibition against potlatching. Other Indians, Christian and
non-Christian, were unwilling to see the custom ended. The latter ap-

parently had some individuals who, like their adversaries, were willing to take pen in hand. The letter which follows is an illustration of this, using the rhetorical language of oration:

Victoria, B.C., September 18, 1899
To Mr. A. W. Powell, Superintendent of Indian Affairs in British Columbia:

Esteemed Sir,—We have been delegated by the chiefs and head men of the tribes Ki-ha-ten, Kit-la-tomic, and Kit-Win-Chilco, residents of Nass River and its tributaries, to express to you our heartfelt thanks for your condoling kindness in thus far protecting us from the threatening attitude of tribes amalgamating with Christianity.

In the treaty on the concession of our lands all our former rights in the usages and customs of the tribes are to be respected. Notwithstanding these are vested rights, which according to the great law-givers cannot be diverted even by Parliamentary enactment, a delegation of our Christian cousins in the month of April last, made application to you to have this treaty stipulation abrogated on the grounds that the potlatch and other customs were consummated with drunkenness, prostitution, and murder. Now, if this is the case, it is in violation of the statute laws of British Columbia, and there is a strong force of Indian Provincial police. Yet but few arrests have been made, and we regret to say that they were all Christians. The last one was fined $6 and allowed to escape. You kindly ignored their application, and your fostering protection has secured us a few months' peace.

On leaving the river, a few days since, we were again confronted by a more serious aspect of hostile demonstration. The Bishop, and Mr. Todd, forming a Christian alliance (of course with no selfish ends in view), are to jump the jurisprudence of British Columbia and bring the powers of Ottawa on the defenceless, and friendless, in condoling kindness, because they cannot convince us that for thousands of years our people all went to hell and still abide in that uncomfortable atmosphere, and we contribute nothing to support the dynasty.

The Christian Indians are in the conglomorate army arrayed against us, and the sympathy of "peace and love" of former missionaries are to be the victims of a general slaughter.

In consideration of "peace and love," we have relinquished the Medicine Towanawas doctrine, the Black Towanawas, the sacred dances, potlatches, our former mode of intercourse, and peacemaking with other tribes.

The only rites which we still celebrate are the invitations to our funerals, of friends and mourners, which we donate to in behalf of the deceased, erecting a monument over the graves of relatives, and gifts are bestowed. We still have dances for amusement, but no potlatch.

In our feeble effort to show the wrongs imposed on us for want of representation in joint council, we would respectfully ask, as a matter of equity, that you appoint a Provincial force of police from the tribes which we have the honour to represent, equal to the Christian police force, that the many drinks in the dark may be brought to light and recorded in the dockets of your criminal courts.

In conclusion, we would say a word of consolation to our persecutors: Turn not the course of the mighty river's pure waters from the mountain's white-capped creation, kissed by the Great Monarch of all living things, in his noonday's love and affection to the little fish that play in its pebbly bottom and smile the welcome advent of the morning Aurora; the parent of their heritage; the divinity of their affections, for he is the noble functionary in evidence of the Great Spirit; our Almighty Providence; an Immaculate and Affectionate God. Darken not the horizon with mysterious delusions of nimbus clouds in the vanity of ostensible civilization, for on the placid bosom of the waters were the happy days of our ancestors spent.

We have the honour to be Her Majesty's most humble subjects, and for the kind regard you have for our welfare we tender, in behalf of our people, their love and gratitude.

Very respectfully,

(Signed)   NES-LES-YAN
                            STE-YAH-WN[10]

The Indian superintendent of British Columbia, A.W. Powell, wrote:

The Kwahkewlths listen to advice, but in the end prefer their own course. They are wedded to old barbarous customs, and regard with suspicion any person who undertakes to change them. . .The most of the past year seems to have been spent by them in idleness at Fort Rupert, where a large number assembled last autumn, for the purpose of holding a series of extensive "potlatches" and where I found them in July, after the most valuable portion of the fishing season, so necessary to them for the usual supply of winter food, had been lost.

Although a great amount of wealth had been given away, their camps were wretched in character and appearance. Owing to the great number huddled together in their large comfortless sanctuaries, there was much sickness and many deaths during the winter. . .I have instructed the agents not to permit, on any account, the congregation of so many, and for such a purpose, on another occasion.[11]

In 1884 legislation was passed in Parliament outlawing the potlatch. The law read: "Every Indian or other person who engages in or assists in celebrating the Indian festival known as the potlatch. . .is guilty of a misdemeanour and shall be liable to imprisonment for a term of not more than six months and not less than two months. . . ."

This did not stop potlatching, however, as Indian Agent reports in succeeding years indicate. Protests against the law now began to be heard. In February, 1887, a group of twenty-four Indians from the Cowichan agency appealed to the Prime Minister's office:

We the undersigned Indians of the Cowichan agency beg respectfully to ask you to use your influence to have the clause of the Indian Act forbidding the "Potlach" and "Tamanawas" Dances repealed.

In asking this we would point out that these are two of our oldest customs, and by them we do not injure anyone.

We cannot read like white people and the dances are our winter amusements.

When our children grow up and are educated they perhaps will not wish to dance.

Some only of us dance now, and we do not wish to teach others, but when one is seized with the ("Quellish") dance he cannot help himself and we believe would die unless he danced. On Saturdays and Sundays we will not dance as this offends the Christian Indians.

The lands of our fathers are occupied by white men and we say nothing.

We have given up fighting with each other.

We have given up stealing and many old habits, but we want to be allowed to continue the "Potlach" and the Dance. We know the hearts of most of the Coast Indians are with us in this. We therefore ask you to have the law amended, that we may not be breaking it when we follow customs that are dear to us.[12]

For the Indians this meant that obligations and responsibilities would go unfulfilled and unmet. Potlatching went underground and the language of the law was sufficiently imprecise so that it wasn't easy to make convictions when arrests were made. Most convictions in the 1920's and 1930's led to suspended sentences. Anti-potlatch-law protest among Indians and whites eventually resulted in the revocation of the legislation in 1951. One factor which contributed to the solidarity of the protest was that by about 1900 some missionaries had accommodated themselves to it, and so Christian Indians and non-Christian or nominal Christians continued to take part in potlatching.

In addition to the importance of the potlatch for establishing and retaining status, the role attributed to it among the Kwakiutl by Helen Codere, other interpretations have been applied. Wayne Suttles concludes that among the Coast Salish,

> . . .the drive to attain high status is clearly not the explanation of the potlatch. Nor is the production of surplus. Nor the co-operation achieved by the potlatching community. The potlatch is part of a larger socio-economic system which enables the whole social network, consisting of a number of communities, to maintain a high level of food production and to equalize its food consumption within and among communities.[13]

Stuart Piddocke, writing about the Southern Kwakiutl, says that redistribution of food was a prime aspect of the potlatch due to the threat of food scarcity due to local variations in food supplies. Philip Drucker and Robert Heizer, in a more recent work, discount this argument and assert that ". . .it is clear that the potlatch must be regarded as a formal procedure for social integration, its prime purpose being to identify the membership of the groups and to define the social status of this membership."[14]

The potlatch provided a formal means of retaining social cohesion even when the potlatch seemed to be at its most extreme due to circumstances created by the impact of the white newcomers.

Forrest LaViolette has suggested that there is among the Kwakiutl and other West Coast Indians an attitude toward social status, wealth, and labour which coincides with the "Protestant ethic" of much of the white society. It is argued that the correspondence of the two cultures in these attitudes and values has given the West Coast Indians an advantage in fitting into aspects of European culture which was not to be found among most other Indians in North America. These similarities, it is further asserted, have made possible adaptation of European culture by the Kawkiutl from a period of voluntary culture change into a period of involuntary culture change. Perhaps another way of stating this would be to say that the Indians of the West Coast have adapted elements of non-Indian culture which are congruent with their own—a phenomenon which we have observed elsewhere.

The mid-nineteenth century saw a shift in the balance of power in British Columbia. Prior to that time the position of the Indian was strong enough to retain the initiative. After the mid-century, areas of white settlement grew, and as they did, the Indian found himself more and more hemmed in and restricted. He was not without recourse. Acts of individual violence and the threat of group violence were always present. As we have stated, much of the conflict had to do with the land. The Indians resisted encroachment on their land and protested to the authorities. Correspondence flowed between Indians and Victoria and New Westminster, the capitals of the two colonies of Vancouver Island and British Columbia respectively; the two colonies were united in 1866. Governor James Douglas, formerly of the Hudson's Bay Company, attempted to follow the traditional British policy of signing treaties and setting aside reserves. However, the cost of such an approach was laid at the feet of the colonial assembly and they were unwilling to pay it. Furthermore, the settler-controlled assembly was equally reluctant to see large tracts of land allotted to the Indians. After Douglas's retirement the Indians found themselves dealing with a more difficult situation. Their aboriginal title was denied, and they were treated on the basis of "whatever the traffic will bear." There occurred a repetition of what had occurred in the East early in the nineteenth century when Indians were no longer a military threat. The friction and pressure on the land followed the pattern of white settlement. In this way it moved from the southwest corner of the mainland and the southern tip of Vancouver Island northward and into the interior, and the process of infringement and resistance and protest was repeated over and over again as the pressure reached successive Indian communities.

The Indians of the southern interior of British Columbia were primarily of the group known as Interior Salish. These consisted of peoples such as the Shuswap, Lilloet, Thompson, and Okanagan. In aboriginal times they fished the rivers which drained the interior and formed the tributaries and mainstreams which flowed into the Pacific Ocean. Seasonal fishing was augmented by hunting game. Like the coastal people they were hard hit by epidemic diseases. Estimates of population figures are not available before about 1835. Their population for that year has been estimated at 13,500. This compares with 8,500 for the Tsimshian; 10,700 for the Kwakiutl; 12,000 for the Coast Salish. By 1885 the populations for all these people had fallen by another fifty per cent or more. To what extent the populations in 1835 represent a decline from the late eighteenth century is not clear, though it probably had declined.

This more remote impact of whites was followed by the arrival of white settlers in growing numbers after the mid-nineteenth century. First miners and then settlers, farmers, and ranchers impinged on the Indians. The earliest discoveries of gold in the interior of British Columbia were the work of Indians, and they pioneered mining activities. As the news got out and white miners flocked in, the Indians were reduced to the status of labourers for the non-Indians. Friction occurred between encroaching whites and Indians, and occasional acts of violence resulted. Governor James Douglas came to the assistance of the miners. On the other hand, Chinese merchants sometimes acted as suppliers of goods and arms to the Indians. From having discovered and first worked the gold, the Indians were pushed onto the periphery of this industry, and from having been intruded upon they became the "intruders."[15]

With the aid of missionaries protests were registered, but despite these efforts the result was the loss of land and permanent occupation by the newcomers. Indians found jobs with the miners, but also experienced discrimination at their hands. The government refused to sign treaties or recognize an Indian claim, but reserves were created and the Indians were obliged to change their way of life. Agriculture and ranching were added to fishing and hunting as means of subsistence, and increasingly Indians took employment with the whites in a variety of industries, usually as labourers. Roman Catholic missionaries were the dominant Christian evangelists among the Interior Salish.

Although Indian population fell sharply between the late eighteenth century and the mid-nineteenth century, Indians remained sufficiently numerous and remote in particular localities that they constituted vital and continuing communities. Under the influence of traders, missionaries, and administrators, in approximately that chronological order, they developed their resistance to the threat to their land. This resistance kept them very much in the attention of the government. In British Columbia there is published historical material which takes the story down to the present time. In part this derives from the fact that the Indians have continued to be "relevant" to British Columbia (or at least to part of it), without interruption, so that their history in some ways calls attention more immediately to the re-emergence in the public attention of the Indian.

One of the reasons for this would seem to be that the issues and techniques which were important in British Columbia were an important segment of, if not a microcosm of, the general pattern of development of Indian protest in Canada. Because settlement in British Columbia has been so recent, and particularly in the northern part of the province, there has been a kind of telescoping effect of the processes which are observable in a more attenuated form in other parts of the country.

In British Columbia the evolution from periodic and localized protest to province-wide protest developed within a relatively short period of time. In the volume published by the British Columbia government in the mid-1870's, *Papers Related to the Land Question, 1850-1875*, we see the first localized, scattered protests evolving out of pressures on the land due to the coming of white settlers. By the early twentieth century, Indian leaders were taking their protest to England (albeit without apparent success), and before 1920, a province-wide organization had emerged.

A close-up view of the background and life-experience of one Indian group which took an active part in the early twentieth century land protest is provided by an examination of the Squamish, a sub-group of the Salishan-speaking peoples who are the southernmost of the West Coast Indians. In aboriginal times they made their living, as did all others of this vast area, by means of hunting, fishing, and gathering, rather than by the practice of agriculture. The food obtainable by these methods was abundant. The searches of the Squamish for new and better food sources brought them down Howe Sound and onto the north shore of Burrard Inlet, in what is now North Vancouver, by the mid-nineteenth century. The settlement became known as Mission Reserve No. 1 from the presence of the mission and school established by the Oblate Fathers (Oblates of Mary Immaculate) and the Little Sisters of the Child Jesus.

The village layout followed a pattern common among West Coast Indians. Houses were arranged in rows facing the beach. The houses of the more prominent members of the community tended to be in the most easily defended position in a village. Pictures of the Mission Reserve village in the 1880's show this practice, as do photographs of Indian villages on other parts of the coast from aboriginal times. The reserve was created informally at first in the mid-1860's. About a decade later, after British Columbia became part of the Dominion, the management of Indians passed to the federal authority. This development introduced a period of more than fifty years of federal-provincial and Indian-government controversy in which land was the major bone of contention.

The settlement had begun as a camping site for the Squamish coming down from Howe Sound. There, through the efforts of Chief Snat, the Squamish acquired thirty-five acres as the original Reserve No. 1. At this time, November 25, 1869, Snat gave the population of the village as fifty families and sixteen single men. Indians claimed that Snat had as early as 1862 attempted to acquire the land, as Crown lands were then available to whites by pre-emption. However, in order to discourage Indians, a series of requirements was laid down which conflicted with Indian practice in the use of land. Pre-emptors were required to clear a stated amount of land over a five-year period and to bring a portion of this land under cultivation. It may be that this was a calculated step, based on a knowledge of Indian use of land as a range for hunting, fishing, and the gathering of wild fruits, vegetables, and roots, rather than for agriculture or domestication of animals. It effectively stopped Indian land pre-emption. By the time of the British Columbia Pre-emption Act of 1870, Indians were excluded from claiming Crown land. However, the government of British Columbia continued to create reserves for Indians. For some time the population of whites in the area remained sparse, and it was not until the arrival of the railroad in the mid-1880's that the population expanded markedly.

When it did, the colonists showed scant sympathy for the Indians' desire to retain their land.

During the early period of contact, Squamish people travelled the Burrard Inlet area, taking jobs in white settlements, in longshoring, and lumber camps and mills. Some of them took work in New Westminster, the capital of the mainland colony of British Columbia. The growing familiarity with white culture, gained through work and travel, is generally credited with bringing about the next important phase in Squamish history, the coming of the Oblate Fathers, and the subsequent conversion of the group to Roman Catholicism.

The first contact between the Squamish and the Oblates is said to have occurred at the request of Chief Snat. The Squamish Indians, according to this semi-legendary account, had reached a point where they were causing considerable disruption in New Westminster, and official concern was growing over the problem. Rumour had it that drastic steps would be taken to discipline the Squamish; these included the threat that the village at Mission Reserve No. 1 was to be bombarded. In his concern, Chief Snat asked the Oblate Fathers to come and Christianize the Squamish and thereby avert the supposedly impending catastrophe. Christianity was thus regarded as having saved the Squamish from possible annihilation. This story probably has a germ of historical truth in it; bombardment of a village was not unknown, but it was very rare.

The relationship which was created between the Squamish and the Oblates was a deep one, and has been lasting. The priest who answered the call to come over was Father Leon Fouquet. Fouquet was known to the political authorities, and was considered by whites to be a capable leader of the Indians. His approach to them fits with that generally accepted at the time, and still voiced by the Rev. A. G. Morice in his *History of the Roman Catholic Church in Western Canada* in 1910. Believing that the Indians enjoyed a good spectacle and participation in gala affairs, he directed his religious and secular activities to supply numerous occasions for the elaborate gratification of these presumed Indian traits. That the secular authorities agreed with this approach is illustrated in the August 31, 1864, dispatch of British Columbia Governor Frederick Seymour, to the Secretary of State for the Colonies, Lord Newcastle. Seymour wrote:

> On the departure of Sir James Douglas, who has been known to the Indians as a great chief,—the principal authority in this territory,—for upwards of forty years, an impression was allowed to arise among them that their protector was withdrawn and would have no successor. The Fraser River Indians uttered many lamentations over their deserted condition, and it became desirable for me to make myself know to the natives and show them that I had succeeded to all the power of my predecessor, and to his solicitude for their welfare. With this object I invited the Catholic priests and others to bring in all the Indians who were willing to come to New Westminster and meet me on the Queen's birthday. About three thousand five hundred Indians attended the summons. They came by water, and the priests marshalled the procession of

canoes, which formed an extremely striking scene as they rounded a point of the Fraser and approached my house. They landed at the site selected for a public park, where luncheon was provided at the expense of the government. I joined them in the afternoon when the enclosed addresses were exchanged between the chiefs and myself.[16]

This celebration was practised for several succeeding years with similar events and pageantry. Seymour's account is of interest because it indicates the relation of the priests to the Indians. To appearances the Indians were enthusiastic participants in a certain segment of Western civilization. Other descriptions of these holidays tell of canoes bearing sixty temperance (meaning "abstinence," usually) flags, which bore the words "Religion, Temperance, Civilization" in gold letters. Apparently both the secular and the religious authorities accepted such a display as being significant in Indian life and as illustrating the cultural change Indians had undergone. Whatever the Indians intended by their participation in these displays, they obviously made a deep impression upon the whites present.

The assumptions behind the pageantry described above were elaborated upon and applied to the daily round of life among the Indians. Father Pierre Paul Durieu, a Frenchman, came to the Northwest in the 1850's. His first work was in the Oregon Territory, where he worked among the Yakima, Tulalip, and perhaps the Swinomish Indians. He later was transferred to the Vancouver area, where he worked for many years until his death in 1899. In 1875 he was created a bishop and consecrated at New Westminster.

Father Morice says of Bishop Durieu that he understood Indian psychology and that the Indians' "psychic make-up" differed from that of the white men far more than the two differed physically. From this conviction, according to Morice, Durieu evolved a system for dealing with the Indians which reproduced on the Pacific Coast his version for Indians of the Church of the first centuries of the Christian era. Durieu's system was in fact a kind of theocratic indirect rule. With the priests acting as the ultimate authority, and through their advice and direction, Indian authorities were designated to regulate society at the local level. Indian offices consisted of chiefs, Eucharistic chiefs being the highest, sub-chiefs, watchmen, policemen, catechists, chanters, and sextons, although all of these categories did not exist at every village.

Social control was in the hands of the highest local chief and his aides. They acted as judges in cases of misconduct, with the priest reserving the right to preside over hearings. Watchmen acted as the eyes of the court, and guilty parties were turned over to the policemen for punishment; policemen and watchmen formed one category.[17] Punishment was both psychological and physical. The priests and judges capitalized upon the importance of shame as a means of social control in the aboriginal culture, and in this they were close to the mark; punishments might be such as to draw public attention to the offender, in church on Sunday morning, for example. The good will of society was of great importance to the people, and children were traditionally warned against committing any shameful act which might bring their names into disrepute. Other punishments, of white origin, varied from the assignments of prayers to be said, to flogging, according to the nature of the offence. The priests were the final authority. The ultimate in punishment was excommunication, with all the dire spiritual consequences that denial of the sacraments was believed to bring. The existence of a final authority beyond the Indian authorities was counter to the aboriginal culture, in which leadership was based upon wealth and respectability rather than physical or even spiritual power. Kinship obligation had bolstered political control, and a leader retained his position through sharing his wealth and acting in conformity with traditional codes. His weapon had been social pressure alone, rather than more formal impersonal authority and office.

The religious requirements of the system were to learn one's prayers, catechism, and hymns; to observe Sunday as the Sabbath; and to participate in church ritual, especially the liturgy. A man who failed to attend Mass and make his communion at appointed times was subject to punishment. Secular goals included the preservation and strengthening of aboriginal patterns of early marriage, incest rules, and respect for elders. The priests encouraged the Indians to build new houses and to keep them washed periodically with disinfectant and painted, to plant gardens and fruit trees. The white-painted churches along the coastlines came to dominate the life of the village. Prohibitions included primitive dances, potlatches, patronage of shamans, alcohol, and gambling, all of which represented, with the exception of alcohol, a broad spectrum of traditional behaviour. Natural disasters and epidemics were held to be evidence of moral failure and resulting divine displeasure.

The adaptive aspect of the system was important in its maintenance. Honours in the new state were accorded to persons who had been of prestige in the old culture, though position, commendation, and titles. Wealth could still be used for demonstrating status, through gifts to the Church. Feasts took place instead of potlatches, and gifts were given as dowries. Pageantry and festivities took the place of winter ceremonies and gambling. Elaborate tableaux and processions were provided, as we have seen. Edwin Lemert observes:

> The fervor and histrionic versatility with which the Salish peoples particpated as actors and spectators in these activities amazed even the priests, and leaves little doubt of the psychic usefulness of this pageantry to the natives. Although the gatherings were mass spectacles, tribal identities remained intact, with competitive participation and honorific expenditures figuring conspicuously in the interaction.[18]

The decline of the system was caused by increased white contact—especially with the completion of the railroad in Vancouver in 1886—the secularization and anti-Roman Catholicism encountered among whites, use of English as *lingua franca*, increased government supervision of Indians, and change in Oblate personnel.

The attitude of the missionaries toward whites whom they felt to be corrupting the Indians can best be demonstrated by quoting from Father Morice, who was himself an Oblate missionary in the Pacific Northwest. He says, "Sadly did the poor Indian stand in need of religious ministrations, especially after their first contact with the unscrupulous whites, as a rule single men of the coarsest description, who abounded in their midst in the early sixties."[19] He quotes a letter from Father Fouquet to the same effect: "The unfortunates had learned to add to their coarse vices the foul habits which accompany the scum of a degraded civilization."[20] No clearer statement of the protective aspect of the missionaries' intention is needed.

The cultural impact of the system is testified to by Roman Catholic and non-Roman Catholic observers alike, both insisting that while the system lasted the Indians under its influence conformed to white standards of living. Newspaper accounts describe the enthusiasm with which Indians participated in religious festivals. Morice recounts the visit of the Archbishop of Montreal to Mission Reserve No. 1, and the favourable impression he formed of it. The Indian Agents reported to Ottawa at the turn of the century the eagerness of the Squamish for education and their devotion to Roman Catholicism and steady progress toward Westernization. Accounts from Indian informants support official reports. Older informants recall that their parents kept neat, clean houses, and dressed their children in clean clothes. One informant told with pride of how Bishop Durieu stayed with his family when on a visit to the Squamish. He regarded this as demonstration of the cleanliness with which his mother kept their house. Another informant recalled that the Indian Agent sometimes brought whites to his home to show it as an example of cleanliness. She also told of seeing her mother stand behind the curtained window, rocking the baby to keep it quiet until the white men tired of knocking and went away. All in all, the Squamish village at the Mission Reserve No. 1 was considered a model of "civilization."

The Squamish settlements on the north shore of Burrard Inlet grew into moderately prosperous communities during the decades of the 1870's and 1880's. Census records of the Indian Affairs Branch show slowly rising population figures by the opening of the twentieth century. The Indians were no longer dying out, though it was to be several more decades before knowledge of this fact became general, as had been the case of the Prairies. The economy of these communities continued, as in aboriginal times, to be based chiefly upon fishing, hunting, and logging, with the addition of stevedoring, rather than upon agriculture, despite the efforts of government and Church to promote the latter. Indian Agents for the area consistently reported that they found the villagers industrious and law-abiding. By the end of the nineteenth century the villagers were largely Roman Catholic. Under the leadership of the Oblate Fathers, the agents reported, the villagers were regular in their religious duties and in church attendance,[21] a tribute to Oblate thoroughness.

The agents reported that they found the younger members of Squamish society attentive to the advice of their elders and chiefs. There is praise for these older men, for their good sense, and for advising their people ". . .wisely and in the right direction,"[22] suggesting that the young were being advised to adapt themselves to white culture and to conform to its laws and customs.

The Squamish erected the church at the Mission Reserve No. 1 in the 1860's, building it themselves under the guidance of the Oblate Fathers. St. Paul's Mission Church became a landmark on Burrard Inlet. Three decades later, the Squamish wanted to add a school; there was no Roman Catholic school nearby, and they refused to attend any other.[23] The school was built, as the church had been, by the Indians themselves. In 1899, with the aid of the Oblate Fathers, they succeeded in getting teaching sisters of a French order, the Little Sisters of the Child Jesus to come and run the school.[24]

The Indian Affairs Department Annual Report of 1900 contains the report of the principal of the school for the first year of its operation. The school was a two-storey frame building, located behind the village in an elevated position on the inland side. It contained four classrooms, a dining hall and kitchen on the lower floor, and dormitory facilities and a chapel on the upper floor. Outbuildings included a woodshed, laundry, and stable. On the twenty-one acres set aside for the school grounds, a garden was laid out to provide fresh produce for the school, and exercise for the boys, who had the task of caring for it. Agriculture was thought by the school authorities to be a mark of "civilization," and therefore training in agriculture was considered to be a civilizing influence—a familiar refrain. As a boarding school, despite the fact that most of the students lived within a few miles of it, the school fitted the familiar pattern for Indian schools in Canada during the period. As we have seen, boarding schools were planned to separate the child from home influence, which might retard the process of assimilation—an end which the schools were intended to effect—as thoroughly and as quickly as possible.

The children dressed in the required uniforms. The boys wore sailor suits. They received instruction in reading, writing, arithmetic, spelling, geography, and singing, and were also given religious instruction, attending daily prayer services every morning and evening. Instruction was all in English. Regular attendance at Mass in St. Paul's Church was required on Sundays and Holy Days. Visits home were permitted every other weekend, the boys alternating with the girls in the use of this privilege. Presumably this procedure was intended to preserve at home the segregation of the sexes which was practised in the school. Ordinarily the children were not allowed to go home on weekdays. During their free time, the boys played games, such as baseball and football, practised running and swimming, and raced their canoes. Girls played quiet games thought proper for young ladies-to-be; they skipped rope, drew on slates, and dressed dolls. They also did housework, and learned to sew, darn, and knit.

Visitors to the school seem to have been pleased with what they saw, as Father Emile Bunoz, O.M.I., the school's first principal, reported to the Indian Affairs Office in 1900.[25] The children attending the school gained the reputation of being deeply interested in gaining an education.[26] Demand for admittance was such that in the summer of 1903 additions were made to the school to increase accommodations.[27]

In 1906, a Squamish delegation led by Chief Joe Capilano went to England to present a petition to Edward VII. The petition, which obtained no results, claimed that: first, Indian land title in British Columbia had never been properly extinguished, despite James Douglas' promise that it would be; second, whites had settled on their lands against the Indians' wishes; third, all appeals to the Canadian government had been in vain; and fourth, the Indians not only had no vote, but were not consulted by the Indian Agents on matters which gravely concerned them. Andrew Paull later referred to this trip as "the beginning of enquiries into the land question."[28] Coming at a time when the Durieu system was on the wane, it marked the beginning of a new series of influences, among them Protestant missionaries and other white "friends of the Indians," and of the period of the growth of Indian organizations and the agitation over the land question. From priestly supervision to government administration the Squamish passed into a new phase of Indian activity.

There occurred in British Columbia the combination of a live and clear issue (the land question) with a cultural adjustment which created a number of sufficiently Westernized individuals who through their experience had learned to manipulate Western forms of protest and whose reaction was along a spectrum from advocates of assimilation (who were also active in Indian organizations and on behalf of Indians; e.g., The Rev. Peter Kelly) to men like Andrew Paull who were feeling their way to a new synthesis which they had not yet formulated and which is only being formulated in recent years. The twin poles of total assimilation and total maintenance of indigenous culture in a contact situation represent theoretical alternatives which are never realized. Between them lies the range of what actually occurs and what is really a third alternative: cultural adjustment and/or synthesis. This can vary in many degrees along the spectrum between the imaginary poles. The usual idea is that they are not "poles" but a beginning (in the past) and an end (in the future). Actually of course the "past" (indigenous cultural pattern) continues in time, perpetuated from generation to generation through influences especially powerful during infancy and early childhood, and the "future" recedes infinitely.

In the meantime, despite the efforts and intentions of the missionaries, educators, and government officials, what seems to have occurred was further cultural synthesis. From the contact of the two cultures the

Indians developed something which was new and unique and was neither Western nor traditional but contained in a new form elements of each. This synthesis was no more static than the previous culture had been but was and is continuing to change and be reshaped. Its newness does not deny continuity; on the contrary it is rooted in continuity. Nobody exposed to the pressure of confrontation with "European" society could remain the same, but early training has not entirely been supplanted, and cultural community patterns are expanded to include new situations. This synthesis becomes part of the definition of the culture and thus continues along with whatever changes are occurring in the majority culture.

In various parts of Canada missionaries tried to foster cultural synthesis. They did this because they wanted to further the cause of their religion, and there is no doubt that, at least in the lives of some of the people whom they taught, this religious experience was genuine and operative. Jesuits and other Roman Catholic orders had long practised adaptations and innovations intended to be congenial to the people being evangelized. In the mid-nineteenth century the Church Missionary Society, the major evangelical Anglican mission organization working in Canada and around the world, was developing the idea of indigenous Christian churches. Unlike the Roman Catholics, they hoped for a native clergy and laity independent and with forms suited to their individual cultures but in communion with Canterbury. The Roman Catholic Church, on the other hand, did not train Indians for the clergy. The Methodists, of course, had many prominent clergy who were Indians or *Métis*—John Sunday, Peter Jones, Peter Kelly, W. H. Pierce, and Eugene Steinhauer.

Not every feature of these missionary efforts is attractive to the modern mind, of course (and how much the less to the Indians to whom they were applied), and some of the end results were probably not foreseen. Nevertheless, not a few men who were to become articulate in the cause of Indian protest and resistance to encroachment gained experience in forms of non-Indian public affairs in part through the medium of church activities. Others gained experience through their activities in labour organizations.

The crystallization of protest at the provincial level in British Columbia took place when the Allied Tribes of British Columbia, advised by the controversial lawyer and cleric the Rev. Arthur E. O'Meara, hoped to present their case to the Judicial Committee of the Privy Council. This body was in the early twentieth century the highest court in the British Empire. The government of British Columbia had not signed treaties for the land taken in most of British Columbia, as we have seen, and the Indians distrusted the federal government. They were asked to relinquish their claims to the land in advance of a finding in the courts, and they refused. Finally they switched their tactic and agreed to go before a Special Joint Committee of Parliament. They seem to have interpreted this as a step before going on into the courts, whether in Canada or in Britain. Unfortunately for the Indians the Special Joint Committee, composed among others of prominent politicians from British Columbia, not only decided that the Indians had no claim, but told them to stop the protest and gave the British Columbia Indians $100,000 a year in lieu of treaty money. This was in 1927. The two main Indian figures involved were the Rev. Peter Kelly and Andrew Paull; they acted as spokesmen at the investigations in Ottawa. Their competence apparently surprised the legislators, judging by the compliments which they drew, although some of the remarks may have also been intended to sweeten the bitter pill of rejection of their claims.

The Indians were deeply discouraged. The Allied Tribes organization collapsed. A development that had begun sporadically as local protests in the mid-nineteenth century and gained momentum through the activities of people like Chief Joe Capilano, the Rev. Peter Kelly, and Andrew Paull, had resulted in drawing together Indians from various tribes of British Columbia. One of the staunchest elements in the protest was the Nishga peoples of the Nass River. The Nishga Petition (1913) protesting loss of land and threats to their land had been a central feature of the more general protest of the Allied Tribes. There followed the 1930's and the depression. A new organization was formed, the Native Brotherhood of British Columbia. Acting as a rallying group, primarily, for the northern coastal Indians, it has continued into the 1970's. The land protest in British Columbia is as alive today as far as the Indians are concerned, as it was in 1927. The Nishga peoples still provide a major voice in the land claims of the Indians of British Columbia.

The most recent phase of the history of Canadian Indians as outlined in this book begins during the middle 1940's, though it may be said to reach a demarcation point with the Indian Act revision of 1951. This is not to say that the revisions were radical, but rather that they reflected the growing pressure of Indians and a gradual changing of mood by the government. Indian organizations had been in existence for several decades already; as far back as the second decade of the twentieth century, as we have seen, a number of tribes had come together to protect their land claims under the designation "Allied Tribes of British Columbia," and had carried their protest to Ottawa and to a Special Joint Committee of Parliament there. Several provincially based organizations came into existence in the 1940's, when the Indians of British Columbia, Alberta, Saskatchewan, and Ontario, for example, were organized—sometimes with the support of white friends, as the Allied Tribes of British Columbia had been.

The origins of the Native Brotherhood of British Columbia go back to 1931, when Indians from the northern coast of British Columbia met to discuss common problems. Steps were taken to present a petition to the Minister of the Interior, dealing with educational welfare needs and calling attention to growing restrictions of Indian hunting, trapping, fishing, and taking of timber.[29] The organization received some inspiration from the Alaska Native Brotherhood, with which British Columbia Indians were familiar.[30] Many years later, a Native Brotherhood of British Columbia leader recalled its origins in a homely story. The sea was rough, he recounted, and the fishermen could not go out. They sat on the beach, Haidas and Tsimshians together, talking about their problems, and sifting sand between their fingers. As they sat through the days of this enforced leisure, the realization of their common problems came to them, and one evening when they were joined by Alfred Adams, a Haida from Massett, he told them that they must unite, act together, and speak with one voice. As the men talked on through the night, Adams finally said, "My good friends, it is near morning—come back tomorrow and we will talk some more for I am sure we have another beach day coming."[31]

During the rest of the decade, the Native Brotherhood of British Columbia grew, spreading from the northern coast to all of the coastal tribes and to some of the interior tribes as well. Alfred Adams became its president, remaining in that office until 1944, and most of its leadership was drawn from the north, especially Tsimshians. The exact date of its founding varies in different accounts, and apparently the organization was slow in taking shape so that several meetings are said to have been the beginning.

In 1936, another Indian organization, the Pacific Coast Native Fisherman's Association, was organized at Alert Bay, primarily of Kwakiutls, with Dan Assu as its president. The impetus here was a strike, during which the Indians struck at the request of whites and then were abandoned, as they felt, when the whites (and some other Indians) withdrew from the strike just before the fishing season ended. The aims of the group were directed toward solving problems met by Indians in the fishing industry. One declared purpose was to help Indians retain their identity, and to this end the group demanded that white unions release Indian members. This the unions refused to do.[32] Still another group of the same type was the Nimpkish Fisherman's Association, formed on the west coast of Vancouver Island. Based upon the co-operative system, the experiment ultimately failed except at Nootka, where it received guidance from the Roman Catholic Church.[33] The formation of all three of the above-mentioned groups indicates the unsettled feelings, the search for solutions, and the new stirring among Indians, even though some of the groups were short-lived.

During the late 1930's the Pacific Coast Native Fisherman's Association was approached by the Native Brotherhood of British Columbia, and ultimately, in 1942, the group was led into the larger organization, mostly through the influence among the Kwakiutl of Andrew Paull. Philip Drucker says of this feat that it was accomplished ". . .through a use of rapid and adept parliamentary maneuvers, requesting appropriate motions and gavelling them through. At the same time it is certain that the Kwakiutl saw the advantage of joining the northern groups to achieve a common aim."[34] As we have seen, the Native Brotherhood of

British Columbia was primarily an organization drawn from northern tribes, and these were primarily Protestant.

Another organization, this time on national scale (in intent at least), grew out of the efforts of Andrew Paull, who was a Roman Catholic (his family had come under the tutelage of the "Durieu system" and he had been educated in the school at Mission Reserve No. 1) and a Squamish Indian; and this group was primarily based among the southern and interior groups where his influence was strongest. The North American Indian Brotherhood, as the new group came to be called, began on a humble scale, reportedly in late June 1943. Among those present besides Paull was Dan Assu of the Pacific Coast Native Fisherman's Association; Paull had gone to Ottawa as Business Agent of the Native Brotherhood of British Columbia to attend a conference on fish prices, and afterwards, he and Assu met in Montreal with Indians from various eastern reserves, including Caughnawaga. The organization then founded, and first called the Brotherhood of Canadian Indians, was composed solely of non-treaty Indians. Later attempts to bring in treaty Indians of the Prairie provinces were largely unsuccessful, as will be seen below. Andrew Paull became president of the new organization; in this role, and in the ensuing years, Paull was able to appear before various government bodies and officials as a national spokesman for Indians. It has been suggested by several observers that after leaving the Native Brotherhood of British Columbia for the North American Indian Brotherhood, Paull spoke more and more on behalf of Roman Catholic Indians.[35] At any rate, here again, as with fishing problems, were ties which crossed aboriginal culture lines and bound members of different backgrounds together because of new factors.

When in 1946 a conference of Saskatchewan Indians was assisted into existence by the C.C.F. government of that province, Paull made a strong appeal for their support for the membership of the newly-forming provincial group in the North American Indian Brotherhood. Members of the Indian Association of Alberta were also present, to give the support of its leadership to the founding conference. The attempt to unify Saskatchewan Indians also had the encouragement of the Indian Affairs Department, according to one informant. There had been at this time three groups already existing in Saskatchewan: the North American Indian Brotherhood, the Protective Association for Indians and Their Treaties, and the Saskatchewan Indian Association. The North American Indian Brotherhood leader in Saskatchewan, John Tootoosis, was a leader at the conference and at first attempted to aid Paull in swinging the group into his organization. His failure to do so may have been due to the firm hand held upon proceedings by members of the government in Saskatchewan, and other public figures present, nearly all of them non-Indians. Ultimately Tootoosis was elected the first President of the New Union of Saskatchewan Indians, and Paull, after coming before the conference one last time in order to pass the hat for his return fare, went home. He occasionally referred darkly, when recalling this experience, to the influence of the C.C.F. in the formation of the Union of Saskatchewan Indians.

The accounts of the origins, intertwining relationships and varying fortunes of these and similar Indian organizations yield some basis for generalization. Frequently these groups were not strongly grounded at the local level. Thus they tended, as was said of one in particular, to be "all head and no tail." This, it may be noted, was a criticism sometimes levelled against incipient nationalist movements in Africa and Asia. Their "mission boys," "trousered blacks," and "wogs" (Westernized Oriental Gentlemen) were ridiculed as self-seeking. Nevertheless these provincially based groups in Canada spoke loudly and obtained the ear of Ottawa. When after World War II the attitude of Canada began to change, Indians were included. They were not always the first to profit by the change; in British Columbia, Canadians of Chinese and East Indian descent got the vote earlier than native Indians and Japanese-Canadians on the grounds that the two former peoples had been allies of Canada in World War II. Prior to the era which followed World War II, the few Indians who achieved more than an elementary level of Western education were offered enfranchisement if they wished or the continuation of their Indian status. Apparently few thought in terms of conducting activities on any larger theatre for the retention of Indian identity or self-consciousness than that of their own people. Thus, although they continued to think of themselves as Indians, their stance lacked the militancy and assertiveness which is to be found in the thinking of some of the Indians of today.

Not until the last two or three decades have these men and women begun to declare popularly their intention to find an alternative to assimilation. This quest for an alternative has borrowed from the ideas and vocabulary of colonial or ex-colonial peoples in other parts of the non-Western world. They assert that they are taking a harder look at Western civilization.

Prior to this new situation it seemed easier to categorize those who tended toward assimilation and those who did not. Adaptation was seen as "transition." Individuals might move into greater harmony with the dominant society, or if not, then they at least presaged the evolution of their fellow Indians toward that goal. Viewed in the light of the new Indian self-consciousness some of these "transitional" figures may be more fruitfully seen as a new type. They can be regarded as representing a line of thinking which in their day was frustrated from crystallizing its categories more clearly because they lacked the knowledge and/or framework for thus interpreting their views.

Such a person was Andrew Paull. During his own lifetime he was sometimes regarded as too conservative, even retrogressive by his counterparts in other Indian organizations. His own analysis of his role caused him occasionally to oppose such steps as the vote for Indians, for fear of the effect this might have on Indian identity. His Indian critics saw this position as retrograde. Neither assimilationist nor clearly adaptationist, he was not easily classifiable; in the context of the last decade or so he may be more clearly understood as a precursor of much of the present militant self-consciousness.

The need for unity, while recognized by emerging Indian leaders, has been hard to make workable. Indians have found that even organizations of, by, and for themselves are not enthusiastically supported. Tribal and even inter-tribal rivalries, as well as personalities and program differences, frequently have frustrated their efforts to speak with a single voice. Organizations have a tendency to be the creations of crisis and therefore spasmodic in nature. "Passing the hat" to enable an individual or small group to go and protest some particular grievance has been a recurring procedure. However, it would be inaccurate to assert of these groups that they have existed only in the persons of their leaders, even in the case of the least popularly based, and they have articulated the frustrations and expectations of many Indians.

In some cases they have been aided by white humanitarians, particularly in creating their organizations and in their early phases. As John Collier aided American Indians, Octavian Hume aided in the creation of what became the Indian Congress Party in colonial India; in the same way men like Arthur E. O'Meara and James Teit figured in the formation of Indian organization in British Columbia.

The leaders of these organizations gradually came to realize that they would be heard only when they imitated the techniques of the white man and made demands through means the white society would accept. The creation of pressure groups by minority group organizations is itself an aspect of acculturation. As the Indians came to define their identity in their new situation vis-à-vis the white man, they were also being introduced to the vocabulary and media with which to express it, not only to whites but to other Indians. The antecedents of this experience have already been adumbrated. It was done through participation in churches and other white institutions and organizations. A variety of names may be cited of men who were active in the 1940's and 1950's and into the 1960's in some cases: John Tootoosis, John Callihoo, Henry Jackson, Andrew Paull, Peter Kelly, Telford Adams. To these names could be added others. Most of these men are now dead or no longer active, and a new generation, even two generations have emerged. The names listed are those of pioneers of the "Indian movement" or resurgence. The younger men have been referred to as "militants." Among all these men, going back to the mid-1940's, two streams of thought have predominated. There are those who are oriented toward assimilation, and those who call for the retention of Indian identity and the continuation of the Indian practice of adaptation. The militants emphasize the Indian identity, using, as we have already observed, the language of nationalism, and indeed speaking of "Indian nationalism."

A tentative scheme for categorizing the growth of organizations might be: one, *ad hoc* organizations created to deal with specific concerns; two, provincial organizations rising out of a recognition of wider common problems; and, three, in the last twenty years, approximately, a number of organizations seeking nationwide membership and influ-ence which are concerned with Indian problems on a national level. The North American Indian Brotherhood, the National Indian Council, and the Canadian Indian Youth Council, illustrate the third category, though there has been a wide divergence in the aims and activities of these organizations. The most recent of these is the National Indian Brotherhood. Organizations based on provinces have been recognized at the national level in that they have been consulted in Ottawa from time to time on matters relating to Indians, such as proposed changes in the Indian Act. In addition, some of their leaders have achieved a degree of national recognition or at least have been organized beyond the bound-aries of their native provinces for their work in matters relating to Indians.

Over the first half of the twentieth century, then, a number of Indian organizations have emerged. Some of them have been touched upon above. The 1940's and 1950's saw an expansion of their numbers. These were usually provincially based. At the same time some Indian figures realized the desirability of forming nationwide organizations, and steps were taken in that direction as well; one of these was the North American Indian Brotherhood formed by Andrew Paull. Com-mon problems and the need for a unified voice were recognized, and Paull's organization presaged later efforts. Problems of leadership, re-gional support, grass-roots support, finances, programs and questions of effectiveness were all part of the environment in which Paull's organiza-tion attempted to operate. Unfortunately for their effectiveness, Indian organizations have tended to be crisis-oriented; that is, when a crisis arises they come into existence or are galvanized into new life and when the crisis is resolved or simply passes away, whether resolved or not resolved to suit the Indian, the organizations decline and/or disappear. Factors such as the geographical dispersion of the Indians, lack of nationally accepted leaders, isolation, the educational limitations of leaders and constituents, poverty, and lack of mass support have all contributed to this pattern.

The geographically dispersed nature of the population precludes the creation of an Indian province and the smallness of their numbers re-duces their voting power except on the local level. "The simple absence of an exciting goal to political activity has denied Indians the possession of dynamic incentives to participation in a united political organization which have been available to the indigenous inhabitants of the former empires in Africa and Asia. . . ."[36] the "Hawthorn Report" states. It continues:

> The nature of Indian organizations has been such that the Indian Affairs Branch and the two post-war Joint Committees of the Senate and House of Commons have been baffled by the difficulty of determining the following of the spokesmen who have claimed to speak for certain groups. In a number of

instances the view presented by one organization before the Joint Committee was subsequently repudiated by a group of Indians for whom the organization claimed to speak.[37]

The two most recent efforts to overcome the difficulties cited have been first, the National Indian Council, and then the National Indian Brotherhood.

The National Indian Council had as its purpose ". . .to promote unity among Indian people, the betterment of people of Indian ancestry in Canada, and to create a better understanding of Indian and non-Indian relationship." To achieve this end it created travelling exhibits of Indian art, put on Indian Princess pageants, helped in planning the Indian Pavilion at Expo '67, and in other ways tried to present to non-Indians a favourable impression of the Indian.

The National Indian Council leadership tended to be drawn from middle-class and/or urban Indians. Because they saw as one of their main objectives the unifying of Indians, they hoped to create one organization which embraced those who were legally Indians and those who identified themselves as Indians though they were not legally recognized as such under the Indian Act, including *Métis*. One of the most important figures in the National Indian Council during the first years of its existence (it lasted from 1961 to 1968), was William Wuttunee, a Cree lawyer in Calgary. The goal of Indian unity proved to be beyond the grasp of the National Indian Council.

They were themselves rent with discord and were suspect in the eyes of many other Indians. The election of a new president, Phil Thompson, in 1966 was followed by a decision to call for a joint meeting of the National Indian Council with representatives from existing Indian organizations in the hopes of forming a nationwide association. Some National Indian Council members still hoped to include Indians and *Métis* in a common organization. This hope was to prove unrealizable, but the delegates met in February 1968. Representatives of six provincial organizations and two *Métis* organizations were present. No delegates came from British Columbia, Quebec, Prince Edward Island, or Newfoundland. Rather than prevent the Indians from forming a united organization, the *Métis* delegates agreed to withdraw. Out of this meeting emerged the National Indian Brotherhood. By 1971 organizations representing Indians of British Columbia, Quebec, and the Northwest Territories had adhered to the National Indian Brotherhood. The National Indian Council dissolved itself. [38]

Published two years before the formation of the National Indian Brotherhood, the "Hawthorn Report" asserted: "Indian organizations have not yet developed to the point where they can be relied on as representative of the views of Indians either regionally or nationally."[39] The National Indian Brotherhood and the provincial organizations are aware of the problem of representativeness. The situation may raise questions of the following nature: What is a syntheis of Indian and non-Indian organization techniques? How effective do

Indian organizations have to be, to be effective in the terms of the Indians wish, and how effective do they have to be to be listened to by the government and the others they are intended to persuade and influence? How much pressure can they bring to bear, in any case?

The "Hawthorn Report" (Part I) calls attention to the colonial situation of the Indians in Canada, and the Indian Affairs Branch is referred to explicitly as the colonial ruler. Corroborating the remarks of Diamond Jenness, discussed above, the report has emphasized the responsibility of the colonial ruler for the Indians' isolation from positions in the decision-making process of their own affairs. The Branch was a "version of colonialism" and a "quasi-colonial government."[40] The era of self-reliance for the Indians was too distant for any other policy than that of keeping peaceful and placid wards. When changes did come, they were not the result of the aggressiveness of the Indians, but due to the benevolence of white elements who had undergone a change of attitude in the post-war years. This follows, the report asserts, from the character of Indian organizations, lacking a definite constituency either regionally or nationally. Despite this fact, it is noted, the government called on leaders of these organizations for consultation when major legislation concerning Indians was being considered, and such groups were represented on the new Regional Advisory Councils created in 1965.[41]

Following the White Paper of 1969 the Indians expressed themselves. The issuance of this government "proposal" was met by a strong and negative response. Prior to the publication of this paper, in which general proposals and their rationale were presented, the Indians had been in a number of consultation sessions with government officials. The Indians asserted that during these sessions they had set out the matters which were of greatest concern to them such as land claims, treaty rights, hunting and fishing rights, control of finances, band membership and other matters. When the White Paper appeared the Indians charged that the government had ignored the presentations made in the consultation sessions and had proceeded to act without regard for Indian opinions. Numerous Indians spoke out, as did church bodies and individuals and organizations which concerned themselves with Indians.

Mr. Dave Courchene, President of the Manitoba Indian Brotherhood, gave some of his observations to an Anglican General Synod:

> Your government recently announced their new Indian policy, their grand design for Indian emancipation, for Indian assimilation. This new policy was not developed with Indian participation, co-operation or consideration. It is a white man's white paper on Indians, conceived in isolation and as far as Indians are concerned aborted at birth.
>
> No single action by any Government since Confederation has aroused such a violent reaction from Indian people—never have Indians felt so bitter and frustrated as they do today.[42]

Mr. Harold Sappier, President of the Union of New Brunswick Indians, called the actions an "arrogant act of paternalism" and stated:

"the department is not only saying that they know what questions Indians will ask but they also have all the answers for him." Further, "...there is a definite indication that this policy is not a 'proposal' but a scheme which is devised to force native people, and the general public, into the belief in the infallibility of the 'Great White Father.'"[43] Then Sappier asserted:

> The Maliseet and Micmac people of New Brunswick, along with their "blood-brothers" across this country have always made it abundantly clear of their deep feelings about their aboriginal and treaty rights. We are not going to be swayed by the vague assurances such as those contained in the new Policy Statement.[44]

The statement on the White Paper issued by the National Indian Brotherhood charged that the "Hawthorn Report" which had been commissioned by the government and had called for the retention by the Indians of a unique status—"Citizens Plus"—had been ignored; that in the consultations no indications had been given that the government was contemplating turning Indian Affairs over to the provinces. The government policy statement was prepared unilaterally, they charged. The National Indian Brotherhood reasserted that the "question of Indian lands" was "of primary importance to the Indian people." In this context British Columbia, the Maritimes, Quebec, and the two northern territories were mentioned.

The National Indian Brotherhood statement also raised doubts about the implications for Indians of the Mid-Canada Corridor, which they noted "...runs through the heart of what are presently Indian lands." The statement declares:

> We view this as a policy designed to divest us of our aboriginal, residual and statutory rights. If we accept this policy, and in the process lose our rights and our lands, we become willing partners in cultural genocide. This we cannot do.[45]

The National Indian Brotherhood statement bore the signature of its president, Chief Walter Dieter, and those of the President of the Manitoba Indian Brotherhood, the Director of the Federation of Saskatchewan Indians and President of the Association of Urban Indians, a representative for British Columbia Indians who was Director of the National Brotherhood (Victoria), the president of the Association of Quebec Indians and Chairman of the National Indian Committee on Rights and Treaties, the President of the Union of Ontario Indians, the Secretary of the Indian Association of Alberta, and the Chairman of the National Native Communications Society as well as other executives of Indian organizations.

Harold Cardinal, in his book *The Unjust Society*, which appeared not long after the government's policy statement, attacked the government's proposals. On the first page of the book, he called it a "thinly disguised programme of extermination through assimilation." He continues:

179

For the Indian to survive, says the government in effect, he must become a good little brown white man. The Americans to the south of us used to have a saying: "The only good Indian is a dead Indian." The MacDonald-Chrétien doctrine would amend this but slightly to, "The only good Indian is a non-Indian." [46]

In June 1970, approximately one year after the White Paper was publicly issued, the Indian Chiefs of Alberta presented to the government their own statement, which they entitled *Citizens Plus*, taking the phrase from the "Hawthorn Report" and quoting the context—"Indians should be regarded as 'Citizens Plus', in addition to the normal rights and duties of citizenship, Indians possess certain additional rights as charter members of the Canadian community." The paper has sometimes been referred to as the "Red Paper." Under the title "The Counter-Policy," the Alberta chiefs stated, "Retaining the legal status of Indians is necessary if Indians are to be treated justly. Justice requires that the special history, rights, and circumstances of Indian People be recognized."[47] They called for the acceptance of diversity and pluralism in Canada's cultural life and insisted that Indian children learn Indian history and customs. They charged the government with divide-and-rule tactics in its "policy statement" and with attempting to bribe the Indian. They recalled that the treaties were solemn agreements in which "Indian lands were exchanged for the promises of the Indian Commissioners who represented the Queen."[48] The missionaries who were present had lent "the authority and prestige of whiteman's religion"[49] to convince the Indians to sign. These agreements therefore could not be unilaterally abrogated nor should they be ignored.

They called for a reorganization of the Indian Affairs Department, recognition and clarification of the Indian treaties, and suggested they be taken to the International Court of Justice at the Hague for impartial interpretation. They rejected the idea of repealing the Indian Act but called for a review of it once the question of treaties was settled. The Indian Act was called paternalistic. They rejected the proposal that Indian Affairs be turned over to the provinces, and proposed economic development but denied that it was necessary to give up Indian identity in order to achieve such development. Indian Affairs needs to alter its outlook, the chiefs noted, and ". . .change to a smaller structure closely attuned to the well-being of Indian people."[50]

Another important aspect to which they gave attention was the creation of an Indian Claims Commission. This body would "help modernize treaties," investigate the claims of Indians whose lands were taken without treaties, examine present reserve boundaries for purposes of adjustment, and attempt to mitigate the restrictions on Indians growing out of legislation such as the Migratory Birds Convention Act. In conclusion, *Citizens Plus* looked for a peaceful solution to all these problems and the avoidance of violence deriving from pent-up bitterness and frustration felt by Indians. After expressing this reaction to the White Paper, *Citizens Plus* discussed some of the historical basis of treaties, land cessions, and other specific concerns, e.g., schools, hunting, trapping, fishing, economic development. Specific proposals were submitted to deal with these categories of concern.

The recency of these developments restricts the historian's perspective on them, but the developments on the provincial and national level do seem to be paralleled by similar growth of participation, enthusiasm, "reawakening" on the local level to a new sense of community, asserted more positively and expressing itself in a variety of channels. One example of the preservation of Indian community structure and identity is given in Claudia Lewis's study of a "typical" Coast Salish community, *Indian Families of the Northwest Coast: The Impact of Change*; her description is worth quoting at length:

> ...in 1968 the Camas Indian does indeed remain an Indian, bolstered by a large network of kin who make up his "community," bound through ties of blood, not of propinquity, and through ties of common purpose, resulting in affirmation of Indian identity and unity. Regarding this concept of "community," let me point out that the subdivision and the plan to "straighten up" the roads in Village 1 should not lead anyone to assume that the old pattern of Camas life is necessarily on its way out. True, parts of Village 1 may in time take on more of a superficial resemblance to the residential areas of the town. But there is no sign that the widespread kinship network, always of fundamental importance to the Camas, is losing its functions or its viability; no sign that the local neighborhood is assuming more significance than the "neighborhood" made up of the related groups residing up and down the coast. Indeed, in addition to the large gatherings for winter dancing, and in lesser degree for Shaker activities, Suttles points to the importance of still another mechanism for cementing traditional loyalties and bringing local groups together—the summer canoe race weekends, important at present in certain of the Salish vicinities.
>
> At the same time, while the Indian is strengthening his identity through traditionally Indian activities, we have seen that he is acquiring new skills and experience in making joint efforts of many kinds, using the techniques of co-operating in councils, committees, associations, conferences. Some of these are local efforts—the band council and its committees, and the nursery school—with membership limited to Camas Indians; others, such as the Southern Vancouver Island Tribal Federation and the leadership conferences and workshops bring him into contact with Indians from other reserves, who may be either kin or non-kin. And the Mika Nika Club leads him into direct action with whites. [51]

It is a commonplace that each generation rewrites history. The study of history offers numerous and varied examples of this assertion. Illustrations of this phenomenon in academic historical writing are increasingly available in the Asian and African fields. Much of this work is being done by Asian and African scholars trained in the academic traditions of the West. One historian has called this the "decolonization of history." Not all of the work done, however, has been of consistent level, nor has it been based on academic training or with a view to an academic audience in every case. Immanuel Wallerstein finds that in some cases revisions of the history of new countries will be characterized more by enthusiasm and nationalistic intention than by scholarship and dispassionate analysis. Out of this new history emerges new heroes, new events of significance, new information, and especially a new view of history.

It would not be stretching a point to say that something like this phenomenon is occurring in Canada among Canadian Indians. We are more familiar with the fact that it is occurring with French Canadians and the United States Negroes. In the case of the Canadian Indian, it has for the most part not yet been taken up by academic historians. Nevertheless Canadian Indian writers are building an interpretation of Indian history. They are synthesizing the variety of Indian cultures into a concept of an "Indian way of life," and using this as an interpretive device for the formulation of an Indian view of Indian history. Their forum is most often the news media, especially television, newspapers, magazines, and a few volumes of essays, poetry, and Indian stories and legends. From them one may hear, see, or read beginnings of the new history of Indians in Canada.

Historians and anthropologists are rewriting Indian history in the United States. Less work of this kind has been done in Canada. Professor Wilson Duff's *Indian History of British Columbia* is a step in this direction. G.F.G. Stanley examined "The Indian Background of Canadian History" in a brief article over a decade ago. His book, *The Birth of Western Canada*, has two chapters on the Indians in the second Riel uprising. A. G. Bailey's study of European-Algonkian relations explores some aspects of early contacts *(The Conflict of European and Eastern Algonkian Cultures, 1504-1700—A Study in Canadian Civilization).* Professor B. G. Trigger has done considerable work on the history of the Hurons in contact with the French. Few if any general or survey works have yet been written on the history of the Canadian Indian, either by an academic or a non-academic writer, Indian or otherwise. The majority of the efforts at revision so far essayed in the news media have been those mostly of articulate young Indians and a few non-Indian journalists who have lent their pens to this concern.

What have these writers found on Indian history in the existing studies? What does the Indian find about the history of himself and his forebears? A recent study of about fifty prominent and not so prominent Canadian histories, many of them standard college surveys of Canadian history, suggests answers. Ignorance, prejudice, and dishonesty have characterized the Canadian historians' treatment of Indians. Historians persist in down-grading the Indian. These are some of the conclusions of a survey of Canadian history books by James Walker, in "The Indian in Canadian Historical Writing."[52] The vocabulary of negative, derogatory, and pejorative terms is cited as an illustration. References to torture, scalping, and harsh treatment of their womenfolk by Indians are part of the picture given of Indians by which the reader is "...fed an impression of the Indian as a man of obvious inferiority to whites."[53] His contributions to Canadian life are relegated to outdoor sports equipment or the arts and crafts shop of today.

The general approach to the Indian, Walker finds, is to squeeze him in between "The Flora and Fauna, the Land and Latitude."[54] The impression frequently left is that the white man came to an empty continent. When the Indian is dealt with he is part of the fur trade, the Anglo-French rivalry, the War of 1812, or the westward expansion and the opening up of lands to settlers. Except for the treaties beginning in 1871 and the Indian rising in 1885, the Indians almost completely drop from the Canadian story after the War of 1812. The activities of Big Bear and Poundmaker are treated as important because they effect the French-English dichotomy. The two founding races do not include Indians.

Walker finds that William Kingsford's *The History of Canada*, written in 1888, presents a still typical attitude when the latter asserts that the study of the Indian "is totally independent of the History of Canada except so far as it bears upon the relations of the European and Indian races."[55] Much of the responsibility for this type of treatment is laid upon the sources. "Generally speaking the times in which these early accounts were written make ignorance and prejudice inevitable. Their greatest historical value is probably in teaching about the men who wrote the narratives, rather than about the subject. . . .To confine oneself to Jesuit, fur trader or explorer relations is to adopt an outlook and limitation that are no longer excusable or necessary."[56]

Imbalance and over-generalizing are two chief faults. Comparable actions by whites and Indians are accorded widely varying presentation. Thus acts of brutality by Indians are portrayed as general to all Indians, while similar acts by whites are not so treated, though the evidence suggests otherwise. Walker observes that in effect the historical image of the Indian has been martyred for the sake of the historical image of the Jesuit martyrs.[57] He ends his essay on the gloomy note that the more recent histories seem to consider the Indian "less worthy of an independent place in Canadian history" than do some of the earlier accounts: "Only. . .Stanley Ryerson. . .tries to explain the Indian viewpoint, and expressly rejects the terms 'savagery' and 'barbarism'."[58] This negative image is what the revisionists desire to shatter to bits.

In other parts of the world men of letters have played a prominent part in the creation of national cultures. They, together with historians, have constituted the nucleus from which national culture movements grow. The job of the "historian" in this case is to create and disseminate the idea that despite local and regional differences within, the traditional cultures are essentially similar, and that this similarity is the product of a common historical background. The myths and legends of the traditional culture which are told about and written down strengthen the belief of the members of the culture in "the supreme validity of their culture" and in their own superiority as heirs of great men.[59]

Historians and their books help to create national stereotypes. They "tend to emphasize the distinctive character of their own nationality and many of them are inclined to exalt it as superior to others, at least in some respects. . . ."[60]; an example of this is cited by Florian Znaniecki in the case of India where the emergence of nationalism was from its inception influenced by the intellectual leaders who compared the history of Hindu civilization with that of Europe and exalted the former as representing the highest spiritual values in contrast to the latter. The European culture was found to be essentially materialistic. The Indian writers called for a pairing of European and Hindu cultures to get a proper balance. Similar arguments appear in early twentieth-century China. Some Canadian Indians are calling for a similar mixture.

Nationalists, Immanuel Wallerstein finds, create, discover, recover, and rediscover values at variance with those of the colonial administrators and colonizers, and these values are carried into the independence period. History legitimizes the new system of values which emerges, but to do this history must be new. It must be rewritten, since the old history was that imposed by the colonialists and tended to downgrade or deny the history of the colonized. In the process of rewriting history from the viewpoint of the colonized or formerly colonized, there is a "revalorization" of heroes. Figures who had formerly, that is in the histories written by the colonizers, been "rebels," "barbarians," "disturbers of the peace," are interpreted in a new light and are seen to be the forerunners of native resistance, nascent patriots, and proto-nationalists. "Alien history" is pulled down and discredited, and "national history" replaces it. The past of the indigenes thus justifies, strengthens, and reassures the leadership and their followers in the era of change. Psychologically, the new history serves to ease the process of modernization, Wallerstein asserts, "by offering the glorification as reassurance about the present."[61] The intellectuals, the leadership group, are those who have had the greatest exposure to the colonizers' version of history, and are therefore in greatest need of this reassurance. They, Wallerstein says, are the cement which asserts most strongly the traditional values, "especially the glories of past history."[62] The anthropologist's work has not been helpful in West Africa to correct the bias in the earlier European-centred histories. Wallerstein believes that this is due to what he calls "the antihistorical and primitivistic bias that influenced much ethnological research."[63]

The re-written history validates change by placing it in a respected and status-conveying context. Changes are made more acceptable because viewed in their new context they are less drastic and upsetting, and therefore less disruptive of the traditional culture and values. Sometimes in the new history, Wallerstein thinks, the "rigor of evidence" is less important than the social function of the doctrines which are advanced.[64]

Certain questions can be asked. Are there indications that Indians have seen in the history books the same things that Walker has seen? Do they reject the received version of Indian history; that is, the version which tells the story in a way which they regard as being derogatory?

Are they rewriting it, "re-valorizing" Indian figures and finding in their traditional culture values which are not only worth preserving but which are adjudged by them to be superior to those of the dominant culture? Is this "history" helping to create a "national culture" among Indians? And is it helping to create an Indian identity in Canada?

In order to answer the above questions, other sources must be consulted for evidence of the Indian view of the Indian's past. The recent upsurge of interest in Indians has provided an opportunity for a growing number of Indians to give their views. An examination of these statements as reported in the news media or as presented directly through the news media provides some answers. Beginning in the late 'sixties the number of books by Indians has been growing. Whether those whose views are aired or published are the "nucleus" of the national culture movement, of which Znaniecki writes, will be a matter for future students to decide. At least they are the people who are increasingly heard by Indians and non-Indians, and many hold leadership posts in Indian organizations and/or organizations concerned with Indians. Increasingly Indians have publicly voiced their distress and outrage because of the way they are portrayed in school books. They have called for rewriting of history books to expunge words like "savage" and to give an "accurate and fair account of the role played" by Indians and *Métis* in Canada's history.

The prominent *Métis* leader, Howard Adams, made these comments several years ago:

> He said that underlying all the conference discussions was the Indian need for a personal and group identity. "The Indian seeks as with most Canadians, a real cultural identity. Because we are so oppressed, because our culture has been so eroded and distorted, our search for identity is so urgent." He attributed this to "an unconscious white supremacy society." and said: "In our schools we are being brainwashed to believe we are shy, retiring, and lack self-confidence. The brain-washing deprives us of developing our leadership qualities."
>
> Indians shouldn't condemn the white society, he said, but they should recognize it and deal with it. Indians should be able to hire their own teachers and control their own reserves. The Indian language should be used at official meetings on the reserves. If a white government official comes there, he should bring along an interpreter.
>
> Indians should promote their own language and culture; but one of the problems is that the true history of Canada's Indians has never been written. "Who wrote the history of the Indians? It was the white man. It is largely an interpretation of the aboriginal Indian. Scalpings, massacres, and so on were never part of the Indian culture. This we are learning now. For example, the Iroquois Confederacy was designed to make war impossible."[65]

At the same time Indians call attention to the destruction of Indian culture which followed the white man's coming and they contend that too little attention is given to this side of the European's "achievements" in the New World. Failure to live up to the tenets of the Christianity they wanted the Indian to believe in is frequently noted, and various and damning criticisms have been levelled against the life imposed on children in the church-run, government-supported, residential schools. Indians charge that in these institutions they have had their language and customs ridiculed and have been submitted to psychological and physical punishment to force them to abandon their traditions. Indians argue that the treaties their ancestors signed were not arrived at in circumstances fair to Indians, and in any case promises have been made to the Indians, including those made in conjunction with the treaties, which have not been honoured. The integrity, fair play, and justice of the government are thereby called into question. This is a view of Indian administration sharply at variance with that presented by Indian administration officials. These are criticisms which they have long felt and expressed among themselves and are now increasingly making known to the non-Indian population.

In these and other ways Indians have called into question the presumption of benevolence and philanthropy in which many non-Indians have viewed their treatment of Indians. Mrs. Ethel Brant Monture, author, lecturer, and descendant of Joseph Brant, has observed that history books have portrayed Indians as murderers, ". . .instead of looking at us as a people struggling to hold an identity in our land against the incoming hordes." [66] Historians, she charged, haven't told things they should have, and many things they have told are inaccurate. They have not known how to teach Indian history. For example, she and others have referred to the Indians' pharmacopoeia and technical "know-how" and of the assistance this knowledge was to the newcomers; a specific example is that of the saving of Cartier's crew from death by scurvy through an Indian prescription—an infusion of Vitamin C-rich pine needles.

In many cases those who are voicing the criticism and condemnations are those who are among the best educated and who are apparently the most capable of operating successfully outside of the Indian community. These are the people who are attempting to redefine Indianness and to consolidate their linkages with the general Indian population. They are assuming positions of leadership in organizations, writing and editing books and through various media giving expression to their views. Several books of the last few years illustrate this point: Harold Cardinal's *The Unjust Society*, Waubageshig's *The Only Good Indian*, and Wilfred Pelletier's *Two Articles*.

The evidence is that increasingly Indians are calling into question and rejecting the image of them conveyed in many books. They are asserting the dignity and validity of their past. They are censuring the white invaders for their behaviour and questioning the values of a society that could do such things. There has been an acceleration of condemnatory language as they do so. In examining their experiences with the non-Indian population, some Indians have found that these serve to bind their various peoples together. Ethnic and regional differences, as well as economic development and differences in acculturation, still exist, however. Their impact on efforts at forming effective organizations have already been touched on. On the other hand, there is evidence of an increasing sense of common identity as well.

Conferences and seminars which bring together Indians from across the country reinforce this tendency. Meetings of Indian leaders in Ottawa and elsewhere provide opportunities for sharing of knowledge, exchange of experiences and plans. The existence of a language—English—common to most is important. Whether these developments can be labelled steps toward the creation of a "national culture" is difficult to say and not as important as the fact that linkages are being made and common analyses, definitions and formulations are being shared. These help to create a unity of view about past and present.

Some Indians think that the multi-cultural society ideal should have a place for Indians. The Canadian Indian Youth Council issued a statement several years ago asserting that, while the council opposed racism, it wanted to demonstrate the validity of Indian culture and "attempt to find means to fit the Indian society into the Canadian mosaic," so that Indians can become a part of the "mainstream of society", "without the threat of becoming a lost people without any identity."

The answer to all questions about Indian ideas concerning their own history as posed above is "Yes." It is a tentative "Yes," to some of the questions, but definitely "Yes." It remains to be seen whether this affirmation will become stronger and more noticeable. There are some indications that it will.

Over the centuries from about 1500 to the present, Indians have moved from a position of autonomy to one of loss of control in most if not all of the major areas of their lives. In the spheres of religion, economics, politics, technology, and social and cultural life, they have experienced a sequence of losses which has resulted in the reduction of control in the shaping of their own affairs. Survival of cultural attributes has sometimes meant going "underground" to perform rites or retain customs. Their economies were altered by their linkage to the white man's extractive economic purposes in the case of the fur trade. As they became more deeply involved in the trade and turned more of their time and attention to acquiring pelts, they restricted the time given to their indigenous technology and art forms. In some cases this followed an initial period of florescence. The lure of the new technology and its products drew them closer to the vortex which eventually forced drastic changes on their economic, social, and political life.

When in the early nineteenth century the large influx of white settlers had begun to transform hunting grounds into cultivated land, the Indians in those areas found themselves numerically overwhelmed and their services as military allies no longer needed. The main economic activity of the newcomers was farming, and most of the Indians had had no experience with this new mode of life. They became peripheral to the main economic purposes of those areas where the settlers located. They also became comparatively and absolutely (through disease particularly) less significant in the total interests of the populace of these areas. In the mid-nineteenth century in eastern Canada and the Maritimes local self-government meant the transfer of control of Indian affairs to the interests of the white settler population. Their land was in demand and the Indians were moved into areas physically peripheral to white settlement. This coincided with the initiation or acceleration of efforts to change their culture. By this train of events the Indians suffered further losses of control over their own destinies. They had become foreigners to be assimilated in the land of their ancestors. The repetition of the pattern first developed in the Maritimes is observable across the country, with prairies peoples settled on reserves by the 1870's, and the beginning of white influx in British Columbia during the gold rush of the 1850's and '60's. The white man and his culture became the mainstream of man's experience in the geographical space now called Canada.

The mid-twentieth century has confirmed the reports of a growing Indian population. Many reserves are no longer able to provide a livelihood for all their people, and Indians are moving into the cities. Assimilation, the long-time goal of Indian administration, some writers hope may now take place in the urban centres.

Some Indians have asserted their desire to regain the control of their own lives and of the facilities which will make this possible. Since World War II, but having its roots in the decades prior to that time, there has been a growing demand that the initiative be passed for the Indian's present and future back to the Indian himself. A variety of mechanisms have been proposed as the means by which this can be and should be done. Indian control of the Department of Indian Affairs, reserves as municipalities, creation of a public corporation dealing with Indian matters, are some ideas put forward by Indians and others. These are not calls to "turn back the clock." The Indians are slowly developing organizations to articulate their ideas about themselves and their future role.

Indian commentators today are still faced with the question of how to survive as a distinctive people within an urbanized, aggressive non-Indian majority. Much still depends on the degree of variety that will be the pattern in the future. Indians have experienced an acceleration of factors working for their disappearance as communities. That Indians will disappear in the foreseeable future is unlikely, but their future seems likely to be as fraught with threats to their survival as has been their past, perhaps more so. Their efforts to strengthen themselves for greater vitality, creativity, and survival will influence what is to come.

FOOTNOTES:

[1] Joyce Wike, "The Effect of the Maritime Fur Trade on Northwest Coast Indian Society," (Ph.D. Dissertation, Columbia University, New York: 1951), p. 91.

[2] F. W. Howay, "Indian Attacks Upon Maritime Traders of the North-West Coast, 1785-1805," *Canadian Historical Review*, Vol. 6 (1925), pp. 287-309.

[3] George I. Quimby, "Culture Contact on the Northwest Coast, 1785-1795," *American Anthropologist*, Vol. 50 (1948), pp. 250-251. Quoted from Meares' account published in 1790.

[4] *Ibid.*, p. 251.

[5] Philip Drucker, *Cultures of the North Pacific Coast* (San Francisco, Calif: 1965), contains an account of the migration of nine tribes of Tsimshian to Fort Simpson (about 4,000 people) the better to participate in "a middleman's profit with little effort." (p. 121).

[6] Helen Codere, *Fighting With Property: a Study of Kwakiutl Potlatching and Warfare 1792-1930*, American Ethnological Society Monograph 18 (Seattle: 1966), pp. 93-94.

[7] *Ibid.*, p. 97.

[8] *Ibid.*, p. 126.

[9] Helen Codere, "Kwakiutl," in Edward H. Spicer (Ed.), *Perspectives in American Indian Culture Change* (Chicago: 1961), p. 457.

[10] *Daily Columbian*, September 15, 1899.

[11] Canada, *Annual Report of the Department of Indian Affairs for 1882* (Ottawa: 1883), pp. 161-162.

[12] From a letter to Sir John MacDonald in 1887 as quoted in *The Struggle for Survival* by F. E. La Violette, (University of Toronto Press: 1961), p. 57.

[13] Wayne Suttles, "Affinal Ties, Subsistence, and Prestige among the Coast Salish," *American Anthropologist*, Vol. 62, No. 2 (April, 1960), p. 304.

[14] Philip Drucker and Robert F. Heizer, *To Make My Name Good* (Los Angeles, Calif.: 1967), p. 8.

[15] T. A. Rickard, "Indian Participation in the Gold Discoveries," *British Columbia Historical Quarterly*, Vol. 2, No. 1, (January, 1938).

[16] "British Columbia Dispatches" (Collection of photostatic copies of correspondence between governors of British Columbia and the Secretary of State for Colonies: Special Collections, University of British Columbia Library), Seymour to Newcastle, pp. 52-53.

[17] Quoted from an account by Father Lejeune in *The Kamloops Warrior*, May, 1898, by Kay Cronin, *Cross in the Wilderness* (Vancouver: 1960), p. 176.

[18] Edwin M. Lemert, "The Life and Death of an Indian State," *Human Organization*, Vol. XIII, No. 3 (Fall, 1954), p. 25.

[19] A. G. Morice, *A History of the Catholic Church in Western Canada from Lake Superior to the Pacific Coast* (Toronto: 1910), Vol. II, p. 309.

[20] *Ibid.*, p. 301. This is a familiar missionary complaint from other parts of the world as well.

[21] *Department of Indian Affairs Reports*, Report of 1898, p. 217.

[22] *Ibid.*, Report of 1891, p. 217.

FOOTNOTES:

[23] *Ibid.*, Report of 1898.

[24] *Ibid.*, Report of 1900, p. 420.

[25] Father Bunoz wrote a defence of the Durieu system: Morice says that he came to Vancouver in 1895 as director of a new seminary. (Morice, *op. cit.*, p. 393.)

[26] *Department of Indian Affairs Reports*, Report of 1905, p. 211.

[27] *Ibid.*, Report of 1904, p. 277.

[28] Letter to the Editor by Andrew Paull, *The Vancouver Province*, February 21, 1955.

[29] Philip Drucker, *The Native Brotherhoods: Modern Intertribal Organizations of the Northwest Coast* (Washington, D.C.: 1958), Bureau of American Ethnology, Bulletin No. 168, p. 106.

[30] Personal interview with the Rev. Peter Kelly, June 30, 1960.

[31] *The Native Voice*, February, 1960, p. 5, article by Guy Williams.

[32] Percy H. Gladstone, *Industrial Disputes in the Commercial Fisheries of British Columbia* (unpublished Master's thesis, University of British Columbia, 1959), p. 253. Note Appendix A, "Native Indians and the Fishing Industry of British Columbia," (pp. 230-258).

[33] *Ibid.*, pp. 255-256.

[34] Drucker (1958), p. 108.

[35] Interview with F. E. Anfield, August 17, 1960. See also H. E. Hawthorn, C. Belshaw, and S. Jamieson, *The Indians of British Columbia*, (Berkeley: 1958), p. 476, for a reference to Paull's role in organizing these particular Indians.

[36] H. B. Hawthorn, (Ed.) *A Survey of the Contemporary Indians of Canada, A Report on Economic, Political, Educational Need and Policies*, Vol. 1 (Ottawa: 1966), p. 365. See especially Chapter XVIII, "The Politics of Indian Affairs." For some helpful comments on this topic I am indebted to Mr. Ron Bakker.

[37] *Ibid.*

[38] I am indebted to Mr. Leonard S. Mandamin's unpublished paper, "The National Indian Council: The Successful Failure," for the information in this section. He was present at the 1968 meeting as a delegate representing the "Canadian Indian Workshop." Mr. Mandamin was at one time President of the Canadian Indian Youth Council. *See Minutes of Meeting of Representatives of Provincial Native Organizations and Executive of the National Indian Council, February 3-4, 1968*.

[39] Hawthorn (1966), p. 382.

[40] *Ibid.*, p. 368.

[41] *Ibid.*, p. 383.

[42] Anglican Church of Canada, *Bulletin 201—Recent Statements by the Indians of Canada, General Synod Action 1969, Government Responses, Suggested Resource (n.p.: January, 1970), p.9*.

[43] *Ibid.*, p. 25.

[44] *Ibid.*

[45] *Ibid.*, p. 28.

[46] Harold Cardinal, *The Unjust Society* (Edmonton: 1969), p. 1.

FOOTNOTES:

[47] Indian Chiefs of Alberta, *Citizens Plus* (n.p.: June, 1970), p. 4.

[48] *Ibid.*, p. 7.

[49] *Ibid.*, p. 8.

[50] *Ibid.*, p. 19.

[51] Claude Lewis, *Indian Families of the Northwest Coast, The Impact of Change* (Chicago: 1970), pp. 218-219. (The Suttles reference is from the article by Wayne Suttles, *The Persistence of the Intervillage Ties Among The Coast Salish*, (Ethnology 2, October 1963), p. 520.

[52] James Walker, "The Indian in Canadian Historical Writing," Unpublished Manuscript. This paper in a revised form was delivered to the Canadian Historical Association Annual Meeting, June 1, 1971.

[53] *Ibid.*, p. 4.

[54] *Ibid.*, p. 11.

[55] *Ibid.*, p. 14, quoted from Kingsford.

[56] *Ibid.*, p. 21.

[57] *Ibid.*, p. 26.

[58] *Ibid.*, p. 29.

[59] Florian Znaniecki, "The Origin of National Culture Societies," reprinted from *Modern Nationalities: A Sociological Study* (Urbana: 1952) in Warren J. Cahnman and Alvin Boskoff (Eds.), *Sociology and History: Theory and Research (New York: 1964)*, p. 298.

[60] *Ibid.*, p. 300.

[61] Immanuel Wallerstein, "The Search for National Identity in West Africa: The New History," originally published in Présence Africaine (1960), in Cahnman and Boskoff (Eds.), *op. cit.*, p. 306.

[62] *Ibid.*, p. 308.

[63] *Ibid.*, p. 305.

[64] *Ibid.*, p. 310.

[65] *Indian-Eskimo Association of Canada Bulletin*, Vol. 8, No. 5 (Toronto: December, 1967), p. 2.

[66] *Kitchener-Waterloo Record*, November 22, 1967, p. 59.

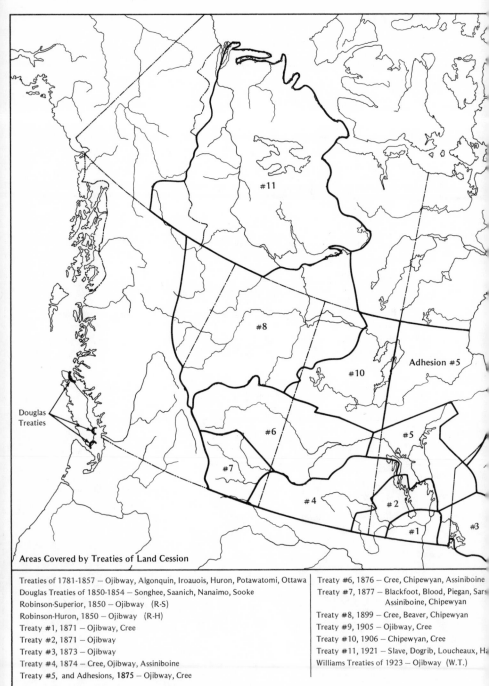

Areas Covered by Treaties of Land Cession

Treaties of 1781-1857 — Ojibway, Algonquin, Iroauois, Huron, Potawatomi, Ottawa
Douglas Treaties of 1850-1854 — Songhee, Saanich, Nanaimo, Sooke
Robinson-Superior, 1850 — Ojibway (R-S)
Robinson-Huron, 1850 — Ojibway (R-H)
Treaty #1, 1871 — Ojibway, Cree
Treaty #2, 1871 — Ojibway
Treaty #3, 1873 — Ojibway
Treaty #4, 1874 — Cree, Ojibway, Assiniboine
Treaty #5, and Adhesions, 1875 — Ojibway, Cree

Treaty #6, 1876 — Cree, Chipewyan, Assiniboine
Treaty #7, 1877 — Blackfoot, Blood, Piegan, Sars
                                  Assiniboine, Chipewyan
Treaty #8, 1899 — Cree, Beaver, Chipewyan
Treaty #9, 1905 — Ojibway, Cree
Treaty #10, 1906 — Chipewyan, Cree
Treaty #11, 1921 — Slave, Dogrib, Loucheaux, Ha
Williams Treaties of 1923 — Ojibway (W.T.)

Note: The ethnic groups are the main ones involved in the areas. In some cases one or two other groups, in small numbers, may have been involved.
     This is more likely in the western treaties than in Ontario.

#9

R-S

R-H

W.T.

1781—
1857

W.T.

Figure 14.
Chief Yellowbird
presenting the Red
Paper to Prime Minister
Trudeau in 1970.

Figure 15.
George Manuel, president
of the National Indian
Brotherhood, on South
Pacific tour.

Figure 16.
Omer Peters, past
president of the
Union of Ontario Indians.

Figure 17.
The founder of the Federation of Saskatchewan
Indians. Seated, Mr. Dave Ahenakew, Chief Joe
Dreaver, Chief Angus Morasty. Standing, Chief William
Kingfisher, Chief John Tootoosis, Chief John Gambler.

Figure 18.
Walter Dieter, a
past president of the
Manitoba Indian
Brotherhood.

Figure 19.
The late Alfred
Adams, one of the
founders of the
Native Brotherhood
of British Columbia.

Figure 20.
Walter Currie, a
past president of
the Indian-Eskimo
Association of
Canada.

Figure 21.
Harvey McCue,
Director of Indians
in the City, an Action
Research Project of the
Union of Ontario Indians.

Figure 22.
Harold Cardinal, author
of *The Unjust Society*
and spokesman for the
Indians of Alberta.

Figure 23.
Jackson Beardy, a Cree artist,
with part of his collection of
paintings depicting the stories
and legends of his people.

Figure 24.
Gerald Tailfeathers
making one of his
quick sketches on the
Indian reserve near
Cardston, Alberta.

Figure 25.
Mrs. Jean Goodwill
of the Department of
Indian Affairs and
Northern Development.

197

Selected Bibliography.

A. BOOKS

Beattie, Jessie L., *The Split in the Sky*. Toronto, The Ryerson Press, 1960.

Blair, E. H., ed. *The Indian Tribes of the Upper Mississippi Valley and Region of the Great Lakes*. New York, Kraus Reprint Co., 1969.

Blake, Freeman, *History of the Indians in British North America*. Washington, Government Printing Office, 1870.

Brebner, J. B., *New England's Outpost, Acadia before the Conquest of Canada*. New York, Columbia University Press, 1927.

Burpee, Lawrence J., ed., "The Journal of Anthony Hendry, 1754-55," in *Transactions of the Royal Society of Canada*, Sec. II, 3rd Series, Vol. I, 1907.

Burpee, Lawrence J., ed., "The Journal of Matthew Cocking, 1772-73," in *Transactions of the Royal Society of Canada*, Sec. II, 1908.

Cameron, William, J., *New Zealand*. Englewood Cliffs, Prentice-Hall, Inc., 1965.

Cardinal, Harold, *The Unjust Society*. Edmonton, M. G. Hurtig Ltd., Publishers, 1969.

Chance, Norman A., ed., *Conflict in Culture: Problems of Developmental Change Among the Cree*. Ottawa, Canadian Research Centre for Anthropology, St. Paul University, 1968.

Codere, Helen, *Fighting with Property*. Seattle, American Ethnological Society, University of Washington Press, 1966.

Codere, Helen, "Kwakiutl," in Edward H. Spicer, ed., *Perspectives in American Cultural Change*. Chicago, University of Chicago Press, 1961.

Collier, John, *From Every Zenith*. Chicago, The Swallow Press Incorporated, 1963.

Cronin, Kay, *Cross in the Wilderness*, Vancouver, 1960.

Crouse, N. M., *La Verendrye, Fur Trader and Explorer*, Toronto, The Ryerson Press, 1956.

Driver, Harold E., *Indians of North America*, Chicago, University of Chicago Press, 1969.

Drucker, Philip, *Cultures of the North Pacific Coast*. San Francisco, Chandler Publishing Co., 1965.

Drucker, Philip and Heizer, Robert F., *To Make My Name Good*. Los Angeles, University of California Press, 1967.

Duff, Wilson, *The Indian History of British Columbia*, Vol. 1, *The Impact of the White Man*. Victoria, Queen's Printer, 1965.

Eccles, W. J., *The Canadian Frontier 1534-1760*. Toronto, Holt Rinehart and Winston of Canada Ltd., 1969.

Garfield, Viola E. and Wingert, Paul S., *The Tsimshian Indians and their Arts*. Seattle, University of Washington Press, 1950.

Geographic Board of Canada, *Handbook of Indians of Canada*. Ottawa, Government Printer, 1913.

Hagan, William, *American Indians*, The Chicago History of American Civilization. Daniel J. Boorstin, ed., Chicago, University of Chicago Press, 1961.

Hamilton, James C., *The Georgian Bay*. Toronto, Arbuthnot Brothers and Co., 1893.

Hanke, Lewis, *Aristotle and the American Indian*. Bloomington, Indiana University Press, 1959.

Hanks, Lucien M. Jr., and Jane R., *Tribe Under Trust*. Toronto, University of Toronto Press, 1950.

Head, Sir Francis Bond, *A Narrative*. London, 1839.

Hinden, Rita, *Empire and After*. London, Essential Books Ltd., 1949.

Hodgetts, J. E. *Pioneer Public Service — An Administrative History of the United Canadas, 1841-1867*. Toronto, University of Toronto Press, 1955.

Honigmann, J. J., *Ethnography and Acculturation of the Fort Nelson Slave*. New Haven, Department of Anthropology, Yale University, 1946.

Hughes, Katherine, *Father Lacombe, The Black-Robe Voyageur*. Toronto, McClelland and Stewart Limited, 1920.

Innis, Harold, *The Fur Trade in Canada*. Toronto, University of Toronto Press, 1962.

Jacobs, Wilbur, *Wilderness Politics and Indian Gifts: The Northern Colonial Frontier, 1748-1763*. Lincoln, University of Nebraska Press, 1966.

Jameson, Anna Burwell, *Winter Studies and Summer Rambles in Canada*, James T. Talman and Elsie McLeod Murray, eds. Toronto, McClelland and Stewart Limited, 1923.

Jenness, Diamond, *Indians of Canada*. Ottawa, The Queen's Printer, 6th edition, 1963.

Jessett, Thomas E., *Chief Spokan Garry*. Minneapolis, T. S. Denison and Co. Inc., 1960.

Johnston, Charles M., *The Valley of the Six Nations*. Toronto, University of Toronto Press, 1964.

Josephy, Alvin, Jr. *The Patriot Chiefs*. New York, Viking Press, Inc., 1960.

Jury, Wilfred and Elsie M., *Sainte-Marie Among the Hurons*. Toronto, Oxford University Press, 1954.

Kane, Paul, *Wanderings of an Artist*. Edmonton, reprinted by M. G. Hurtig Ltd., Publishers, 1968.

Kinietz, W. Vernon, *The Indians of the Western Great Lakes, 1615-1760*. Ann Arbor, University of Michigan Press, 1940.

Klinck, Carl F., ed., *Tecumseh — Fact and Fiction in Early Records*. Englewood Cliffs, Prentice-Hall Inc., 1961.

LaViolette, F. E., *The Struggle for Survival*. Toronto, University of Toronto Press, 1961.

LaViolette, Gontran, *The Sioux in Canada*. Regina, The Marian Press, 1944.

Lewis, Anna, *Chief Pushmataha*. New York, Exposition Press, Inc., 1959.

Lewis, Claudia, *Indian Families of the Northwest Coast: The Impact of Change*. Chicago, University of Chicago Press, 1970.

Lewis, Oscar, "Mexico Since Cardenas," in Richard Adams and others, *Social Change in Latin America Today*. New York, Harper & Row, Publishers, Inc., 1960.

Marriott, McKim, "Cultural Policy in the New States," in Clifford Geertz, ed. *Old Societies and New States*. New York, The Free Press of Glencoe, 1963.

Mason, J. A., *Notes on the Indians of the Great Slave Lake Area*. New Haven, Department of Anthropology, Yale University, 1946.

MacNutt, W. S., *The Atlantic Provinces: the Emergence of Colonial Society 1712-1857*. Toronto, McClelland and Stewart Limited, 1965.

MacLean, John, *Canadian Savage Folk — The Native Tribes of Canada*. Toronto, reprinted by Coles Publishing Co., Ltd., 1971.

McLean, John, *The Indians: Their Manners and Customs*. Toronto, reprinted by Coles Publishing Co., Ltd., 1970.

McLennan, J. S., *Louisbourg from Its Foundations to Its Fall, 1713-1758*. Sydney, Fortress Press, 1957.

Mellor, G. R., *British Imperial Trusteeship*. London, Faber and Faber Ltd., 1951.

Miller, Harold, *New Zealand*. London, Hutchinson's University Library, 1955.

Mooney, James, *The Ghost Dance Religion*. Chicago, University of Chicago Press, 1965.

Morice, A. G., *A History of the Catholic Church in Western Canada from Lake Superior to the Pacific Coast*, Vol. II. Toronto, The Mission Book Co., Ltd., 1910.

Morris, Alexander, *The Treaties of Canada with the Indians of Manitoba and the Northwest Territories*. Toronto, reprinted by Coles Publishing Co., Ltd., 1971.

Morris, J. L., *Indians of Ontario*. Toronto, Ontario Government Department of Lands and Forests, 1943. (Reprinted 1964).

Nagler, Mark, *Indians in the City*. Ottawa, Canadian Research Centre for Anthropology, St. Paul University, 1970.

Neill, Stephen, *A History of Christian Missions*. London, Penguin Books Ltd., 1964.

Nix, James E., *Mission Among the Buffalo*. Toronto, The Ryerson Press, 1960.

Osgood, Cornelius, *Contributions to the Ethnography of the Kutchin*. New Haven Department of Anthropology, Yale University, 1936.

Owen, Roger C., Deetz, James J. and Fisher, Anthony D., eds., *The North American Indian*. New York, The Macmillan Company, 1967.

Parkman, Francis, *The Conspiracy of Pontiac*. New York, The Macmillan Company, 1962.

Perham, Margery, *The Colonial Reckoning*. London, William Collins Sons & Co. 1963.

Phelan, J. L., *The Hispanization of the Philippines*. Madison, 1959.

Price, Sir A. Grenfell, *White Settlers and Native Peoples*. Melbourne, 1950.

Quimby, George I., *Indian Culture and European Trade Goods: The Archaeology of the Historic Period in the Western Great Lakes Region*. Madison, University of Wisconsin Press, 1966.

Quimby, George I., *Indian Life in the Upper Great Lakes, 11000 BC to AD 1800*. Chicago, University of Chicago Press, 1960.

Robertson, Heather, *Reservations are for Indians*. Toronto, James, Lewis & Samuel, Publishers, 1970.

Robinson, Kenneth, *The Dilemmas of Trusteeship*. London, Oxford University Press, 1965.

Rosberg, Carl G. and Nottingham, John, *The Myth of "Mau Mau": Nationalism in Kenya*. New York, Praeger Publishers, Inc., 1966.

Saum, Lewis O., *The Fur Trader and the Indian*. Seattle, University of Washington Press, 1965.

Scott, Duncan Campbell, *The Administration of Indian Affairs in Canada*. Toronto, Canadian Institute of International Affairs, 1931.

Scott, Duncan Campbell, "Indian Affairs, 1763-1841," in Adam Shortt and A. G. Doughty, eds., *Canada and Its Provinces*, Vol. 4., Toronto, Publishers' Association of Canada, Ltd., 1914.

Scott, Duncan Campbell, "Indian Affairs, 1840-1867," in Adam Shortt and A. G. Doughty, eds., *Canada and Its Provinces*, vol. 5., Toronto, Publishers' Association of Canada, Ltd. 1913.

Spicer, Edward H., *Cycles of Conquest: the Impact of Spain, Mexico, and the United States on the Indians of the Southwest, 1533-1960*. Tuscon, University of Arizona Press, 1962.

Stanley, George F. G., *The Birth of Western Canada*. Toronto, University of Toronto Press, 1960.

Steele, S. B., *Forty Years in Canada*. Toronto, McClelland, Goodchild and Stewart, Ltd., 1915.

Thompson, Laura, *Culture in Crisis*. New York, 1950.

Toynbee, Arnold J., *A Study of History*. London, Oxford University Press, 1946.

Trigger, Bruce G., *The Impact of Europeans on Huronia*. Toronto, The Copp Clark Publishing Company, 1969.

Van Stone, James, *The Snowdrift Chipewyan*. Ottawa, Department of Northern Affairs and National Resources, 1963.

Wallace, Paul A. W., *The White Roots of Peace*, rev. ed. Long Island, Ira D. Friedman, Inc., 1968.

Wallerstein, Immanuel, ed., *Social Change: The Colonial Situation*. New York, Wiley, John & Sons, Inc., 1966.

Wallerstein, Immanuel, "The Search for National Identity in West Africa: The New History," in Warren J. Cahman and Alvin Boskoff, eds., *Sociology and History: Theory and Research*. New York, The Free Press of Glencoe, 1964.

Wallis, Wilson D. and Wallis, Ruth Sawtell, *The Micmac Indians of Eastern Canada*. Minneapolis, 1955.

Warren, William W., *History of the Ojibway Nation*. Minneapolis, Ross & Haines, Inc., 1970.

Woodruff, William, *Impact of Western Man — A Study of Europe's Role in the World Economy, 1750-1960*. London, Macmillan & Co. Ltd., 1966.

Young, Egerton Ryerson, *By Canoe and Dog Train*. London, 1894.

Znaniecki, Florian, "The Origin of National Culture Societies," in Warren J. Cahnman and Alvin Boskoff, eds. *Sociology and History: Theory and Research*. New York, The Free Press of Glencoe, 1964.

B. Articles and Reports

Aborigines' Protection Society, *Report on the Canadian Indians*. London Aborigines Protection Society, 1839.

Aborigines' Protection Society, *Ninth Annual Report*. London, The Aborigines' Protection Society, 1846.

Anderson, J. W., "Eastern Cree Indians." *Historical and Scientific Society of Manitoba Papers*, Series III, No. 11, (1956), p. 31.

Anglican Church of Canada, *Bulletin 201 — Recent Statements by the Indians of Canada*. Toronto, 1970.

Bailey, Alfred, *The Conflict of European and Eastern Algonkian Cultures 1504-1700*. New Brunswick Museum Monographic Series #2, 1937.

"British Columbia Dispatches." (Collection of photostatic copies of correspondence between governors of British Columbia and the Secretary of State for the Colonies,) deposited in Special Collections Division, University of British Columbia Library, Vancouver, 1864.

Canada, *Annual Report of the Department of Indian Affairs for 1882, 1891, 1898, 1900, 1904 and 1905*. Ottawa, The Queen's Printer.

Canada, Parliament, "Special Joint Committee of the Senate and House of Commons appointed to examine and consider the Indian Act," *Minutes of the Proceedings and Evidence*, Nos. 1 — 506, Select and Standing Committees of the Senate and House of Commons, Vol. VI, Ottawa, 1946.

Canada, Parliament, "Special Joint Committee of the Senate to continue and complete the examination and consideration of the Indian Act," *Minutes of the Proceedings and Evidence*, Nos. 21-41 Select and Standing Committees of the Senate and the House of Commons, Vol. II, pts. 1 and 2, 1947, Ottawa, 1947. Nos. 1-5, Vol. II, 1948, Ottawa 1948.

Drucker, Philip, *The Native Brotherhoods*, Bureau of American Ethnology, Bulletin No. 168, Washington, 1958.

Garfield, Viola E., *Tsimshian Clan and Society*. University of Washington Publications in Anthropology, Vol. 7, No. 3, (February, 1939), pp. 167-340.

Gladstone, Percy H., *Industrial Disputes in the Commercial Fisheries of British Columbia*. Unpublished Master's thesis, University of British Columbia, 1959.

Hickerson, Harold, "The Southwestern Chippewa." *American Anthropological Association Memoirs 92*, Vol. 64, No. 3, Pt. 2 (1962), pp. 82-83.

Hickerson, Harold, "The Sociohistorical Significance of Two Chippewa Ceremonials." *American Anthropologists*, Vol. 65, No. 1, (1965) pp. 74-75.

Hlady, Walter M., "Indian Migrations in Manitoba and the West." *Historical and Scientific Society of Manitoba Papers*, Series III, No. 17, 1960-61.

Hutton, Elizabeth, *Indian Affairs in Nova Scotia, 1760-1834*. Nova Scotia Historical Society, Collections, 1963.

Indian Chiefs of Alberta, *Citizens Plus*. Edmonton, 1970.

Jenness, Diamond, *The Indian Background of Canadian History*. Department of Mines and Resources Bulletin #86, Anthropological Series #21, Ottawa, 1937.

Lewis, Oscar, *The Effects of White Contact Upon Blackfoot Culture*. Monographs of the American Ethnological Society, A. Irving Hollowell, ed., Seattle, 1942.

Mandelbaum, David G., *The Plains Cree*. The Anthropological Papers of the American Museum of Natural History, Vol. XXVII, Pt. II, New York, 1940.

Report on the Affairs of the Indians in Canada, *Journals* Appendix EEE, Section I, "History of the Relations Between the Government and the Indians," Ottawa, The Queen's Printer, 1844.

Sanders, Douglas and others, *Native Rights in Canada*. Toronto, Indian-Eskimo Association of Canada, 1970.

Stanley, George F.G., "The Indian Background of Canadian History." *Canadian Historical Association Annual Report of 1952*.

Tooker, Elisabeth, *An Ethnography of the Huron Indians 1615-1649*. Bureau of American Ethnology, Bulletin No. 190, Washington, 1964.

Van Stone James, *The Changing Culture of the Snowdrift Chipeyan*. Ottawa, National Museum of Canada, Bulletin 209, Anthropological Series 74.

Walker, James, *The Indians in Canadian Historical Writing*. Unpublished manuscript delivered to Canadian Historical Association Annual Meeting, June 1, 1971.

Wike, Joyce, *The Effect of the Maritime Fur Trade on Northwest Coast Indian Society*. Unpublished Ph.D. dissertation, Columbia University, 1951.

C. Periodicals

Ahenakew, Edward, "An Opinion of the Frog Lake Massacre." *Alberta Historical Review*, Vol. VIII, No. 3, (1960), pp. 10-11.

Botting, Douglas, "Demoralized Indians of Brazil." *The Geographical Magazine*, Vol. XXXIX, No. 12, (April, 1967), p. 1002.

Daily Columbian, September 15, 1889, Victoria.

Duff, Wilson, "The Fort Victoria Treaties." *B.C. Studies* No. 3, (Fall, 1969), pp. 3-57.

Fraser, William, "Big Bear, Indian Patriot." *Alberta Historical Review*, (Spring 1966), p. 15.

Howay, F. W. "Early Days of the Maritime Traders on the North-West Coast." *Canadian Historical Review*, Vol. 4, (1923).

Howay, F. W., "Indian Attacks upon Maritime Traders of the North-West Coast 1785-1805" *Canadian Historical Review*, Vol. 6, (1925), pp. 287-309.

Indian-Eskimo Association of Canada, *Bulletin*, Vol. 8, #5, (December, 1967), p. 2.

Jenness, Diamond, "Canada's Indians Yesterday, What of Today." *Canadian Journal of Economics and Political Science*, Vol. 20, No. 1, (February, 1954), pp. 45-100.

Kitchener-Waterloo Record, November 22, 1967, p. 59.

Lemert, Edwin M., "The Life and Death of an Indian State." *Human Organization*, Vol. XIII, No. 3, (Fall, 1954), pp. 23-27.

Liebon, Elliot and Trudeau, John, "A Preliminary Study of Acculturation Among the Cree Indians of Winisk, Ontario." *Arctic*, XV, (September, 1962).

MacFarlane, R. O., "British Indian Policy in Nova Scotia to 1760." *Canadian Historical Review*, Vol. 19, (June, 1938), pp. 154-167.

MacInnes, T.R.L., "History of Indian Administration in Canada." *Canadian Journal of Economics and Political Science*, Vol. 12, Toronto, 1946.

McNickle, D'Arcy, "Indian and European: Indian-White Relations from Discovery to 1887." *The Annals of the American Academy of Political and Social Science*, Vol. 311, Philadephia, 1957.

Paull, Andrew, "Letter to the Editor," *The Vancouver Province*, February 21, 1955.

Quimby, George I., "Culture Contact on the Northwest Coast, 1785-1795." *American Anthropologist*, Vol. 5, (1948), pp. 250-251.

Richard, T. A., "Indian Participation in the Gold Discoveries." *British Columbia Historical Quarterly*, Vol. 2, No. 1, (January, 1938).

Stanely, George F. G., "The First Indian Reserves in Canada." *Revue d'Histoire de l'Amerique Française*, Vol. 4, No. 2, (September, 1950).

Stanley, George F. G., "The Indians in the War of 1812." *Canadian Historical Review*, Vol. 31, No. 2, (June, 1950).

Suttles, Wayne, "Affinal Ties, Subsistence and Prestige Among The Coast Salish." *American Anthropologist*, Vol. 62, No. 2, (April 1960), p. 304.

"The Story of the Ahenakews." *Saskatchewan History*, Vol. 17, No. 1, (Winter 1964), p. 22.

Thomas, Robert K., "Pan-Indianism." *Midcontinent American Studies*, Vol. 6, No. 2, (1965), pp. 78-83.

Trigger, Bruce G., "The French Presence in Huronia: The Structure of Franco-Huron Relations in the first half of the 17th Century." *Canadian Historical Review*, Vol. 49, (1968).

Williams, Guy, article in *The Native Voice*, Vancouver, February, 1960.

Index

206

Const 1795 bad of 1789

physiocrats - in France - both like
            Adam Smith

— there are material society that must change
its material wealth thru agriculture